DESSERTS, CAKES & PASTRIES

LAROUSSE

Gastronomique

— RECIPE COLLECTION—

DESSERTS, CAKES & PASTRIES

With the assistance of the Gastronomic Committee
President Joël Robuchon

CLARKSON POTTER/PUBLISHERS
NEW YORK

First published in Great Britain by Hamlyn, a division of Octopus Publishing
Group Ltd, London, in 2004. The recipes in this book were previously printed
in *Larousse Gastronomique*, published in the United States by Clarkson
Potter/Publishers, a division of Random House, Inc., New York, in 2001.

Library of Congress Cataloging-in-Publication Data is available upon request.

ISBN-13 978-0-307-33603-3
ISBN-10 0-307-33603-4

Printed in China

10 9 8 7 6 5 4 3 2

Gastronomic Committee

President

Joël Robuchon

Members of the Committee

Michel Creignou, *Journalist*

Jean Delaveyne, *Chef, founder of Restaurant Le Camélia, Bougival*

Éric Frachon, *Honorary president, Evian Water SA*

Michel Guérard, *Chef, Restaurant Les Prés d'Eugénie, Eugénie-les-Bains*

Pierre Hermé, *Confectioner, Paris*

Robert Linxe, *Founder, The House of Chocolate, Paris and New York*

Élisabeth de Meurville, *Journalist*

Georges Pouvel, *Professor of cookery; consultant on cookery techniques*

Jean-François Revel, *Writer*

Pierre Troisgros, *Chef, Restaurant Pierre Troisgros, Roanne*

Alain Weill, *Art expert; member of the National Council of Gastronomy*

Contributors

Marie-Paule Bernardin
Archivist

Geneviève Beullac
Editor

Jean Billault
Member of the College of Butchery

Christophe Bligny
Paris College of Catering

Thierry Borghèse
Chief Inspector of Consumer Affairs

Francis Boucher
Confectioner

Pascal Champagne
Barman, Hotel Lutetia; Member, French Association of Barmen

Frédéric Chesneau
Project manager

Marcel Cottenceau
Former technical director, College of Butchery

Robert Courtine
President, Marco-Polo Prize

Philippe Dardonville
Secretary-general, National Union of Producers of Fruit Juice

Bertrand Debatte
Officer of the Bakery, Auchamps

Jean Dehillerin
President and managing director, E. Dehillerin SA (manufacturers of kitchen equipment)

Gilbert Delos
Writer and journalist

Christian Flacelière
Journalist

Jean-Louis Flandrin
Professor emeritus, University of Paris VII; Director of studies,
E.H.E.S.S. *(College of Social Sciences)*

Dr André Fourel
Economist

Dominique Franceschi
Journalist

Dr Jacques Fricker
Nutritionist

Jean-Pierre Gabriel
Journalist

Thierry Gaudillère
Editor, Bourgogne Aujourd'hui *(Burgundy Today)*

Ismène Giachetti
Director of research, C.N.R.S. (National Centre for Scientific Research)

Sylvie Girard
Cookery writer

Catherine Goavec-Bouvard
Agribusiness consultant

Jo Goldenberg
Restaurateur

Catherine Gomy
Agribusiness certification officer, French Association of Standardization

Bruno Goussault
Scientific director, C.R.E.A. (Centre of Food and Nutrition Studies)

Jacques Guinberteau
Mycologist; Director of studies, I.N.R.A. (National Institute of Agriculture)

Joseph Hossenlopp
Director of studies, Cemagref (Institute of Research for Agricultural and Environmental Engineering)

Françoise Kayler
Food critic

Jacques Lacoursière
Writer

Josette Le Reun-Gaudicheau
Teacher (specializing in seafood)

Paul Maindiaux
Development officer, Ministry of Agriculture

Laurent Mairet
Oenologist

Jukka Mannerkorpi
Cookery editor

Pascal Orain
Manager, Bertie's Restaurant

Philippe Pilliot
Secretary-general, Federation of French Grocers; Editor, Le Nouvel Épicier *(The New Grocer)*

Jean-Claude Ribaut
Cookery correspondent, Le Monde

Isabelle Richard
Bachelor of Arts

Michel Rigo
Deputy head, National Federation of Fruit Brandies

Françoise Sabban
Master of ceremonies, E.H.E.S.S. (College of Social Sciences)

Jacques Sallé
Journalist

Jean-Louis Taillebaud
Chef, Ritz-Escoffier (French School of Gastronomy); Ritz Hotel, Place Vendôme, Paris

Claude Vifian
Chef and professor, College of the Hotel Industry, Lausanne

Leda Vigliardi Paravia
Writer and journalist

Jean-Marc Wolff
College of the Hotel Industry, Paris

Rémy Yverneau
Secretary-general, National Federation of Makers of Cream Cheese

Contents

Useful information

How to use this book

The recipes are divided into two main chapters: Desserts, and Biscuits, cakes, pastries & sweet breads. Within these chapters, entries are grouped by type of dish and then by main ingredient in A–Z order. The third chapter, Basic recipes & classic additions, has recipes for the batters, custards, pastry, sauces and so on referred to in the first two chapters.

When an entry refers to another recipe, it may be found by first referring to the relevant section and then to the food or dish type. A comprehensive index of entries lists the entire contents.

Weights & measures

Metric, imperial and American measures are used in this book. As a general rule, it is advisable to follow only one set of measures and not to mix metric, imperial and/or cup quantities in any one recipe.

Spoon measures

Spoon measures refer to standard measuring utensils. Serving spoons and table cutlery are not suitable for measuring as they are not standard in capacity.

¼ teaspoon = 1.5 ml
½ teaspoon = 2.5 ml
1 teaspoon = 5 ml
1 tablespoon = 15 ml

Oven temperatures

Below are the standard settings for domestic ovens. However, ovens vary widely and manufacturer's instructions should be consulted. Individual ovens also perform differently and experience of using a particular appliance is invaluable for adjusting temperatures and cooking times to give the best results. Those working with commercial cooking appliances will be accustomed to using the higher temperatures attained. Many chefs' recipes refer to glazing or cooking in a hot oven for a short period: as a rule, the hottest setting for a domestic appliance should be used as the equivalent.

Temperatures and timings in the recipes refer to preheated ovens.

If using a fan-assisted oven, follow the manufacturer's instructions for adjusting timing and temperature.

Centigrade	Fahrenheit	Gas mark
110°C	225°F	gas ¼
120°C	250°F	gas ½
140°C	275°F	gas 1
150°C	300°F	gas 2
160°C	325°F	gas 3
180°C	350°F	gas 4
190°C	375°F	gas 5
200°C	400°F	gas 6
220°C	425°F	gas 7
230°C	450°F	gas 8
240°C	475°F	gas 9

Introduction

Larousse Gastronomique is the world's most famous culinary reference book. It was the vision of Prosper Montagné, a French chef who was responsible for the first edition published in Paris in 1938. His aims were to provide an overview of 20th-century gastronomy and its history, as well as a source of reference on the more practical aspects of cookery. Twenty-three years later the first English edition was published and it immediately became the culinary bible of chefs, cooks and food aficionados.

A new English edition of this monumental work was published in 2001. Completely revised and updated, it reflected the social and cultural changes, together with advances in science and technology, that have dramatically influenced our ideas about food, the way we cook and how we eat.

Distilled from the latest edition, in one convenient volume, is this collection of over 500 recipes for desserts, biscuits, cakes, pastries and sweet breads, together with 60 recipes for sauces, custards, icings, preserves, pastry and creams. Whether your interest is in the great traditions of French cuisine or in the wide spectrum of food as the international subject it has become, the recipes reflect the diversity of the world of cooking in the 21st century.

DESSERTS

Desserts & sweet puddings

Almond blancmange (modern)

Blanch and skin 450 g (1 lb, 3 cups) sweet almonds and 20 bitter almonds (or use all sweet almonds). In a blender purée the almonds with 1 litre (1¾ pints, 4⅓ cups) hot water; when the liquid is milky and the almonds are very fine, strain the mixture through muslin (cheesecloth). Sprinkle 25 g (1 oz, 4 envelopes) gelatine over 5 tablespoons almond milk and leave to swell. Heat the remaining almond milk with 100 g (4 oz, ½ cup) sugar, stirring frequently. When the sugar has dissolved and the liquid is almost boiling, stir into the gelatine, and continue stirring until the gelatine has melted. Pour the almond blancmange into a 1.15 litre (2 pint, 5 cups) mould, leave until cold, then refrigerate until firmly set.

Almond blancmange (traditional)

Blanch 450 g (1 lb, 3 cups) sweet almonds and about 20 bitter almonds. Leave them to soak in a bowl of cold water, which renders them singularly white. Drain in a sieve and rub in a napkin to remove the skins. Pound in a mortar, moistening them, little by little, with 1½ tablespoons water at a time, to prevent them from turning into oil. When they are pounded into a fine paste, put into a bowl and dilute with 1.15 litres (2 pints, 5 cups) filtered water, added a little at a time. Spread a clean napkin over a dish, pour the almond mixture into it and, with two people twisting the napkin, press out all the almond milk. Add to the milk 350 g (12 oz, 1½ cups) sugar and rub through a fine sieve. Strain the liquid through a napkin once again and add 25 g (1 oz plus 4 grains) clarified isinglass a little warmer than tepid – or use 25 g (1 oz, 4 envelopes) gelatine dissolved in warm water. Blend with the blancmange. Pour into a mould and place in a container with crushed ice.

- *variations:* to make rum blancmange, add ½ glass rum to the mixture described above. To make a Maraschino blancmange, add the same amount of Maraschino.

To serve this dessert in small pots, prepare two-thirds of the quantity given in the recipe; you will, however, need less gelling agent, as when the blancmange is served in small pots it should be more delicate than when it is to be turned out.

Blancmanges can also be flavoured with lemon, vanilla, coffee, chocolate, pistachio nuts, hazelnuts and strawberries. Whipped cream can also be incorporated for a richer mixture.

Almond crêpes

Prepare some sweet crêpe batter and leave it to stand. Meanwhile, make some confectioner's custard (pastry cream), adding 75 g (3 oz, ¾ cup) ground almonds to each 600 ml (1 pint, 2½ cups) custard. Cook the pancakes and fill them with the almond cream. Roll them up, arrange them in an ovenproof dish, dust with caster (superfine) sugar, and brown them quickly in a preheated oven at 230°C (450°F, gas 8).

Almond milk jelly

Soak 3 leaves of gelatine in a little water. Alternatively ¾ oz, 1½ envelopes of dissolved powdered gelatine may be added to the hot milk. Blanch 250 g (9 oz, scant 2 cups) sweet almonds and 15 g (½ oz, 1 tablespoon) bitter almonds in 500 ml (17 fl oz, 2 cups) water for 2 minutes – or use all sweet nuts. Drain and skin the almonds and pound them thoroughly in a mortar, adding a few drops of iced water to prevent the nuts turning into oil. When the paste is completely smooth, strain the gelatine liquid into the almond paste (reserving the leaves) and stir.

Stretch some muslin (cheesecloth) over a bowl and carefully pour the mixture on to the cloth. Twist and squeeze the muslin to obtain 500 ml (17 fl oz, 2 cups) almond milk. Pour the milk into a saucepan. Crush the leaves of gelatine and add to the almond milk, together with 200 g (7 oz, 1 cup) caster (superfine) sugar. Bring slowly to the boil, stirring continuously. Then strain through a fine sieve. Spoon into individual dishes or into a ring mould. Chill the jelly until set.

American pudding

Put in a large bowl 75 g (3 oz, ¾ cup) stale breadcrumbs, 100 g (4 oz, 1 cup) plain (all-purpose) flour, 100 g (4 oz, ⅔ cup, firmly packed) brown sugar and 75 g (3 oz, ⅓ cup) chopped beef suet. Add 100 g (4 oz, ⅔ cup) finely diced crystallized (candied) fruit, 1 tablespoon blanched finely shredded orange zest and the same amount of lemon zest. Bind the mixture with 1 egg and 3 yolks. Add a generous pinch of cinnamon, the same amount of grated nutmeg and 1 liqueur glass of rum. Mix well and pour into a buttered and floured charlotte mould. Cook in a bain marie in a preheated oven at 200°C (400°F, gas 6) for about 50 minutes until firm. Leave to cool and turn out on to a serving dish. Serve with rum-flavoured zabaglione.

Apple and rice charlotte

Butter a charlotte mould. Line the bottom and sides with a layer of cold milky rice pudding to which an egg yolk and a stiffly whisked egg white have been added. Fill the mould with a well-reduced apple purée. Cover with a layer of rice pudding and place the mould in a bain marie. Bring to the boil on top of the cooker (stove) and then place the bain marie in a preheated oven at 220°C (425°F, gas 7) and cook for 40 minutes. Turn out on to a serving dish and coat with a hot blackcurrant sauce.

Apple and walnut crêpes

Make some sweet crêpes. Lightly brown some thin slices of apple in butter and sprinkle them with sugar. Cover a quarter of each crêpe with the apple slices and a few peeled moist walnuts. Fold the crêpes into four and sprinkle with more sugar. The crêpes may be flamed with Calvados or with another fruit liqueur if desired.

Apple charlotte (1)

Peel and core 3 kg (6½ lb) apples and cut into quarters. Slice them thinly and place in a shallow frying pan with 800 g (1¾ lb, 3½ cups) caster (superfine) sugar and 150 g (5 oz, ⅔ cup) butter. Place the pan over a brisk heat, stir the ingredients quickly with a wooden spatula, add a vanilla pod (bean) and reduce to a thick purée.

Butter a cold charlotte mould and dust it lightly with caster sugar. Slice a loaf of bread. Remove the crusts and cut the slices into 8 heart-shaped pieces and 16 very thin strips, 4 cm (1½ in) wide and the exact height of the mould. Dip the pieces in 100 g (4 oz, ½ cup) melted butter. Place the 8 hearts in a rosette in the bottom of the mould and arrange the 16 strips around the sides of the mould, so that they overlap with no gaps. To make it easier to unmould the charlotte, brush the strips that are lining the inside of the mould with some beaten egg: this coating will stiffen the lining during cooking.

Mix the well-reduced apple purée with 200 ml (7 fl oz, ¾ cup) thick sweetened apricot purée and pour into the mould. Cook in a preheated oven at 220°C (425°F, gas 7) for 25–30 minutes. Leave to stand for a short time before turning out; serve hot.

Apple charlotte (2)

For 20–22 sponge fingers (ladyfingers), prepare a syrup with 200 (7 oz, generous ¾ cup) granulated sugar and 175 ml (6 fl oz, ¾ cup) water. Flavour the syrup (by addding 2 tablespoons of rum, for example). Line the bottom of a charlotte mould with sponge fingers that have been cut into a point and then steeped in the syrup. Line the sides of the mould with sponge fingers that have been cut to the height of the mould and soaked in syrup. Place them tightly together (cut-side down).

Peel and slice about 12 apples. Melt 1 tablespoon butter in a shallow frying pan, add the apples, 250 g (9 oz, generous 1 cup) caster (superfine) sugar, 1 vanilla pod (bean) and a little grated lemon rind. Cover and leave to cook for 5 minutes. Remove the lid from the pan and cook for a further 10 minutes, stirring occasionally. Then add 4 tablespoons apricot jam (preserve). Remove the vanilla pod and pour the purée into the lined mould. Cover with pieces of sponge finger. Place in a preheated oven at 190°C (375°F, gas 5) and bake for 30–40 minutes. Take the charlotte out of the oven, leave it to stand for about 15 minutes and then turn it out of the mould. Coat it with a hot apricot sauce.

Apple charlotte with brown sugar

Peel, core and quarter 4 Belle de Boskoop or Granny Smith apples. Remove the crusts from 10 slices of white bread and fry in 65 g (2½ oz, ¼ cup) butter.

Drain and use to line the bottom and the sides of a charlotte mould. Melt about 75 g (3 oz, ⅓ cup) butter in a frying pan, add 200 g (7 oz, 1¼ cups) soft brown sugar, then the apple quarters, and cook for 10 minutes, stirring from time to time. Flame with 1½ tablespoons warmed Calvados. Heap this mixture in the mould and bake in a preheated oven at 200°C (400°F, gas 6) for 30 minutes. Cool under a press, then turn out and serve with custard cream.

Apple compote

Prepare a syrup with 350 g (12 oz, 1½ cups) granulated sugar to 600 ml (1 pint, 2½ cups) water. Peel the apples, cut them into quarters, remove the cores and cover them with lemon juice. Boil the syrup, add the apples and remove as soon as they are tender. Serve either warm or cold.

Apple crown à la normande

Peel and core some dessert (eating) apples, and poach in a vanilla-flavoured syrup. Leave to cool in the syrup, then drain. Prepare an egg custard flavoured with Calvados, and cook in a plain ring mould in a bain marie. Leave to cool, then turn out on to a serving dish. Arrange the apple halves in the centre in a dome. Decorate with very thick Chantilly cream using a piping (pastry) bag with a fluted nozzle. Serve with an apricot sauce flavoured with Calvados.

Apple crumble

Into a food processor put 150 g (5 oz, 1¼ cups) plain (all-purpose) flour, add 150 g (5 oz, ⅔ cup) butter cut into pieces, and 150 g (5 oz, ⅔ cup) caster (superfine) sugar. Process until the mixture looks like breadcrumbs. Peel and core 1.5 kg (3¼ lb) apples. Cut into quarters, arrange in an ovenproof dish and cover with the crumble mixture. Cook for 35 minutes in a preheated oven at 200°C (400°F, gas 6). Serve with custard or thick crème fraîche.

Apple délicieux

Prepare and bake 675 g (1½ lb) apples on a baking sheet in a preheated oven at 190°C (375°F, gas 5). Reduce the pulp to a purée and allow to cool. Beat 5 egg yolks with 100 g (4 oz, ½ cup) caster (superfine) sugar until the mixture becomes light and foamy. Whisk the 5 whites stiffly and fold a little at a time into the egg mixture alternately with the apple purée and 65 g (2½ oz, ⅔ cup) dried white breadcrumbs. Empty the mixture into a buttered and floured soufflé dish and cook in a preheated oven at 190°C (375°F, gas 5) for 40–45 minutes. Dust with sugar and serve very hot.

Apple flamusse

Put 65 g (2½ oz, ⅔ cup) plain (all-purpose) flour in a mixing bowl. Make a well in the centre and add 75 g (3 oz, 6 tablespoons) caster (superfine) sugar, a generous pinch of salt and 3 beaten eggs. Mix with a wooden spoon until smooth. Gradually add 500 ml (17 fl oz, 2 cups) milk and mix well. Peel 3 or 4 dessert (eating) apples and cut them into thin slices. Arrange them on a buttered pie plate so that they overlap. Pour the batter mixture over the top and cook in a preheated oven at 150°C (300°F, gas 2) for 45 minutes. When cooked, turn the flamusse over to serve, and sprinkle the apples generously with caster sugar.

Apple fritters

Core the apples with an apple corer, peel and cut into rounds about 3 mm (⅛ in) thick. Sprinkle with lemon juice and macerate for 30 minutes in Cognac or Calvados. Drain, dip in batter and deep-fry in hot oil. Drain the fritters. Dust with caster (superfine) sugar and arrange on a napkin. Fritters may also be served dusted with icing (confectioner's) sugar and glazed in a hot oven or under a grill (broiler).

Apple gratiné

Make 1 litre (1¾ pints, 4⅓ cups) syrup per 1 kg (2¼ lb) apples, using 500 g (18 oz, 2¼ cups) sugar per 1 litre (1¾ pints, 4⅓ cups) water. Peel some firm dessert (eating) apples, cut them in half and poach gently in the syrup, making sure that they do not disintegrate. Drain and leave to cool.

Peel and core some apples, cut into quarters and weigh. For 500 g (18 oz) apples, allow 300 g (11 oz, ⅓ cups) sugar. Put the apples and sugar in a preserving pan with 2 tablespoons water. Cook gently until the apples crush under a spoon. Rub them through a strainer over a bowl. Put the purée back into the pan, bring to the boil, stirring continuously, and cook until the purée reaches a temperature of 106°C (223°F). Use the conserve to line a buttered ovenproof dish, then arrange the apple halves on top. Mix some fine breadcrumbs with half as much ground almonds. Scatter liberally over the apples, sprinkle with melted butter and brown in a preheated oven at 220°C (425°F, gas 7).

The syrup in which the apples have been cooked can be strained and used to cook apples or other fruit.

Apples flamed with Calvados

Pommes flambées au calvados Peel some apples, core them and arrange in a buttered ovenproof dish. Sprinkle with sugar and melted butter and cook in a preheated oven at 220°C (425°F, gas 7) until just tender. Arrange the apples in a silver timbale or flameproof dish and heat it. Sprinkle with warmed Calvados and set alight.

Apple soufflés

Cut 8 large dessert (eating) apples in half, core them and then scoop out half the pulp without piercing the skin. Cook the pulp for 5 minutes with

2 tablespoons water, without stirring, in a covered saucepan. Then add 300 g (11 oz, 1⅓ cups) caster (superfine) sugar to the pulp and continue cooking, stirring to obtain a very smooth purée. Sprinkle the inside of the fruit halves with 100 ml (4 fl oz, ½ cup) brandy and add another 100 ml (4 fl oz, ½ cup) brandy to the apple purée. Stiffly whisk 5 egg whites and fold them into the apple purée. Arrange the apple halves in a well-buttered ovenproof dish, use a spoon or piping (pastry) bag to fill them with apple purée and sprinkle with 50 g (2 oz, ⅓ cup) icing (confectioner's) sugar. Cook in a preheated oven at 230°C (450°F, gas 8) for 10–12 minutes until browned. Serve immediately. The apples soufflés may be served on a caramel sauce, made by adding single (light) cream to caramel, or a caramel dessert sauce based on a custard, flavoured with light caramel. Diced red, yellow and green apple makes an attractive decoration.

Apples with cream and kirsch

Peel and core crisp sweet dessert (eating) apples, sprinkle them with lemon juice and cook them in boiling vanilla-flavoured syrup until transparent. Drain and leave to cool. Mix very cold fresh double (heavy) or whipping cream with a quarter of its volume of very cold kirsch, then whip until the whisk leaves a trail. Pour this over the apples.

Apples with honey and salted butter

Peel, halve and core 8 dessert (eating) apples. Pour 250 g (9 oz, ¾ cup) liquid acacia honey into a flameproof baking dish, spreading it evenly. Place this dish over a brisk heat until the honey has browned. Remove from the heat and arrange the apple halves in the dish with their curved sides underneath and a small knob of salted butter in each. Cook in a preheated oven at 240°C (475°F, gas 9) for 10 minutes. Serve immediately.

Apricot compote

Halve the apricots, remove the stones (pits) and extract and blanch the kernels in boiling water. Cook the fruit for about 20 minutes in syrup: use 350 g (12 oz, 1½ cups) granulated sugar to 600 ml (1 pint, 2½ cups) water. Arrange the apricot halves in a fruit bowl with half a kernel on each; pour the syrup over them.

Apricot compote (baked)

Place some apricot halves in an ovenproof dish. Sprinkle them with sugar and bake in a preheated oven at 180°C (350°F, gas 4) for about 20 minutes. Serve in a fruit dish.

Apricot croquettes

Cook 500 g (18 oz) apricots in syrup, drain, dry and cut into large dice. Add 400 ml (14 fl oz, 1¾ cups) very thick confectioner's custard (pastry cream). Flavour the apricot mixture with rum and leave to cool completely. Divide into portions of 50–65 g (2–2½ oz).

Mould each portion into a small ball, flatten slightly and roll in flour, beaten egg and fresh breadcrumbs. Deep-fry in oil heated to 175–180°C (347–350°F) and serve with hot apricot sauce.

Apricot fritters

Stone (pit) some ripe apricots and macerate for 30 minutes in sugar and rum (or kirsch or Cognac). Drain thoroughly, dip in sweetened or unsweetened batter and deep-fry in hot oil. Remove the fritters and drain. Dust them with caster (superfine) sugar and arrange on a napkin. Fritters may also be served dusted with icing (confectioner's) sugar and glazed in a hot oven or under a grill (broiler).

Apricot pannequets

Pannequets are sweet or savoury pancakes that can be filled with chopped ingredients, a purée or a cream.

Make a batter with 250 g (9 oz, 2¼ cups) plain (all-purpose) flour, a pinch of salt, 3 beaten eggs mixed with 1 tablespoon caster (superfine) sugar, 250 ml (8 fl oz, 1 cup) milk, 250 ml (8 fl oz, 1 cup) water and 1 tablespoon melted butter. Use the batter to make some fairly thick pancakes (8 are required for this recipe). Pile them in a covered dish and keep hot over a saucepan of boiling water. Make 250 ml (8 fl oz, 1 cup) confectioner's custard (pastry cream) flavoured with rum and add to it 12 very ripe apricots (or drained canned apricots), stoned (pitted) and cut into dice, and 75 g (3 oz, ¾ cup) coarsely chopped almonds. Spread the pancakes with this preparation and roll them up. Arrange them in a buttered ovenproof dish, dust them generously with icing (confectioner's) sugar, and place them in a preheated oven at 230°C (450°F, gas 8) for 8–10 minutes.

Apricots à l'ancienne

Poach large apricot halves in a vanilla-flavoured syrup. Drain them and arrange on a layer of sponge cake which has been soaked with rum and coated with sweet apple purée. Sprinkle the apricots with chopped almonds and sugar, spoon over a little melted butter and bake in a preheated oven at 220°C (425°F, gas 7) until brown on top. Serve with a sauce made of apricot jam (preserve) diluted with a little hot water, sieved and then flavoured with rum.

Apricots bourdaloue

Poach 16 apricot halves in a light vanilla-flavoured syrup. Drain and wipe with paper towels. Two-thirds fill a flameproof dish with cooked dessert semolina. Arrange the apricot halves on top. Cover with a thin layer of semolina and top with 2 crushed macaroons and 1 tablespoon sugar. Place in a very hot oven for a short time to glaze the top. Serve with apricot sauce. Pudding (short-grain) rice may be used instead of semolina and peaches or bananas instead of apricots.

Apricots colbert

Poach apricot halves in a sugar syrup until barely tender, then pat dry. Fill each half with thick cold rice pudding; sandwich the halves together and coat with egg and breadcrumbs. Deep-fry the coated apricots, drain and serve with an apricot sauce flavoured with kirsch.

Apricots condé

Poach apricot halves in a sugar syrup and arrange on both sides of a thick ring of cold rice pudding. Decorate with glacé (candied) cherries and angelica. Insert split blanched almonds between the apricots. Heat the apricot ring in a preheated oven at 160°C (325°F, gas 3) and serve with a kirsch-flavoured apricot sauce.

Apricots flambé

Allow 4–6 poached and drained apricot halves per person; while still hot place in individual dishes. Spoon 2–3 tablespoons of the hot poaching syrup over each portion, warm a scant tablespoon kirsch for each portion and set alight and pour over the fruit.

Attereaux of apricots Pompadour

Thread slices of stale brioche on skewers, alternating with halved apricots, which have been cooked in syrup and thoroughly drained. Dip them in fried custard mixture flavoured with rum or kirsch. Coat them with breadcrumbs and deep-fry quickly in hot oil at 180°C (350°F). Drain on paper towels, sprinkle with caster (superfine) sugar and serve with hot apricot sauce.

Attereaux of pineapple

Peel a fresh pineapple and cut into cubes. Thread the cubes on to skewers, dip them into a fried custard mixture, coat with breadcrumbs and deep-fry.

Baked apples

Make a light circular incision round the middle of some firm cooking apples. Core them and then place them in a large buttered ovenproof dish. Fill the hollow in each apple with butter mixed with caster (superfine) sugar. Pour a few tablespoons of water into the dish. Cook in a preheated oven at 220°C (425°F, gas 7) until the apples are just tender, about 30 minutes. Serve the apples in the dish in which they were cooked.

Baked bananas

Bake unpeeled bananas in a preheated oven at 220°C (425°F, gas 7) for 10–20 minutes. Peel off a third of the skin lengthways to form a boat shape and serve with melted butter and caster (superfine) sugar or with redcurrant jelly.

Baked pears with Sauternes

Make some walnut ice cream with a custard base made from 1 litre (1¾ pints, 4⅓ cups) milk, 150 ml (5 fl oz, ⅔ cup) walnuts ground to a purée with a little milk, 150 g (5 oz, ⅔ cup) caster (superfine) sugar and 6 whole eggs. Peel, core and halve 2 Doyenné du Comice pears. Put 200 g (7 oz, ¾ cup) butter and 300 g (11 oz, 1⅓ cups) sugar in a sauté pan over a medium heat. As soon as the caramel begins to thicken, add the pears, then a bottle of Sauternes and cook slowly until the fruit is tender. Serve with the ice cream.

Baked quinces

Generously butter an ovenproof dish. Peel 4 very ripe quinces and hollow them out carefully with an apple corer. Mix 100 ml (4 fl oz, 7 tablespoons) double (heavy) cream with 65 g (2½ oz, 5 tablespoons) caster (superfine) sugar and fill the quinces with the mixture. Sprinkle the fruit with 125 g (4½ oz, ½ cup) caster (superfine) sugar and bake in a preheated oven at 220°C (425°F, gas 7) for 30–35 minutes, basting several times.

Banana croûtes à la maltaise (1)

Cut from a stale brioche 12 rectangular slices, 6 cm (2½ in) long and slightly wider than a banana. Arrange these slices on a baking sheet, dust with caster (superfine) sugar and glaze in a preheated oven at 230°C (450°F, gas 8). Peel 6 bananas and cut them in half lengthways. Lay these banana halves on a buttered baking sheet, sprinkle them with caster sugar and cook them for 5 minutes in the preheated oven at 230°C (450°F, gas 8).

Make a turban shape on a round ovenproof dish, alternating the bananas and the slices of brioche. Make a thick confectioner's custard (pastry cream) flavoured with orange zest and mixed with split almonds. Fill the centre of the turban with this mixture. Sprinkle the whole preparation with finely crumbled macaroons, moisten with melted butter and brown in the preheated oven. Just before serving, surround the turban with a thin ribbon of apricot sauce flavoured with rum or with a fruit liqueur.

Banana croûtes à la maltaise (2)

Cut a large, day-old brioche into slices, and then cut the slices into rectangles a little longer and wider than the bananas. Arrange them on a baking sheet, sprinkle with sugar, and lightly glaze in a preheated oven at 220°C (425°F, gas 7). Meanwhile peel 6 bananas, cut them in half lengthways, and sprinkle lightly with lemon juice. Place the bananas on a buttered baking sheet and cook in the oven for 5 minutes. Arrange the bananas, alternating with slices of brioche, in a circle in an ovenproof dish. Fill the centre with a confectioner's custard (pastry cream) flavoured with orange zest. Sprinkle the whole dish with finely crushed macaroons and melted butter and brown in the oven. Before serving, decorate with candied orange peel.

Banana fritters

Peel some bananas and cut in half lengthways. Macerate for 1 hour in white or dark rum with sugar. Dip in batter and deep-fry in hot oil. Drain, dust with caster (superfine) sugar and arrange on a napkin.

Banana soufflé

Mix together in a saucepan 1 tablespoon sifted flour and a pinch of salt with 100 ml (4 fl oz, 7 tablespoons) milk, which has been boiled with 2 tablespoons caster (superfine) sugar and ½ vanilla pod (bean) and then cooled. Boil the mixture for 2 minutes, whisking all the time, then remove from the heat and add the pulp of 4 finely sieved bananas, 2 egg yolks and 20 g (¾ oz, 1½ tablespoons) butter. Flavour, if required, with kirsch or rum. Fold in 3 stiffly whisked egg whites. Pour the mixture into a 20 cm (8 in) buttered soufflé mould (or small ramekins) coated with caster sugar. Cook in a preheated oven at 200°C (400°F, gas 6) for 30 minutes for a large soufflé or about 12 minutes for ramekins.

Banana soufflés

Select some firm ripe bananas. Peel off a strip of skin from each and remove the flesh. Sprinkle the flesh with lemon juice, mash and mix with a very small amount of confectioner's custard (pastry cream). Fold in whisked egg whites to prepare a soufflé mixture. Fill the skins with the soufflé mixture. Smooth the surface. Bake in a preheated oven at about 200°C (400°F, gas 6) for 8–9 minutes. Serve immediately.

Bananas à la créole au gratin

Select firm bananas and peel off a wide strip of skin from each. Remove the flesh in one piece, without crushing and sprinkle with lemon juice. Blanch the skins for 2 minutes in boiling water, cool by dipping in cold water and pat dry. Slice the flesh and soak for 30 minutes in lemon juice, sugar and rum. Put a layer of cooked rice pudding mixed with finely chopped crystallized (candied) fruit into each skin. Arrange the banana slices vertically on top and cover with finely crushed macaroons. Coat with melted butter and place under a hot grill (broiler).

A rum-flavoured apricot sauce can be served with the bananas.

Bananas flambé

Peel some firm bananas and cook in butter or a vanilla-flavoured sugar syrup, without allowing them to become soft. Drain. Warm some rum, Calvados, Armagnac or Cognac and pour over the bananas. Set alight and serve.

Bananas in butter

Peel some just-ripe bananas and arrange in a buttered ovenproof dish. Pour some melted butter over and dust with sugar. Bake in a preheated oven at about 200°C (400°F, gas 6) for 15 minutes.

Bavarian cream

A Bavarian cream is a cold dessert made from egg custard, stiffened with gelatine, mixed with whipped cream and sometimes flavoured. Soak 15–20 g

(½–¾ oz, 2–3 envelopes) gelatine in 3 tablespoons cold water. Heat 600 ml (1 pint, 2½ cups) milk with a vanilla pod (bean). Work together 8 egg yolks, 100 g (4 oz, ½ cup) caster (superfine) sugar and a pinch of salt. When the mixture is smooth, strain in the milk, stir well, then add the gelatine and mix. Stir continuously over a gentle heat until the mixture coats the back of a spoon. The mixture must not boil. Pour into a bowl and allow to cool, then refrigerate until the custard is cold and just beginning to thicken.

Chill 350 ml (12 fl oz, 1½ cups) double (heavy) cream and 75 ml (3 fl oz, ⅓ cup) milk in the refrigerator. Then whip together. As soon as it begins to thicken, add 50 g (2 oz, ¼ cup) caster sugar. Fold the cream into the cooled mixture. Brush the inside of a Bavarian cream (or soufflé or savarin) mould with oil, preferably almond oil. Fill to the brim with the Bavarian cream mixture. Cover with lightly oiled paper and refrigerate until firmly set. To loosen the cream, dip the bottom of the mould in hot water, place a serving dish on top of the mould and quickly turn them over together.

- *coffee Bavarian cream:* add 2 tablespoons instant coffee to the milk instead of the vanilla pod.
- *chocolate Bavarian cream:* add 100 g (4 oz, 4 squares) melted plain (bittersweet) chocolate to the milk.
- *lemon or orange Bavarian cream:* add the juice of 2 lemons or oranges.
- *Bavarian cream liqueur:* add about 2 teaspoons liqueur or more depending on its particular strength of flavour.

Bavarian cream à la cévenole

Make a Bavarian cream mixture and add an equal volume of puréed marrons glacés flavoured with kirsch. Brush a round mould with sweet almond oil and heap the mixture into it. Set in the refrigerator, then turn out on to a serving dish. Decorate with piped Chantilly cream and halved marrons glacés.

Bavarian cream à la créole

Grease a mould with sweet almond oil and fill it with alternating layers of rum-flavoured and pineapple-flavoured basic Bavarian cream, separating the layers with finely chopped bananas soaked in rum. Place in the refrigerator for about 3 hours. Then turn it out on to a dish and decorate with Chantilly cream. Sprinkle with chopped pistachio nuts.

Bavarian cream à la normande

Line the base of a suitable mould with a thick layer of the basic Bavarian cream flavoured with Calvados. Leave to set. Prepare an apple purée and stir in sufficient dissolved gelatine to set it. Allow 15 g (½ oz, 2 envelopes) gelatine for 300 ml (½ pint, 1¼ cups) purée. Whip 150 ml (¼ pint, ⅔ cup) double (heavy) cream with 2 tablespoons icing (confectioner's) sugar until thick. Mix the whipped cream with the apple purée, spoon into the mould and top with a layer of the basic Bavarian cream.

Bavarian cream au parfait amour

Finely shred the zest of ½ a lemon and place in a bowl. Add 475 ml (16 fl oz, 2 cups) boiling milk, 6 cloves and 100 g (4 oz, ½ cup) caster (superfine) sugar, stir well, then leave to infuse for 1 hour. Strain the mixture and add 15–20 g (½–¾ oz, 2–3 envelopes) gelatine dissolved in 6 tablespoons hot water and sufficient cochineal or red food colouring to give a pink colour. Chill the bowl and as soon as the mixture begins to set, stir in 125 g (4½ oz, ½ cup) soft cream cheese. Turn into a dish and refrigerate until firmly set.

Bavarois aux fruits

Soak 25 g (1 oz, 4 envelopes) gelatine in 5 tablespoons cold water. Warm 500 ml (17 fl oz, 2 cups) heavy sugar syrup, add the gelatine and stir to dissolve. Cool slightly, then add the juice of 3 lemons and 500 ml (17 fl oz, 2 cups) thick fruit purée (apricot, pineapple, blackcurrant, strawberry, raspberry) and refrigerate until on the point of setting. Whip 450 ml (¾ pint, 2 cups) double (heavy) cream with 50 g (2 oz, ¼ cup) caster (superfine) sugar until softly thick and gently fold this into the half-set fruit jelly. Turn the mixture into an oiled mould and refrigerate until it is firmly set, then turn out. It may be served with a fruit sauce (preferably matching the fruit that is used in the cream).

Beauharnais bananas

Peel 6 bananas and arrange in a buttered ovenproof dish. Sprinkle with sugar and 4 tablespoons white rum. Bake in a preheated oven at 200°C (400°F, gas 6) for 5–8 minutes. Pour some double (heavy) cream over, sprinkle with crushed macaroons and a little melted butter, then glaze in a preheated oven at 240°C (475°F, gas 9). Serve in the baking dish.

Bilberry compote

Dissolve 500 g (18 oz, 2¼ cups) caster (superfine) sugar in 200 ml (7 fl oz, ¾ cup) water. Add a little grated lemon zest, and boil for 5 minutes. Clean 1 kg (2¼ lb, 5 cups) bilberries (huckleberries), add them to the syrup and boil for 8–10 minutes. Drain the bilberries using a slotted spoon and place them in a bowl. Reduce the syrup by one-third and pour it over the bilberries. Serve well chilled. When prepared by this method, the bilberries can be used to make a tart.

Biscuit pudding with crystallized fruits

Soak 125 g (4½ oz, ⅔ cup) currants in rum. In a saucepan, moisten 200 g (7 oz, 2½ cups) crumbled sponge finger biscuits (ladyfingers) with 600 ml

(1 pint, 2½ cups) boiling milk to which 150 g (5 oz, ⅔ cup) caster (superfine) sugar has been added. Work the mixture over the heat, then add 150 g (5 oz, ¾ cup) diced crystallized (candied) fruits, the rum-soaked currants, 3 egg yolks and 125 g (4½ oz, ½ cup) melted butter. Finally, fold in 3 egg whites whisked into very stiff peaks. Butter a smooth, round mould, sprinkle it with breadcrumbs, pour the mixture into it, and cook in a bain marie in a preheated oven at 200°C (400°F, gas 6) for 50–60 minutes. Serve with a pineapple or cherry sauce.

Blackcurrant charlotte (frozen)

To make the ice cream, beat 6 egg yolks and 200 g (7 oz, ¾ cup) sugar until white and fluffy. Add 60 ml (2 fl oz, ¼ cup) blackcurrant liqueur and, if available, some blackcurrants macerated in sugar. Add 6 tablespoons cold milk to 400 ml (14 fl oz, 1¾ cups) very thick, cold double (heavy) cream and whip until the cream stands in peaks. Mix the whipped cream with the blackcurrant mixture and pour into a container. Place in the freezer until it is slightly set.

Line the base and sides of a charlotte mould with sponge fingers (ladyfingers) dipped in blackcurrant syrup and cut to fit the mould. Fill the mould with alternate layers of blackcurrant ice cream and sponge fingers soaked in the syrup. Finish with a layer of fingers. Weight the top, then place in the freezer. Turn out the frozen charlotte just before serving. It can either be served with custard or decorated with Chantilly cream and blackcurrants cooked in a sugar syrup.

Bricelets vaudois (waffles)

Put 65 g (2½ oz, 5 tablespoons) butter and 100 g (4 oz, ½ cup) caster (superfine) sugar into a mixing bowl and beat into a foamy mixture. Add

1 egg plus 1 yolk, 250 ml (8 fl oz, 1 cup) crème fraîche, a pinch of salt and the grated zest of 1 lemon. Mix together, then add 200 g (7 oz, 1¾ cups) sifted plain (all-purpose) flour. Work together quickly to make a runny batter. Using a ladle or spoon, pour small quantities of the batter into a waffle iron. Close the iron and cook, then remove and serve hot, dusted with sugar or with butter and syrup.

Buttered apples

Core and peel some apples and place them for 2 minutes in boiling water with some lemon juice added to it (or squeeze the lemon juice over the apples). Drain, arrange in a buttered ovenproof dish, sprinkle with caster (superfine) sugar and moisten with a few drops of water. Cover and cook in a preheated oven at 220°C (425°F, gas 7) until tender. Place each apple on a round slice of bread fried in butter. Add a few tablespoons of sugar or golden (corn) syrup and some butter to the cooking juices, stir in until the butter has melted and pour over the apples.

Cabinet pudding

Prepare 600 ml (1 pint, 2½ cups) vanilla-flavoured egg custard. Cut 100 g (4 oz, ⅔ cup) crystallized (candied) fruits into a fine dice. Wash 100 g (4 oz, ⅔ cup) seedless raisins, then moisten them with 3 tablespoons rum. Pour another 3 tablespoons rum over 150 g (5 oz, 2 cups) sponge finger biscuits (ladyfingers) broken into pieces. Butter a charlotte mould and fill it with alternate layers of the sponge fingers, raisins and crystallized fruit. Pour the egg custard over the filling. Place in a bain marie and cook in a preheated oven at 220°C (425°F, gas 7) for about 45 minutes. Leave the pudding until lukewarm before turning it out on to a serving dish. Serve with a vanilla custard cream or an apricot sauce.

Caramel cream with honey

Make a caramel with 50 g (2 oz, 3 tablespoons) honey and 50 g (2 oz, ¼ cup) sugar and use to line the bottom and sides of a charlotte mould. Mix together 8 eggs and 350 g (12 oz, 1 cup) honey with a spatula. Pour 1 litre (1¾ pints, 4⅓ cups) boiling milk on to the egg and honey mixture, mix well and pour it into the mould. Cook in a bain marie in a preheated oven at 180°C (350°F, gas 4) for 1 hour.

Caribbean brioche

Hollow out a large brioche mousseline in the same way as for brioche with raspberries. Cut the brioche removed from the inside into cubes and brown these in butter. Reduce the syrup from a can of pineapple by three-quarters and flavour with rum. Cut the pineapple into large dice. Cut some firm ripe bananas into thin slices and heat these with the pineapple dice in butter; place the fruit in the reduced syrup. Add the cubes of brioche, mix together, and fill the brioche with the mixture. Replace the top and heat in the oven.

Charlotte à la Chantilly

Line the bottom and sides of a charlotte mould with 18–22 sponge fingers (ladyfingers). Prepare some Chantilly cream with 500 ml (17 fl oz, 2 cups) double (heavy) cream blended with about 3 tablespoons mixed crystallized (candied) fruits. Fill the mould with the mixture and refrigerate until ready to serve. Turn out on to a serving dish and decorate with crystallized fruits. The crystallized fruits may be replaced with strawberries or raspberries.

Charlotte à la valentin

Cook 1 kg (2¼ lb, 3 cups) raspberry jam (preserve) until it is almost caramelized. Cover a round sheet (the detachable bottom of a flan ring, for example) with a layer of sponge fingers (ladyfingers) and spread with a coating of jam; build up the cake with alternate layers of sponge fingers and jam. Trim the shape with a very sharp knife so that it forms a round cake. Pour the remaining jam over the top of the cake and spread it evenly over the whole surface with a metal spatula. Leave to cool thoroughly and then place the cake on a sheet of gold embossed paper.

Make a meringue with 4 egg whites and 250 g (9 oz, generous 1 cup) caster (superfine) sugar and decorate the cake with it. Sprinkle the meringue with 100 g (4 oz, 1 cup) flaked almonds then place the cake in a preheated oven at 230°C (450°F, gas 8) to colour it. Chill the cake in the refrigerator until ready to serve.

Charlotte majestic

Butter a charlotte mould. Decorate the bottom with crystallized (candied) fruits and then line the mould with sponge fingers (ladyfingers). Prepare a Bavarian cream of the desired flavour and pour into the mould. Cover with sponge fingers and place in the refrigerator. To turn out, quickly dip the mould in hot water.

Chartreuse crêpes

Prepare a sweet crêpe batter. Fifteen minutes before making the crêpes, prepare the filling. Beat 50 g (2 oz, ¼ cup) butter to a soft paste and add 50 g (2 oz, ¼ cup) caster (superfine) sugar, 3 crushed meringues and 3 tablespoons green Chartreuse. Add 6 crushed macaroons, the grated zest of 1 orange and 3 tablespoons Cognac to the batter and mix well. Thin the batter with 100 ml (4 fl oz, 7 tablespoons) water and cook the crêpes. Spread each one with the filling and fold in four. Dust with icing (confectioner's) sugar and serve very hot.

Cherries Condé

Stone (pit) the cherries and poach them in syrup. Fill an ovenproof dish with rice cooked in milk, smooth over the top and decorate with some of the drained cherries, candied angelica cut into diamond shapes, and shelled almonds. Purée the rest of the cherries and add enough of the syrup to obtain a very liquid sauce; reduce this sauce until it becomes syrupy. Reheat the decorated rice in the oven. Serve with the cherry sauce.

Cherries flambéed à la bourguignonne

Remove the stalks and stones (pits) from some cherries and cook them with sugar and water, using 350 g (12 oz, 1½ cups) sugar and 3 tablespoons water per 1 kg (2¼ lb) cherries. Cook gently for 8–10 minutes, then add 2–3 tablespoons redcurrant jelly and reduce for about 5 minutes. Pour into a flambé pan, sprinkle with Burgundy marc, heated in a small saucepan or a ladle, and flame the cherries just before serving.

Cherry compote

For each 1 kg (2¼ lb, 4½ cups) stoned (pitted) cherries, use 300 g (11 oz, 1½ cups) caster (superfine) sugar and 5 tablespoons water to make a sugar syrup. Cook until it has reached the 'large ball' stage. Add the cherries and cook with the lid on for 8 minutes over a low heat. Drain the cherries and place in a bowl. Mix 2 tablespoons kirsch with the syrup and pour over the cherries. Cool before serving.

Cherry compote (baked)

Stone (pit) the cherries, place them in a deep dish and sprinkle with caster (superfine) sugar to taste. Leave for 3–4 hours so the juice runs out, then cover and cook in a preheated oven at 180°C (350°F, gas 4) for about 20 minutes.

Cherry crêpes

Prepare a crêpe batter with 250 g (9 oz, 2¼ cups) plain (all-purpose) flour, 75 g (3 oz, 6 tablespoons) caster (superfine) sugar, a pinch of salt, 3 beaten eggs and 1 egg yolk, gradually adding 500 ml (17 fl oz, 2 cups) milk. Leave to stand for 2 hours at room temperature. Remove the stalks and stones (pits) from 400 g (14 oz, 1⅔ cups) fresh cherries or use 300 g (11 oz, 1¼ cups) cherries preserved in syrup. Cut them in two, mix them with the batter and allow to stand for 2 hours.

Cook the crêpes and keep them hot on a plate over a saucepan of boiling water. Coat each crêpe with a thin layer of orange marmalade – about 200 g (7 oz, ⅔ cup) is required. Roll up the crêpes and arrange them on an ovenproof dish. Sprinkle with caster sugar and glaze in the oven.

Cherry-filled soufflé fritters

Remove the stalks and stones (pits) from some cherries and cook them in syrup. Remove and drain the cherries and reduce the syrup until it coats a wooden spatula. Flavour it with kirsch. Return the cherries to the syrup and coat them thoroughly. Prepare some fritter batter; dip the cherries in the batter and fry. Arrange the fritters in a bowl or compote dish and dust them with icing (confectioner's) sugar.

Chestnut charlotte

Mix 200 g (7 oz, ⅔ cup) chestnut purée with 125 g (4½ oz, ⅓ cup) chestnut preserve and add 2 tablespoons pure malt whisky. Soak 15 g (½ oz, 2 envelopes) gelatine in sufficient cold water to swell, blend with 3 tablespoons double (heavy) cream and then add the chestnut mixture. Mix 150 ml (5 fl oz, ⅔ cup) double cream with 2 tablespoons vanilla sugar, beat well and add the chestnut mixture a little at a time.

Soak 18 sponge fingers (ladyfingers) in a mixture of 2 tablespoons whisky and an equal quantity of syrup and use them to line the bottom and sides of a charlotte mould. Pour the chestnut mixture into the mould and leave to set for at least 6 hours in the refrigerator.

Chestnut compote

Slit the shells of the chestnuts, plunge them into boiling water for 5 minutes and peel them while they are still hot. Make a vanilla-flavoured syrup using 350 g (12 oz, 1½ cups) granulated sugar to 600 ml (1 pint, 2½ cups) water. Cook the chestnuts in this syrup for about 45 minutes. Pour the chestnuts and syrup into a bowl, cool and refrigerate before serving.

Chestnut cream

Make some chestnut preserve (see basic recipes) and put into sundae dishes. Decorate with Chantilly cream piped through a fluted nozzle and top each with a crystallized (candied) violet. If the preserve is prepared especially for this cream, the amount of sugar used may be reduced by a quarter if desired.

Chestnut croquembouche

Take 60 choice roasted chestnuts, peel them carefully and remove any traces of burning. Glaze by dipping them in sugar cooked to the crack stage, one by one, and place them on a smooth round mould, 18 cm (7 in) in diameter and 13 cm (5 in) deep. Assemble the *croquembouche* at the last minute: the moisture in the chestnuts softens the sugar so it loses its consistency and gloss.

Chestnut croquettes

Dip some chestnuts in boiling water and peel them. Cook them in a light syrup – 500 g (18 oz, 2¼ cups) granulated sugar per 1 litre (1¾ pints,

4⅓ cups) water – flavoured with vanilla. Press the cooked chestnuts through a sieve to obtain a purée and thicken it with egg yolks and butter, allowing 5 egg yolks and 50 g (2 oz, 4 tablespoons) butter per 500 g (18 oz, 2¼ cups) chestnut purée. Spread the mixture onto a well-buttered baking sheet and leave to cool completely. When cooled, cut into rectangles of about 50 g (2 oz), cover with egg and breadcrumbs and deep-fry in oil heated to 180°C (356°F). Serve the croquettes very hot with a fruit sauce flavoured with Cognac or Armagnac.

Instead of fresh chestnuts, 500 g (18 oz, 4½ cups) sieved marrons glacés may be used, blended with 400 ml (14 fl oz, 1¾ cups) confectioner's custard (pastry cream) flavoured with rum, Cognac or Armagnac.

Chestnut soufflé

Place 300 g (11 oz) peeled chestnuts in a saucepan with 200 ml (7 fl oz, ¾ cup) milk, 1½ tablespoons sugar and a pinch of salt. Boil for 10 minutes with the lid on, then remove the lid and continue to boil for a further 5 minutes to allow the milk to evaporate. Set 4 whole chestnuts aside and rub the remainder through a sieve or put in a blender or food processor. Blend the purée with 400 ml (14 fl oz, 1¾ cups) double (heavy) cream and place in a bain marie of very hot water.

Butter a 20 cm (8 in) soufflé mould and coat with flour. Whisk 5 egg whites until stiff, together with a pinch of salt. Return the chestnut purée to the heat and, when it is just boiling, remove from the heat and mix in 3 egg yolks. Stir thoroughly. Add one quarter of the stiffly whisked egg whites and mix thoroughly. Crumble 2 of the reserved chestnuts and add them. Carefully fold in the remaining egg whites using a metal spoon. Pour this mixture into the prepared mould and smooth the surface with the spoon. Sprinkle with the 2 remaining chestnuts cut into 12 pieces. Place in a preheated oven at 180°C

(350°F, gas 4). Turn off the oven and leave it to cook for 15–20 minutes without opening the door. Serve immediately with a tangerine sorbet.

Chestnut soufflé Mont-Bry

Boil 100 ml (4 fl oz, 7 tablespoons) milk with 40 g (1½ oz, 3 tablespoons) caster (superfine) sugar and a pinch of salt. Blend 25 g (1 oz, ¼ cup) plain (all-purpose) flour with a small quantity of cold milk in a pan. Add the sweetened milk and cook for 2–3 minutes, stirring constantly. Remove from the heat and blend in 4 egg yolks and 15 g (½ oz, 1 tablespoon) butter, followed by 4 tablespoons sweetened vanilla-flavoured chestnut purée and a few pieces of marron glacé. Whisk 5 egg whites until very stiff and fold carefully into the mixture. Put the mixture into a buttered soufflé dish and bake in a preheated oven at 200°C (400°F, gas 6) for 35 minutes.

Chocolate and strawberry mousse

Melt 500 g (18 oz) plain (dark) chocolate. Separate the whites from the yolks of 8 eggs. Add the yolks, one by one, to the cooled melted chocolate and then blend in 6 tablespoons double (heavy) cream. Place in the refrigerator. Very lightly cook 200 g (7 oz, 1½ cups) strawberries in 6 tablespoons sugar syrup. Drain and leave to cool. Stiffly whisk the egg whites with a pinch of salt. Fold them carefully into the chocolate cream. Serve the mousse in individual moulds, topped with a few strawberries.

Chocolate charlotte

Break 250 g (9 oz, 9 squares) bitter (semisweet) chocolate into pieces and melt them very gently in a bain marie to obtain a smooth paste. Remove from the heat and add 4 egg yolks one by one, mixing well. Then add 2 tablespoons double (heavy) cream. Beat 6 egg whites into very stiff peaks and add 150 g

(5 oz, ⅔ cup) caster (superfine) sugar. Blend the chocolate carefully into this mixture. Line a charlotte mould with sponge fingers (ladyfingers) – 300 g (11 oz) are required. Fill with the chocolate mixture. Place in the refrigerator for at least 4 hours. Turn out the charlotte and serve it with custard cream.

Chocolate custard

Melt 100 g (4 oz, 4 squares) cooking (unsweetened) chocolate in a bain marie with 1 tablespoon milk; when the mixture is quite smooth, add 500 ml (17 fl oz, 2 cups) milk, bring to the boil, then remove from the heat. Whisk 6 eggs with 100 g (4 oz, ½ cup) caster (superfine) sugar until pale and thick. Gradually add the chocolate-flavoured milk, whisking it all the time. Strain the custard into 6 ramekins and cook in a bain marie in a preheated oven at 190°C (375°F, gas 5) for 25–30 minutes. Take the moulds out of the bain marie, leave to cool and chill well.

Chocolate marquise

Chocolate marquise is a glazed dessert halfway between a mousse and a parfait, based on chocolate, fine butter, eggs and sugar and chilled in a mould.

Break 250 g (9 oz, 9 squares) plain (dark) chocolate into small pieces and melt it gently in a covered bain marie. Separate the yolks and whites of 5 eggs. Add 100 g (4 oz, ½ cup) granulated sugar to the yolks, beating the mixture until it becomes light and fluffy. Then add the melted chocolate and 175 g (6 oz, ¾ cup) melted butter and mix well. Whisk the egg whites with a little salt until very stiff, and carefully fold them into the chocolate mixture. Cool a deep sandwich tin (layer cake pan) or charlotte mould under running water and pour the mixture into it, smoothing it down well.

Chill for 12 hours in the refrigerator before removing from the mould. Serve with vanilla flavoured custard cream or Chantilly cream.

Chocolate mousse

Melt 150 g (5 oz, 5 squares) plain (dark) chocolate in a bain marie, remove from the heat and add 75 g (3 oz, 6 tablespoons) butter. When the mixture is very smooth, quickly blend in 2 large egg yolks. Whisk 3 egg whites with a pinch of salt until very stiff, then whisk in 25 g (1 oz, 2 tablespoons) caster (superfine) sugar and 1 teaspoon vanilla-flavoured sugar. Carefully mix the chocolate preparation with the whisked egg whites, using a wooden spatula. Pour into a dish and chill for at least 12 hours.

Chocolate pudding

Soften 150 g (5 oz, ⅔ cup) butter at room temperature and 125 g (4½ oz, 4½ squares) plain (dark) dessert chocolate in a bowl over a pan of simmering water. Work the butter with a wooden spoon in a warm mixing bowl, then beat in 75 g (3 oz, 6 tablespoons) caster (superfine) sugar and 1 tablespoon vanilla-flavoured sugar. When the mixture is white and creamy, add 8 egg yolks, one after the other.

Mix the softened chocolate with 1 tablespoon flour and 1 tablespoon potato flour, then blend it with the mixture. Finally, add 5 stiffly whisked egg whites. Pour into a buttered and floured charlotte mould, place in a bain marie, and cook in a preheated moderate oven at 200°C (400°F, gas 6) for about 50 minutes until firm. Turn out the pudding while still lukewarm and coat with vanilla- or coffee-flavoured custard cream.

Chocolate soufflé

Over a low heat, dissolve 75 g (3 oz, 3 squares) dark (semisweet) chocolate in 1 tablespoon milk taken from a 250 ml (8 fl oz, 1 cup). Then add the remainder of the milk. Sweeten with 75 g (3 oz, ⅓ cup) caster (superfine) sugar and heat until both sugar and chocolate have dissolved and melted. Beat 2 egg yolks with 2 tablespoons caster sugar until the mixture turns thick and white, then incorporate 25 g (1 oz, ¼ cup) plain (all-purpose) flour in a trickle. Gradually pour the boiling chocololate-flavoured milk into the mixture, beating briskly. Pour the mixture into a saucepan and bring to the boil, stirring all the time. Once it has boiled, transfer the mixture to a large bowl and allow to cool.

Butter a 20 cm (8 in) soufflé mould and sprinkle it with 2 tablespoons caster sugar. Whisk 6 egg whites until they are stiff. Incorporate a further 2 egg yolks into the chocololate preparation, then carefully fold in the whites using a metal spoon. Pour the mixture into the mould and cook in a preheated oven at 190°C (375°F, gas 5) for 20 minutes. Then sprinkle the soufflé with icing (confectioner's) sugar and return to the oven for 5 minutes to glaze the surface. Serve immediately.

Christmas pudding

Finely chop 500 g (18 oz, 3½ cups) suet. Wash and dry 500 g (18 oz, 3 cups) seedless raisins, the same amount of sultanas (golden raisins), and 250 g (9 oz, 1½ cups) currants. Finely chop 250 g (9 oz, 1½ cups) candied peel or 125 g (4½ oz, ¾ cup) orange peel and 125 g (4½ oz, ½ cup) glacé (candied) cherries, 125 g (4½ oz, 1 cup) blanched almonds and the zest of 2 lemons. Mix all the ingredients together with 500 g (18 oz, 9 cups) fresh breadcrumbs, 125 g (4½ oz, 1 cup) plain (all-purpose) flour, 1 tablespoon mixed spice, the same amount of cinnamon, half a nutmeg (grated) and a pinch of salt. Add 300 ml (½ pint, 1¼ cups) milk and, one by one, 7 or 8 beaten eggs. Next, add 300 ml (½ pint, 1¼ cups) rum (or brandy) and the juice of 2 lemons. Mix everything together thoroughly to obtain a smooth paste.

Wrap the mixture in floured cloths, shaping the portions into balls, or spoon into a greased pudding basin (heatproof mould). Steam or boil.

Keep the pudding in its cloth or basin for at least 3 weeks, in a cool place. Before serving, steam the pudding for 2 hours, then turn it out, sprinkle it with rum or brandy and serve it flambéed, decorated with a sprig of holly.

Clafoutis

A dessert from the Limousin region of France, clafoutis consists of black cherries arranged in a buttered dish, covered with fairly thick batter and baked. It is served lukewarm, dusted with sugar. As a rule, the cherries are not stoned (pitted) but simply washed and stalked (stemmed), since the kernels add their flavour to the batter during cooking.

Remove the stalks from 500 g (18 oz) washed black cherries, dust them with 50 g (2 oz, ¼ cup) caster (superfine) sugar and leave for at least 30 minutes. Butter a baking tin (pan) and fill it with the cherries. Put 125 g (4½ oz, 1 cup) plain (all-purpose) flour in a mixing bowl and add a pinch of salt, 50 g (2 oz, ¼ cup) caster sugar and 3 well-beaten eggs; mix well; then add 300 ml (½ pint, 1¼ cups) milk and mix thoroughly again. Pour the mixture over the cherries and bake in a preheated oven at 180°C (350°F, gas 4) for 35–40 minutes. When it is lukewarm dust with icing (confectioner's) sugar.

Coffee dacquoise

Dacquoise is a traditional gâteau from south-western France, also called *Palois* (the Dacquois are the inhabitants of Dax, the Palois those of Pau). It consists of two or three layers of meringue mixed with almonds (or almonds and hazelnuts).

Whisk 8 egg whites with a pinch of salt until they form stiff peaks. Then gradually add 200 g (7 oz, 1 cup) caster (superfine) sugar and 2 teaspoons vanilla sugar, whisking continuously, and continue whisking until the meringue is firm and shiny. Gently fold in 150 g (5 oz, 1¼ cups) ground almonds and 75 g (3 oz, ¾ cup) chopped blanched hazelnuts. Butter three 20 cm (8 in) flan (pie) rings, place them on buttered baking sheets and divide the mixture between them. Cook in a preheated oven at 180°C (350°F, gas 4) for about 20 minutes. When the meringue rounds are cooked, turn them out and allow to cool.

Prepare a coffee *crème au beurre* for the filling using 250 g (9 oz, 1 cup) sugar cooked with 100 ml (4 fl oz, 7 tablespoons) water, 8 egg yolks, 250 g (9 oz, 1 cup) butter and 1 tablespoon coffee essence (extract). Toast 100 g (4 oz, 1 cup) flaked almonds. Place the coffee cream in a piping (pastry) bag fitted with a fluted nozzle and sandwich the meringue rounds with thick layers of piped cream. Sprinkle the top with toasted almonds and dust with icing (confectioner's) sugar.

Coffee soufflé

Over a low heat, dissolve 2 tablespoons instant coffee in 1 tablespoon milk taken from a 250 ml (8 fl oz, 1 cup). Then add the remainder of the milk and bring to the boil. Beat 2 egg yolks with 2 tablespoons caster (superfine) sugar until the mixture turns thick and white, then incorporate 25 g (1 oz, ¼ cup) plain (all-purpose) flour in a trickle. Gradually pour the boiling coffee-flavoured milk into the mixture, beating briskly. Pour the mixture into a saucepan and bring to the boil, stirring all the time. Once it has boiled, transfer it to a large bowl and allow to cool. Butter a 20 cm (8 in) soufflé mould and sprinkle it with 2 tablespoons caster sugar. Whisk 6 egg whites until they are stiff. Incorporate a further 2 egg yolks into the coffee preparation, then carefully fold in the whites using a metal spoon. Pour the mixture into the mould and cook in a preheated oven at 190°C (375°F, gas 5) for 20 minutes. Then sprinkle the soufflé with icing (confectioner's) sugar and return to the oven for 5 minutes to glaze the surface. Serve immediately.

Compote du vieux vigneron

Peel 1 kg (2¼ lb) fairly sour apples. Cut them into quarters, remove the pips (seeds) and place them in a heavy based saucepan together with 150 g (5 oz, ⅔ cup) sugar. Cover and stew the apples over a very gentle heat until they disintegrate. Prepare a syrup with 575 g (1¼ lb, 2½ cups) granulated sugar and 750 ml (1¼ pints, 3¼ pints) red wine. Peel 800 g (1¾ lb) pears and an equal quantity of peaches. Cut the pears into quarters and remove the pips. Cut the peaches in half and stone (pit) them. Add the peaches and pears to the boiling syrup together with 2 or 3 cloves and ½ teaspoon powdered cinnamon. Cook for 15–18 minutes.

Add 50 g (2 oz, ¼ cup) butter to the hot apples, mix well and pour into a bowl. When the peaches and pears are cooked, drain them and arrange them on top of the stewed apples. Add 250 g (9 oz) grapes to the boiling syrup, leave for 3 minutes and then drain. Use them to decorate the other fruit. Remove the cloves from the syrup and reduce it until it thickens. Pour it over the compote and allow it to cool completely.

If no grapes are available, soak some raisins in a little weak tea. When they have swollen, use as for fresh grapes.

Compote of prunes

Soak the prunes in tepid weak tea to soften for at least 2 hours. When they are swollen, drain them, stone (pit) them and put in a saucepan. Just cover the fruit with cold water (or red or white wine) and stir in some sugar to taste – a maximum of 100 g (4 oz, ½ cup) per 500 g (18 oz, 4 cups) prunes – 2 tablespoons lemon juice and 1 teaspoon vanilla-flavoured sugar. Bring to the boil, then cook gently for about 40 minutes. Serve lukewarm or cold. When well-reduced and strained, this compote may also be used to fill puff-pastry cases, turnovers or tartlets.

The prunes may be left unstoned (unpitted) and the quantity of water or wine can be increased; the prunes are then served with all their juice.

Cranberry compote

Combine 500 g (18 oz, 2¼ cups) caster (superfine) sugar, the grated zest of ½ a lemon and 200 ml (7 fl oz, ¾ cup) water in a saucepan; slowly bring to the boil, then boil for 5 minutes. Add 1 kg (2¼ lb) washed and stalked cranberries and cook over a high heat for 10 minutes. Remove the fruit from the liquid with a perforated spoon and place in a fruit dish. Reduce the syrup by one-third if the compote is to be eaten straight away, or by half if it is to be kept for a few days in the refrigerator. Pour the syrup over the fruit and allow to cool for 1 hour. Serve with vanilla-flavoured meringues.

Crème brûlée

Slit open a vanilla pod (bean) lengthways and remove all the little seeds using a knife. Place them in a bowl with 3 egg yolks and 50 g (2 oz, ¼ cup) caster (superfine) sugar and mix well with a whisk. Gradually whisk in 300 ml (½ pint, 1¼ cups) single (light) or double (heavy) cream and 60 ml (2 fl oz, ¼ cup) milk. Strain through a chinois. Pour this mixture into small ramekins and place in a bain marie. Cook for 30 minutes in a preheated oven at 190°C (375°F, gas 5). Allow to cool and place in the refrigerator for at least 1 hour.

Sprinkle 100 g (4 oz, ⅔ cup) soft brown sugar on top to cover the custards completely. Place under a very hot grill (broiler) until the sugar has caramelized. Refrigerate before serving.

Crème caramel

Boil 500 ml (17 fl oz, 2 cups) milk with a vanilla pod (bean) split in two. In a mixing bowl, blend 2 whole eggs, 4 egg yolks and 125 g (4½ oz, ½ cup) caster (superfine) sugar; gradually add the boiling milk (having removed the vanilla pod), whisking it quickly. Pour the resulting custard into a caramel-coated mould, place the mould in a bain marie and cook in a preheated oven at 190°C (375°F, gas 5) for about 40 minutes or until the custard is lightly set. Then take the mould out of the bain marie and allow it to cool completely. Turn out on to a dish and cool before serving.

Crêpes à la cévenole

Prepare some sweet crêpes and coat each one with a thin layer of rum-flavoured chestnut cream. Roll up the crêpes and arrange them in a buttered ovenproof dish. Dust generously with caster (superfine) sugar and grill (broil) to caramelize the sugar. Serve with Chantilly cream if desired.

Crêpes à la condé

Prepare a crêpe batter with 250 g (9 oz, 2¼ cups) plain (all-purpose) flour, 3 eggs, 500 ml (17 fl oz, 2 cups) milk, 2 teaspoons dried yeast and 2 tablespoons oil. Let it stand for 2 hours at room temperature. Soak 50 g (2 oz, ⅓ cup) chopped crystallized (candied) fruits in 100 ml (4 fl oz, 7 tablespoons) rum.

Boil 2 litres (3½ pints, 9 cups) water in a saucepan, add 100 g (4 oz, ⅔ cup) short-grain rice, boil for a few seconds and then rinse in cold water. Set aside to drain. Boil 400 ml (14 fl oz, 1¾ cups) milk with a vanilla pod (bean). Remove the pod and add to the milk 75 g (3 oz, 6 tablespoons) caster (superfine) sugar, 25 g (1 oz, 2 tablespoons) butter, a generous pinch of salt and the rice. Bring to the boil, stir and pour into an ovenproof dish. Cover with foil and cook in a preheated oven at 200°C (400°F, gas 6) for 20 minutes.

Cook the crêpes and keep them hot on a plate over a saucepan of boiling water. Remove the rice from the oven, stir and allow it to cool for 5 minutes. Add 3 egg yolks one by one, followed by the crystallized fruits and the rum.

Mix well. Fill the crêpes with the rice mixture, roll them up and arrange them in an ovenproof dish. Sprinkle them with caster sugar and brown lightly for a few minutes in a preheated oven at 230°C (450°F, gas 8).

Crêpes à la frangipane

Make some crêpes and prepare some frangipane cream, using 500 ml (17 fl oz, 2 cups) milk for the cream and an equal quantity for the crêpe batter. Coat the crêpes with the cream and fold into four. Arrange in a buttered ovenproof dish, dust with icing (confectioner's) sugar and lightly caramelize in a very hot oven or under the grill (broiler). Serve very hot.

Crêpes à la russe

Heat 600 ml (1 pint, 2½ cups) milk until lukewarm. Mix a little of the milk with 15 g (2 oz) fresh yeast or 7 g (¼ oz) dried yeast and add to the remaining milk together with 20 g (¾ oz, 1½ tablespoons) caster (superfine) sugar, 200 ml (7 fl oz, ¾ cup) single (light) cream and a large pinch of salt. Blend 400 g (14 oz, 3½ cups) plain (all-purpose) flour with the milk mixture in a deep bowl. Allow the mixture to rise in a warm place for 1 hour. Whisk 2 egg whites into stiff peaks and blend them carefully with the batter using a metal spoon. Cook the crêpes (which swell as they start to brown). Roll them up when they are cooked, arrange them on a warmed serving dish and sprinkle them generously with fine caster sugar. Serve them hot.

Crêpes mylène

Prepare a crêpe batter by mixing 200 g (7 oz, 1¾ cups) plain (all-purpose) flour, 2 whole eggs, 200 ml (7 fl oz, ¾ cup) beer, 2 tablespoons oil, a pinch of salt, the grated zest of 1 lemon and about 200 ml (7 fl oz, ¾ cup) water to thin the batter. Leave to stand for 1 hour at room temperature.

Twenty minutes before cooking the crêpes, make a sauce: put a large knob of butter in a frying pan with 200 g (7 oz, ¾ cup) caster (superfine) sugar, the juice of 2 oranges and 1 lemon, and a small glass of Cognac. Cook over a gentle heat, stirring continuously to obtain a smooth sauce. Keep it warm. Cut 3 peeled pears into fine slices, cook them for a few minutes in boiling syrup and drain them. Toast 100 g (4 oz, 1 cup) flaked (slivered) almonds in a preheated oven at 230°C (450°F, gas 8), stirring them from time to time.

Cook the crêpes and keep them hot on a plate over a saucepan of boiling water. Fill each crêpe with some slices of pear, roll them up and place them in the frying pan with the sauce. Heat for 2 minutes, then pour over a small glass of mirabelle plum brandy and flame over a brisk heat, gently shaking the frying pan. Arrange the crêpes in a warmed serving dish and serve sprinkled with the toasted almonds.

Crêpes normandes

Prepare a crêpe batter with 250 g (9 oz, 2¼ cups) plain (all-purpose) flour, 3 eggs, 300 ml (½ pint, 1¼ cups) milk, 200 ml (7 fl oz, ¾ cup) water, a pinch of salt, 1 tablespoon single (light) cream, 2 tablespoons Calvados and 1 tablespoon melted butter. Leave to stand for 2 hours at room temperature. Peel and slice 2 dessert (eating) apples and toss them in 40 g (1½ oz, 3 tablespoons) butter in a frying pan until they brown lightly. (The apples may be soaked in a little Calvados before they are cooked.) Cool and add them to the crêpe batter. Make the crêpes and pile them up on a serving dish. Sprinkle with caster (superfine) sugar and serve very hot with fresh cream.

Crêpes Suzette

Prepare a crêpe batter with 250 g (9 oz, 2¼ cups) plain (all-purpose) flour, 3 whole eggs, 250 ml (8 fl oz, 1 cup) milk and a pinch of salt. Add the juice of

1 tangerine, 1 tablespoon Curaçao and 2 tablespoons olive oil. Leave to stand for 2 hours at room temperature. Work 50 g (2 oz, ¼ cup) butter with the juice and grated zest of 1 tangerine, 1 tablespoon Curaçao and 4 tablespoons caster (superfine) sugar.

Make some thin crêpes in a heavy-based frying pan (never washed, but wiped each time with clean paper towels). Coat them with a little of the tangerine butter, fold them in four, return them one by one to the frying pan and heat them through. Arrange them in a warmed dish, so that they overlap slightly, to serve.

Crown of croûtes à la Montmorency

Cut stale brioches into slices 1 cm (½ in) thick. Arrange these slices on a baking sheet, dust them with sugar and glaze them in a preheated oven at 230°C (450°F, gas 8). Cover each slice with a thin layer of frangipane cream flavoured with cherry brandy, then arrange them in a crown on a round dish, placing them very close to one another. Fill the centre of this crown with a dome of stoned (pitted) cherries, cooked in a vanilla-flavoured syrup and drained well. Decorate the border of the crown with more cherries. If liked, coat with redcurrant sauce laced with cherry brandy and serve more of this sauce separately.

Crown of croûtes with pears

Cut a brioche or a stale savarin into 4 slices, dust with sugar and glaze in a preheated oven at 230°C (450°F, gas 8). Peel and core 3 apples and 2 pears and cut into thin slices. Put them in a saucepan with the juice of ½ a lemon, 500 ml (17 fl oz, 2 cups) red wine, 150 g (5 oz, ⅔ cup) caster (superfine) sugar, 1 clove and a large pinch of cinnamon. Cook quickly for 15 minutes, then drain the fruits.

Peel 4 pears, leaving them whole, and place them, stalks upwards, in the saucepan containing the cooking syrup. Add some water so that the liquid comes halfway up the fruit. Bring to the boil, then simmer gently for 12 minutes. Remove the clove and leave to cool.

Arrange the croûtes in a crown on a large round dish. Fill the centre with the thin slices of apple and pear, and place the whole pears on top of the croûtes. Warm in a preheated oven at 220°C (425°F, gas 7) and serve with Chantilly cream.

Crown of peaches with Chantilly cream

Prepare an egg or caramel custard or a Bavarian cream in a 1 litre (1¾ pint, 4⅓ cup) ring mould. Bring a mixture of 1 litre (1¾ pint, 4⅓ cup) water and 575 g (1¼ lb, 2½ cups) granulated sugar to the boil, add a vanilla pod (bean) and simmer gently for 5 minutes. Plunge 6 ripe peaches into boiling water for 30 seconds. Drain, peel and remove the stones (pits). Poach the fruit gently in the sugar syrup for 15 minutes, then drain thoroughly.

Unmould the custard (or Bavarian cream) on to a round dish. Arrange the peaches in the centre of the ring and chill. Whip 300 ml (½ pint, 1¼ cups) double (heavy) cream with 100 ml (4 fl oz, 7 tablespoons) very cold milk, 65 g (2½ oz, ⅓ cup) caster (superfine) sugar and 1 teaspoon vanilla sugar. Pipe this whipped cream in a dome over the peaches, using a piping (pastry) bag fitted with a star (fluted) nozzle.

Decorate with glacé (candied) cherries and pieces of angelica.

Curaçao soufflé

Whisk 250 g (9 oz, 1 cup) granulated sugar with 8 egg yolks until the mixture turns pale and thick. Incorporate 100 ml (4 fl oz, 7 tablespoons) Curaçao (or another liqueur), then fold in the whites of 12 eggs very stiffly whisked with a pinch of salt. Pour the mixture into a large buttered soufflé mould coated with sugar, place in a preheated oven at 200°C (400°F, gas 6) and bake for 15 minutes. Sprinkle icing (confectioner's) sugar over the top and return to the oven for 5–6 minutes to glaze the surface. Serve immediately.

Dauphine (or Viennese) fritters

Sift 500 g (1 lb 2 oz, 4½ cups) plain (all-purpose) flour. Set aside three-quarters of the flour, place the remaining quarter in a bowl and make a well in the centre. Put 20 g (⅔ oz) fresh yeast (1½ cakes compressed yeast) in the well and stir with a little warm milk or water. Then add enough warm water so that the mixture can be kneaded into a softish dough. Shape the dough into a ball, make a cross in the top with a knife, cover and leave in a warm place.

Make a well in the remaining flour on the table. Put 4 eggs and 2 tablespoons warm water in the centre of the well and work together to form a dough, pounding it several times. Dissolve 25 g (1 oz, 2 tablespoons) sugar and 15 g (½ oz) salt in a very small quantity of water and add to the dough. Soften 200 g (7 oz, 1 cup) butter and work this into the dough. Then add 2 eggs, one at a time, working the dough continuously. Pound several times, then flatten out on the table and put the yeasted dough in the centre. Mix both doughs together, kneading well. Put in a bowl, cover with a cloth and leave in a warm place to rise for 5–6 hours. Knead the dough again and leave, covered, in a cool place until required.

Divide the dough in half and roll each piece out to a thickness of 5 mm (¼ in). On one half, arrange at regular intervals small blobs of apricot jam (preserve), not more than 4 cm (1½ in) in diameter. Moisten the dough around each blob of jam with water and cover with the other piece of dough. Press down well between the jam to stick the dough together and cut with a plain 5 cm (2 in) diameter pastry (cookie) cutter.

Spread a cloth on a plate. Dust with flour and arrange the fritters on the cloth. Allow to rise for 30 minutes and then deep-fry the fritters in oil at 180°C (350°F). When they have puffed and are light golden on one side, turn and cook the other side. Drain the fritters. Arrange on a napkin and dust with icing (confectioner's) sugar.

Délicieux surprise

Gently melt 125 g (4½ oz, 4½ squares) dark chocolate in a bowl over hot water. Add 1 tablespoon single (light) cream, 20 g (¾ oz, 1½ tablespoons) butter, 1 tablespoon milk and the grated zest of an orange. Keep the sauce hot over the hot water. Cut a large brioche mousseline into 6 thick slices, put them in a dish and sprinkle with 100 ml (4 fl oz, 7 tablespoons) rum. Peel 3 pears, remove the seeds, slice and place on the brioche slices. Whip 150 ml (¼ pint, ⅔ cup) double (heavy) cream with 1 tablespoon very cold milk and slowly add 50 g (2 oz, ¼ cup) caster (superfine) sugar. Cover the brioche and pears with a dome of the whipped cream and pour over the hot chocolate sauce. Serve immediately.

Diplomat pudding

Make a syrup with 100 ml (4 fl oz, 7 tablespoons) water and 100 g (4 oz, ½ cup) caster (superfine) sugar. Bring to the boil and add 50 g (2 oz, ⅓ cup) sultanas (golden raisins). Leave for a few minutes, drain and reserve the syrup. Dice 50 g (2 oz, ⅓ cup) crystallized (candied) fruits and soak in 3 tablespoons rum.

Make a Bavarian cream: soak 15 g (½ oz, 1 tablespoon) gelatine in 3 tablespoons cold water. Boil 500 ml (17 fl oz, 2 cups) milk with half a vanilla pod (bean). Beat 4 large egg yolks with 125 g (4½ oz, ½ cup) caster sugar until the mixture is light and creamy, then add the boiling milk a little at a time, stirring with a wooden spatula. Pour the mixture into a saucepan and cook over a low heat, stirring continuously, until the custard cream is just thick enough to coat the spoon. Stir the gelatine into the custard cream, then press through a sieve. Leave to cool. Whip 200 ml (7 fl oz, ¾ cup) double (heavy) cream until stiff with 1 tablespoon very cold milk and fold into the cold custard.

Strain the rum from the crystallized fruit and add it to the reserved syrup. Use the rum-flavoured syrup to soak 200 g (7 oz) sponge fingers (ladyfingers). Put some of the crystallized fruit in the bottom of a greased mould, cover with a layer of the Bavarian cream, and then with a layer of sponge fingers sprinkled with sultanas and crystallized fruit. Coat with a little apricot jam (preserve). Continue to fill the mould with layers of Bavarian cream, sponge fingers, sultanas, crystallized fruits and apricot jam. Chill for at least 2 hours.

Heat some apricot jam until melted and add to it 3 tablespoons rum. Unmould the diplomat pudding on to a dish and coat it with the apricot sauce or, if preferred, with a little thin custard.

Diplomat pudding (baked)

Coarsely chop 100 g (4 oz) crystallized (candied) fruits. Put in a bowl with 75 g (3 oz, ½ cup) raisins and add 100 ml (4 fl oz, 7 tablespoons) rum. Leave to macerate for 1 hour. Slice a loaf of brioche. Remove the crusts, butter and lightly toast the slices until golden. Butter a 1.5 litre (2¾ pint, 6½ cups) charlotte mould and sprinkle with icing (confectioner's) sugar. Line the bottom with brioche slices and cover with a layer of the drained macerated fruit, reserving the rum. Fill the mould in this way with alternate layers of bread and fruit.

Beat 200 g (7 oz, 1 cup) caster (superfine) sugar, 100 ml (4 fl oz, 7 tablespoons) milk and 1 teaspoon vanilla sugar with 6 eggs and the rum in which the fruit was macerated. Gradually pour this mixture into the mould, allowing the brioche to soak up the liquid. Cook for 1 hour in a bain marie in a pre-heated oven at 150°C (300°F, gas 2), making sure the liquid in the bain marie does not come to the boil. Allow to cool completely. Remove from the mould and serve with crystallized fruit.

Diplomat pudding with prunes

Place 200 g (7 oz, 1¼ cups) dried prunes in a small bowl and add just enough weak tea to cover them. Cover and leave to soak for 24 hours. Place the tea and the prunes in a saucepan, add 4 tablespoons caster (superfine) sugar, bring to the boil and cook gently for 15 minutes. Put 2 egg yolks in another saucepan together with 3 tablespoons caster sugar, 1 tablespoon vanilla sugar and 1 tablespoon cornflour (cornstarch). Slowly add 250 ml (8 fl oz, 1 cup) cold milk and stir over a low heat until the mixture boils and the custard thickens. Set aside to cool.

Drain and stone (pit) the prunes, reserve the cooking liquid and add to it 1 liqueur glass of rum or kirsch. Soak 28 sponge fingers (ladyfingers) in this syrup. Cover the bottom of a greased charlotte mould with some of the soaked sponge fingers, ensuring that the rounded surface of each finger is in contact with the mould. Place successive layers of custard cream, prunes and sponge fingers in the mould, finishing with sponge fingers. Chill thoroughly and turn the pudding out just before serving. Serve with a thin rum- or kirsch-flavoured custard cream.

Elderflower fritters with honey

Put 250 g (9 oz, 2¼ cups) plain (all-purpose) flour into a mixing bowl. Make a well in the centre and add 1 teaspoon salt, 4 teaspoons sugar and 4 egg yolks. Very gently incorporate 325 ml (11 fl oz, 1⅓ cups) light beer to make a smooth dough, but without working it. Allow to rest for 1 hour in a cool place. Heat oil in a deep-fryer to 180°C (350°F). Whisk 4 egg whites until stiff and fold into the mixture very carefully. Dip the flowers of 24 racemes or heads of elderflower into the mixture, holding them by the stem. Turn them between the fingers to remove excess dough and fry them head downwards. Drain on paper towels. Sprinkle the fritters with icing (confectioner's) sugar and pour a little acacia honey over them. Serve hot.

English almond pudding

Cream together 125 g (4½ oz, ½ cup) softened butter and 150 g (5 oz, ⅔ cup) caster (superfine) sugar in a basin. Add 250 g (9 oz, 2 cups) almonds, blanched and finely chopped, a pinch of salt, 1 tablespoon orange-flower water, 2 whole eggs and 2 yolks, and 4 tablespoons double (heavy) cream. Work the mixture well, then pour it into a buttered soufflé dish and cook in a preheated oven at 200°C (400°F, gas 6) for at least 45 minutes. Serve straight from the dish.

English apple pudding

Mix together the following ingredients: 400 g (14 oz, 3½ cups) self-raising flour, 225 g (8 oz, 1½ cups) finely chopped beef suet, 2 tablespoons caster (superfine) sugar, a little salt and 100 ml (4 fl oz, 7 teaspoons) water. Knead thoroughly, then roll out the dough to a thickness of 8 mm (⅜ in).

Butter a 1 litre (1¾ pint, 4⅓ cup) pudding basin (mould) and line it with half of the dough. Fill with finely sliced apples, sweetened with caster sugar and flavoured with the grated zest of 1 lemon and some ground cinnamon. Cover with the remaining dough and press the edges together firmly. Wrap the basin in a cloth and tie it up firmly at the top. Place the pudding on an old saucer in a saucepan with enough boiling water to come halfway up the sides of the basin. Cover and cook for about 2 hours over a gentle heat, topping up with boiling water as necessary. This pudding can be prepared with pears in the same way.

Exotic fruit salad with lime

Peel a very ripe pineapple and dice the flesh. Peel and stone (pit) 3 mangoes and cut the flesh into strips. Peel 3 bananas, slice them and roll (but do not soak) the slices in the juice of 1 lime. Put all these ingredients together in a bowl, sprinkle with 3–4 tablespoons sugar and chill in the refrigerator for at least 3 hours before serving.

Far breton

Thought of as a flan (tart) with prunes this is a baked butter pudding. It may be eaten warm or cold. The French word *far* was originally used for a porridge made with durum wheat, ordinary wheat or buckwheat flour, with added salt or sugar and dried fruit. It was a popular dish throughout Brittany.

Soak 125 g (4½ oz, 1 cup) currants and 400 g (14 oz, 2¾ cups) stoned (pitted) prunes overnight in warm weak tea, then drain them. Make a well in the centre of 250 g (9 oz, 2¼ cups) plain (all-purpose) flour and mix in a large pinch of salt, 2 tablespoons sugar and 4 well-beaten eggs to make a batter. Thin the batter with 400 ml (14 fl oz, 1¾ cups) milk and mix in the currants and prunes. Pour into a buttered tin (pan) and bake in a preheated oven at 200°C (400°F, gas 6) for about 1 hour, until the top is brown. Sprinkle with icing (confectioner's) sugar.

Fig compote using dried figs

Soak the figs in cold water until they swell. Prepare a syrup with half red wine and half water, using 350 g (12 oz, 1½ cups) granulated sugar to 600 ml

(1 pint, 2½ cups) liquid; flavour it with finely grated lemon zest. Bring the syrup to the boil, add the figs and cook very gently for 20–30 minutes.

Fig compote using fresh figs

Peel some white or black figs. Put them in boiling vanilla-flavoured syrup, made with 350 g (12 oz, 1½ cups) granulated sugar to 600 ml (1 pint, 2½ cups) water, and poach for a few minutes only. Drain, reduce the syrup and pour it over the figs.

Fig fritters

Peel and quarter some figs and macerate for 30 minutes in brandy (or liqueur) and sugar. Drain thoroughly, dip in sweetened or unsweetened batter and deep-fry in hot oil. Remove and drain. Dust with caster (superfine) sugar and arrange on a napkin. Fritters may also be served dusted with icing (confectioner's) sugar and glazed in a hot oven or under a grill (broiler).

Figs with raspberry mousse

Peel some fresh ripe figs and cut them into quarters. Make a raspberry mousse by folding in 200 ml (7 fl oz, ¾ cup) Chantilly cream to 250 g (9 oz, 1½ cups) sieved sweetened raspberries. Arrange the fig quarters in a shallow bowl, cover with the mousse and chill for 30 minutes before serving.

Flambéed plums

Stone (pit) some greengages or mirabelle plums and poach them in a vanilla-flavoured syrup until just tender. Drain them and place in a flameproof casserole. Add a little arrowroot blended with water to the cooking syrup, pour a little of this syrup over the plums and heat. Sprinkle with quetsch or mirabelle brandy heated in a ladle, flame and serve immediately.

Flamri

Also known as flamery, this is a baked semolina pudding prepared with white wine instead of milk and served cold. It is coated with a purée of sweetened red fruit.

Place 500 ml (17 fl oz, 2 cups) sweet white wine and 500 ml (17 fl oz, 2 cups) water in a saucepan and bring to the boil. Gradually stir in 250 g (9 oz, 1¼ cups) fine semolina and simmer gently for 25 minutes. Remove from the heat and add 250 g (9 oz, 1 cup) caster (superfine) sugar, 2 beaten eggs and a generous pinch of salt. Then stir in 6 stiffly whisked egg whites. Pour the mixture into a buttered charlotte mould in a bain marie. Cook in a preheated oven at 200°C (400°F, gas 6) for 30 minutes. Allow to cool, then turn out on to a serving dish and coat with a sauce made from a purée of uncooked red fruit that has been sweetened with sugar.

Flaugnarde

Also known as *flangnarde*, *flognarde* or *flougnarde*. A flan made in the Auvergne, Limousin and Périgord regions of France. The name is derived from the Old French *fleugne*, meaning soft or downy. The flan resembles clafoutis and is made with apples, pears or prunes, flavoured with cinnamon, vanilla, rum, brandy, orange-flower water or lemon. It resembles a large pancake and is served lukewarm or cold (Curnonsky recommended the latter), generously sprinkled with icing (confectioner's) sugar and sometimes spread with jam (preserve).

Beat 4 eggs with 100 g (4 oz, ½ cup) caster (superfine) sugar in a bowl until the mixture is light and frothy. Gradually add 100 g (4 oz, 1 cup) plain (all-purpose) flour and a pinch of salt. Slowly beat in 1.5 litres (2¾ pints, 6½ cups) milk. Mix well, then flavour with 100 ml (4 fl oz, 7 tablespoons) rum or 4 tablespoons orange-flower water. Peel and core 3 pears, cut them into thin slices and add them to the mixture. Butter an ovenproof dish, pour in the mixture and dot the surface with small pieces of butter. Bake in a preheated oven at 220°C (425°F, gas 7) for 30 minutes. Serve hot or cold.

Floating island with pink pralines

Make a custard with 500 ml (17 fl oz, 2 cups) boiled milk, 6 egg yolks, 200 g (7 oz, 1 cup) sugar and half a vanilla pod (bean). Pour it into a serving dish and leave to cool completely.

Butter a deep cake tin (pan) that has a slightly smaller diameter than the serving dish. Crush 100 g (4 oz) pink pralines or sugared almonds with a rolling pin and sprinkle three-quarters over the bottom of the mould. Whisk 4 egg whites with a pinch of salt and 8 tablespoons caster (superfine) sugar until very stiff. Fold in the remaining crushed pralines and fill the mould with the mixture. Cook in a bain marie in a preheated oven at 140°C (275°F, gas 1) for 30–40 minutes. Unmould while still hot on to the chilled custard. Decorate with pralines.

Floating islands

A cold dessert consisting of a light egg custard topped with egg whites that have been stiffly whisked with sugar, shaped with a tablespoon and poached either in boiling water or in the milk used to make the custard. In the latter case the dish is more difficult to make successfully and the whites are not as meltingly soft. Floating islands are served drizzled with pale caramel or crushed praline.

Boil 750 ml (1¼ pints, 3¼ cups) milk with a vanilla pod (bean) or 1 teaspoon vanilla sugar. Whisk 8 egg whites to stiff peaks with a pinch of salt, then fold in 3 tablespoons caster (superfine) sugar. Using a tablespoon, gently drop portions of the whisked egg whites into the boiling milk. Turn the whites so that they are cooked all over. Remove after 2 minutes and drain on a cloth. Make an egg custard with the same milk, the 8 egg yolks, and 250 g (9 oz, 1 cup) sugar. When completely cold, pour the custard into a deep dish, place the cooked egg whites on top, and chill until ready to serve. Serve drizzled with caramel.

Fondant-coated or Marquise cherries

Thoroughly drain about 50 cherries (complete with their stalks) preserved in brandy or eau-de-vie. Pat dry, removing any excess liquid. Put 375 g (13 oz) fondant into a small heavy-based saucepan and heat rapidly, adding 4 tablespoons kirsch; mix well with a wooden spatula. When the fondant is liquid, remove from the heat and incorporate 3–4 drops of red food colouring, mixing briskly. Hold each cherry by the stalk and dip it in the fondant; let any excess drip back into the saucepan. Then lay the cherries on a work surface or marble slab sprinkled lightly with icing (confectioner's) sugar to prevent the fruit from sticking. Transfer each cherry to a small paper case.

Alternatively, add colouring to only half the fondant, to give 25 pink and 25 white cherries. (The same method can be used for large blackcurrants preserved in brandy; use pink fondant.)

Four-fruit compote

Use equal quantities of apples, quinces and oranges, together with a few large grapes. Prepare a syrup with 350 g (12 oz, 1½ cups) granulated sugar to 600 ml (1 pint, 2½ cups) water. Peel the apples and quinces, remove the pips (seeds), slice thickly and sprinkle with lemon juice. Plunge the slices of quince in the boiling syrup; 15 minutes later, add the apples. Meanwhile, peel and slice the oranges, removing the pith, and add them to the other fruit 20 minutes after the beginning of the cooking time. Continue to cook for another 10 minutes. Peel and, if possible, remove the pips from the grapes. Add them to the syrup as soon as the pan has been removed from the heat. Allow to cool and chill in the refrigerator.

French bread pudding

Crumble 14 slices of stale milk bread. Pour over the top 4 beaten eggs mixed with 100 g (4 oz, ½ cup) caster sugar (superfine) sugar; add 400 ml (14 fl oz, 1¾ cups) tepid milk, then 4 tablespoons raisins which have been soaked in weak tea, 3 tablespoons chopped crystallized (candied) fruit, the same amount of rum, a pinch of salt and sieved apricot jam (preserve). Mix together well.

Butter a pudding basin (mould) or a charlotte or manqué mould and pour half the mixture into it. Arrange 4 finely sliced canned pears over the surface, then pour in the remaining mixture. Place the mould in a bain marie containing boiling water. Put in a preheated oven at 200°C (400°F, gas 6) and cook for about 1 hour until set. Dip the bottom of the mould in cold water, then turn the pudding out. Serve with blackcurrant sauce.

Fried custard fritters

Boil 500 ml (17 fl oz, 2 cups) milk with 1 tablespoon vanilla-flavoured sugar. In a mixing bowl, beat 5 egg yolks with 100 g (4 oz, ½ cup) caster (superfine) sugar until the mixture is white. Beat in 75 g (3 oz, ¾ cup) plain (all-purpose) flour and gradually add the boiling milk, whisking it well. Pour the mixture into a saucepan, boil over a gentle heat for 3 minutes, stirring all the time, then remove from the heat and leave to cool until lukewarm. Spread the custard evenly over a buttered baking sheet to a thickness of 1.5 cm (⅝ in) and leave it to cool completely. Cut it into rectangles, diamonds or circles, dip these in batter and plunge them into hot oil at a temperature of 170–180°C (338–350°F). Drain and dust with icing (confectioner's) sugar.

Fried custard with crystallized fruits

Macerate 100 g (4 oz, ⅔ cup) diced crystallized (candied) fruits in 100 ml (4 fl oz, 7 tablespoons) Grand Marnier. Prepare some custard for frying as in the previous recipe and blend the fruit with it. Lightly oil a baking sheet and pour the custard on to it to form an even layer, 2 cm (¾ in) thick; leave to cool before putting in the refrigerator for 2–3 hours. Then cut the custard into diamond shapes and coat with beaten egg and breadcrumbs. Fry in hot oil at a temperature of 175–180°C (347–350°F) until lightly browned, then drain on paper towels. Dust with icing (confectioner's) sugar and serve very hot.

Fried rice pavés

Make a thick rice pudding using 125 g (4½ oz, ½ cup) short-grain rice and 600 ml (1 pint, 2½ cups) milk, sweetened to taste (the grains must be completely soft and sticky). Butter a baking sheet and spread with a layer of rice about 1 cm (½ in) thick. Smooth the surface, sprinkle with a little melted butter and leave to cool completely. Cut the rice into 5 cm (2 in) squares.

Stew 800 g (1¾ lb) fruit with a little sugar until reduced to a purée (use apricots, apples, plums, oranges or greengages). Strain the pulp into a pan, add some chopped canned pineapple and boil to reduce by one-third. (Chestnut purée could also be used.)

Spread half of the rice squares with the fruit and top with the remaining squares. Press them together, coat in breadcrumbs and deep-fry in hot oil at 175–180°C (347–350°F) until golden brown. Drain them on paper towels and serve very hot with strawberry sauce or custard cream.

Fritters Mont-Bry

Prepare sweetened semolina as for a dessert, let it cool, then spread it on a buttered baking sheet in a layer 1 cm (½ in) thick. When completely cold, cut it into small rectangles 4 × 5 cm (1½ × 2 in). Boil down some apricot jam (preserve) mixed with rum until reduced by half, then add a salpicon of finely diced walnuts and figs. Coat half the semolina rectangles with this mixture and cover with the remaining rectangles. Dip into batter and deep-fry at 175°C (347°F). Drain on paper towels and dust with caster (superfine) sugar.

Fruit brochettes en papillotes

Peel some oranges, remove the pith and seeds, and cut the segments into pieces; peel some pears, apples and bananas, cut into cubes or slices and sprinkle with lemon juice; cut some fresh or canned pineapple into cubes. Macerate for 30 minutes with sugar to taste and a liqueur or spirit (Curaçao, brandy, rum or Grand Marnier), then thread the pieces on to small skewers, mixing the various fruits. Lay each skewer on a piece of lightly buttered foil or greaseproof (wax) paper and dot the fruit with small pieces of butter. Wrap the brochettes in the foil or paper, lay them on the shelf (rack) in a preheated oven at 240°C (474°F, gas 9), and cook for about 15 minutes. Serve the brochettes in their wrapping. To microwave, use wooden skewers and buttered greaseproof paper, and cook for about 3 minutes on full power.

Fruit mousse

Weigh the pulp of the fruits (for example, strawberries, raspberries, apricots) and rub it through a sieve. Measure the same amount of double (heavy) cream. Prepare a sugar syrup using half as much sugar as fruit pulp. Whisk the cream and quickly add first the syrup, then the fruit purée. Refrigerate.

Fruit salad à la maltaise

Macerate some sliced bananas, stoned (pitted) cherries and cubes of fresh pineapple in Curaçao and sugar. Chill. Put a layer of orange-flavoured ice cream in the bottom of a glass fruit bowl; arrange the drained fruit on top. Decorate with whipped cream and peeled orange segments. Alternatively, the ice cream can be omitted and orange juice mixed with Curaçao poured over.

Fruit salad à la normande

Peel and core a pineapple and cut the flesh into cubes. Peel and slice some bananas. Peel and core some apples, cut them into cubes and sprinkle with lemon juice. Macerate all the fruit in some Calvados mixed with sugar. Chill. Arrange the fruit in a glass bowl and pour the fruit liquid over it. Cover with single (light) or Chantilly cream.

Fruit salad à l'occitanienne

Peel and core some pears, slice thickly and sprinkle with lemon juice. Peel and slice some figs. Peel some large black and white grapes. Arrange the ingredients in layers in a glass bowl, sprinkle with sugar and pour over some Blanquette de Limoux (a sparkling white wine) and a little brandy. Chill for at least 1 hour. Cover with Chantilly cream and decorate with peeled grapes.

Fruit salad with gin

Chill 4 shallow glass sundae dishes. Peel 2 pink grapefruit; detach the segments and skin them completely. Peel 2 papayas, remove the seeds and cut the flesh into thin slices. Peel and slice 4 kiwi fruit. Shell about 20 lychees, removing the stones (pits) if wished, or carefully drain 20 canned lychees.

Remove the dishes from the refrigerator; arrange the grapefruit segments alternately with the slices of papaya, insert slices of kiwi fruit here and there, and arrange the lychees in the centre of each dish. The decoration can be completed with a large raspberry in the middle. Put the filled dishes in the least cold part of the refrigerator.

Squeeze 2 oranges, dissolve 2 tablespoons caster (superfine) sugar in the juice and add 4 tablespoons gin. Just before serving, divide the juice between the dishes. Serve with vanilla-flavoured meringues.

Fruit salad with kirsch and Maraschino

Peel 6 peaches, 3 pears and 2 apples and slice thinly; slice 4 bananas and cut 6 apricots into chunks. Mix all the fruit in a bowl; then add 25 g (1 oz) hulled strawberries, 75 g (3 oz) raspberries, and 125 g (4½ oz) seeded white grapes. Sprinkle with 5–6 tablespoons caster (superfine) sugar; pour over 300 ml (½ pint, 1¼ cups) kirsch and 300 ml (½ pint, 1¼ cups) Maraschino. Gently mix the ingredients together. Surround the bowl with crushed ice and leave to macerate for 1 hour. Then pour the contents into a glass fruit bowl, also surrounded by crushed ice. Decorate with about 50 g (2 oz) strawberries, some grapes and 25 blanched and halved almonds.

Fruit salad with kiwi fruit

Choose the fruit according to the season. Divide oranges and grapefruit into segments, then peel and remove the pith. Peel, core and slice apples and pears, and sprinkle with lemon juice. Peel peaches and melon and cut into cubes; sprinkle the peaches with lemon juice. Hull strawberries and raspberries. Peel and slice the kiwi fruit, which should represent a quarter of the total volume of fruit.

Place all the fruit (except for the raspberries) in a large salad bowl, sprinkle with sugar and moisten with kirsch or another fruit-based liqueur. Leave in a cool place until ready to serve. Add the raspberries at the last moment.

The whole strawberries can be replaced by strawberry purée: put the fruit through a blender, sieve the purée, sweeten with sugar and pour it over the other fruit just before serving.

Fruit soufflé made with sugar syrup

Mix 1 kg (2¼ lb, 4½ cups) granulated sugar with 100 ml (4 fl oz, 7 table-spoons) water and boil until the temperature reaches 140°C (275°F). Then add 1.12 kg (2½ lb) finely sieved fruit purée. Fold in 12 stiffly whisked egg whites and cook in a large soufflé mould in a preheated oven at 190°C (375°F, gas 5) for about 35–40 minutes. Use strawberries and raspberries raw. Cook apricots, cherries, pears and apples with sugar beforehand; apples should be reduced until very dry before being sieved.

Gâteau de crêpes

Make a dozen sweet crêpes. Prepare a Chantilly cream with 200 ml (7 fl oz, ¾ cup) double (heavy) cream, 500 ml (17 fl oz, 2 cups) milk, 1 tablespoon vanilla-flavoured sugar (or a few drops of vanilla extract), and 25 g (1 oz, 2 tablespoons) caster (superfine) sugar. Lay a crêpe on the serving dish and spread with strawberry jam (preserve). Cover with a second crêpe and spread with Chantilly cream. Continue in this way, alternating the layers of jam and cream. Finish with a crêpe. Sprinkle with icing (confectioner's) sugar and trace a pattern of diamond shapes for decoration. Serve immediately.

German bread and fruit pudding

Finely dice 150 g (5 oz, about 5 slices) white bread and fry lightly in butter. Put in a bowl and pour on 200 ml (7 fl oz, ¾ cup) boiled milk. Mix, then add 2 apples cut into small cubes and cooked in butter, 50 g (2 oz, ⅓ cup) diced candied orange peel, 50 g (2 oz, ½ cup) ground almonds and the same amount of seeded raisins, which have been soaked in water and drained. Add 75 g (3 oz, 6 tablespoons) caster (superfine) sugar, 1 tablespoon blanched and finely chopped lemon peel and 3 egg yolks. Mix well, then blend in 3 egg whites whisked into very stiff peaks.

Pour this mixture into a buttered charlotte mould, place in a bain marie, and cook in a preheated oven at 200°C (400°F, gas 6) for about 50 minutes. Turn out the pudding while still lukewarm and coat with a sauce made by mixing 200 ml (7 fl oz, ¾ cup) red wine with 2 tablespoons sieved and warmed apricot jam (preserve).

Glacé cherries filled with almond paste

Prepare some almond paste with 125 g (4½ oz, 1 cup) ground almonds, 250 g (9 oz, 1 cup) sugar, 4 tablespoons glucose powder, 5 tablespoons water and some kirsch. Split 50 glacé (candied) cherries in half, but without separating the halves completely. Shape the almond paste into small balls and insert one into each cherry. Serve on a tray sprinkled with icing (confectioner's) sugar.

Grapefruit salad

Mix grapefruit segments with fine slices of apple sprinkled with lemon juice, chopped celery and a few shredded lettuce leaves. Dress with a little yogurt or a light oil-based dressing.

Gratinée de poires aux pistaches

Bring to the boil 1 litre (1¾ pints, 4⅓ cups) water with 1 vanilla pod (bean) cut in two, 200 g (7 oz, 1 cup) caster (superfine) sugar and 2 tablespoons lemon juice. Peel and core 6 ripe but firm pears. Poach gently. Allow to cool. Make a confectioner's custard (pastry cream) with 250 ml (8 fl oz, 1 cup) milk, 1 vanilla pod cut in two, 20 g (¾ oz, 2½ tablespoons) plain (all-purpose) flour, 3 egg yolks and 70 g (2¾ oz, 5 tablespoons) sugar. Place in a bowl, add 1 tablespoon pear brandy and, when it is almost cold, 3 tablespoons whipped cream. Beat 1 egg yolk with 25 g (1 oz, 2 tablespoons) sugar until the mixture foams and turns a paler yellow. Incorporate 1 tablespoon chopped pistachio nuts and 2 tablespoons whipped cream. Drain the pears and cut them in the shape of a fan but so they are still attached at the stalk end. Cut 1 vanilla pod into matchsticks. Put some confectioner's custard (pastry cream) on to each plate and place a pear fan in the middle. Sprinkle icing (confectioner's) sugar on the pears without going over the edge. Place the plates under the grill (broiler) to brown the fruit. Pour some pistachio cream evenly around the pears and draw marbling patterns with the point of a knife. Now sprinkle the edge of the plate with icing sugar and chopped pistachio nuts. Place a spoonful of ice cream next to each pear, decorate with vanilla matchsticks and serve them immediately.

Grilled bananas

Peel some bananas, brush with melted butter and grill (broil) gently for 15 minutes. Arrange the bananas in a dish, dust with caster (superfine) sugar and coat with sour cream, soft (whipped) cream cheese or a dessert sauce.

Hawaiian cream coupes

Prepare 500 ml (17 fl oz, 2 cups) almond milk jelly or blancmange and keep it in a cool place. Wash, pat dry and hull 300 g (11 oz, 2½ cups) strawberries, cutting large ones in half. Peel and dice the flesh of a fresh pineapple. Line some sundae dishes with the strawberries and diced pineapple and completely cover with the jelly or blancmange. Top with a layer of raspberry coulis – about 100 g (4 oz, ½ cup). Decorate each dish with piped rosettes of whipped cream.

Italian meringue

Put 300 g (11 oz, scant 1½ cups) caster (superfine) sugar and 100 ml (4 fl oz, 7 tablespoons) water in a heavy-based saucepan and boil to the soft ball stage.

Whisk 4 egg whites until stiff. Add the boiling syrup in a thin stream, whisking continuously until is cold. Store in the refrigerator until needed.

Jam crêpes

Make some sweet crêpes and keep them hot. Sieve some apricot, plum or peach jam (preserve) and heat it, possibly adding some rum or a fruit liqueur. Spread the crêpes with jam, roll them up, sprinkle them with caster (superfine) sugar and serve immediately. The crêpes may also be placed for a few moments under the grill (broiler) to caramelize the sugar.

Kaltschale

This is a Russian dessert consisting of a fresh fruit salad that has been macerated in wine and covered with a purée of red fruit (strawberries, raspberries and redcurrants). It is served in a large bowl that traditionally rests on a dish of crushed ice. The word *kaltschale* is German, and its literal meaning is 'cold cup'.

Rub 1 kg (2¼ lb, 7 cups) strawberries and 250 g (9 oz, 2 cups) very ripe redcurrants through a sieve. Bring 1 litre (1¾ pints, 4⅓ cups) light sugar syrup and ½ bottle of champagne to the boil, then allow to cool. Add the syrup mixture to the fruit purée. Peel and remove the seeds or stones (pits) from several different fruits, such as melon or watermelon, apricots, peaches, pears or fresh pineapple. Cut them into thin slices and sprinkle with lemon juice. Place all the fruit in a large bowl and pour the liquid purée over it. Chill until ready to serve. Add some raspberries at the last moment.

Kissel with cranberries

Kissel is a Russian dessert made from sweetened red fruit purée thickened with arrowroot or flour and sometimes flavoured with white wine. Kissel can

71

be served warm or cold with crème fraîche. Put 1 kg (2¼ lb, 9 cups) cranberries through a vegetable mill. Mix with 2–2.5 litres (3½–4¼ pints, 9–11 cups) water, pour the mixture through a cloth into a bowl and wring out the cloth thoroughly to extract the maximum quantity of juice. Alternatively, purée the fruit and water in a blender. Mix 50 g (2 oz, ½ cup) potato flour, cornflour (cornstarch) or tapioca into the juice and pour into a saucepan. Add 200 g (7 oz, 1 cup) caster (superfine) sugar and bring to the boil. Stir constantly until the mixture thickens. Pour into a fruit bowl and serve either warm or cold.

Langues-de-chat mousse

Butter a charlotte mould and line the bottom and sides with langues-de-chat biscuits (cookies). Melt 250 g (9 oz) chocolate over a low heat with 2 tablespoons water and 200 g (7 oz, 1 cup) caster (superfine) sugar. Remove from the heat and add 200 g (7 oz, 1 cup) butter and 4 egg yolks, then fold in 4 egg whites, stiffly whisked. Fill the mould with this preparation. Cover the top with langues-de-chat and refrigerate for at least 2 hours. Turn out and serve with coffee-flavoured whipped cream.

Lemon crêpes

Add the grated zest of 1 lemon to 500 ml (17 fl oz, 2 cups) milk. Bring to the boil and leave to cool. Make a crêpe batter with the lemon-flavoured milk, 250 g (9 oz, 2¼ cups) plain (all-purpose) flour, 3 eggs, and a pinch of salt. Strain and let it stand for at least 1 hour at room temperature. Add 25 g (1 oz, 2 tablespoons) butter to the batter and thin with 100 ml (4 fl oz, 7 tablespoons) water. Make the crêpes and keep them hot on a plate over a saucepan of boiling water. Fold the crêpes in four, arrange them on a buttered serving dish and dust generously with caster (superfine) sugar.

Lemon mousse

Beat together 2 egg yolks and 5 tablespoons sugar. When the mixture is foamy, add 2 tablespoons cornflour (cornstarch) and then the heated juice of 6 limes and 2 lemons. Bring the mixture to the boil, stirring all the time. Stiffly whisk 2 egg whites and fold into the mixture. Pour this mousse into ramekin dishes and serve chilled with a salad of blood oranges and pink grapefruit.

Lemon soufflé

In a saucepan, work 100 g (4 oz, ½ cup) butter into a soft paste with a wooden spoon. Add 100 g (4 oz, ½ cup) caster (superfine) sugar and 100 g (4 oz, 1 cup) plain flour (all-purpose flour), then moisten with 300 ml (½ pint, 1¼ cups) hot milk and mix well. Bring to the boil, stirring all the time, then beat until the mixture leaves the sides of the pan clean. Remove from the heat and beat in the juice of 2 lemons and 5 egg yolks, then fold in 6 egg whites whisked into stiff peaks and 2 tablespoons blanched and finely chopped lemon peel.

Turn the mixture into a buttered 1.5 litre (2¾ pint, 6 cup) pudding basin or soufflé mould, place in a bain marie, and cook in a preheated oven at 200°C (400°F, gas 6) for 40 minutes until well risen and golden brown. Serve with a lemon-flavoured custard cream.

Liège waffles

Take 500 g (18 oz, 4½ cups) sifted strong plain (bread) flour. Mix 15 g (½ oz, 1 cake) fresh (compressed) yeast or 1½ teaspoons dried yeast with 120 ml (4½ fl oz, ½ cup) tepid water and blend with a quarter of the flour. Leave to rise until doubled in size. Then add the rest of the flour, a generous pinch of salt, 125 g (4½ oz, generous ½ cup) caster (superfine) sugar, 4 beaten eggs and 200 g (7 oz, scant 1 cup) softened butter. Mix well.

Work the dough with the palm of the hand. Divide it into balls, each the size of an egg. Roll into sausage shapes and leave to stand on a floured board for 30 minutes. Heat a waffle iron and, if necessary, grease it. Put a piece of dough between the plates, close the waffle iron and leave to cook. Repeat with the remaining dough. Serve the waffles lukewarm or cold, sprinkled with icing (confectioner's) sugar.

Lime soufflé

Boil 120 ml (4½ fl oz, ½ cup) milk together with the zest of 1 lime. Whisk together 50 g (2 oz, ¼ cup) granulated sugar, 2 egg yolks, 25 g (1 oz, ¼ cup) cornflour (cornstarch) and 120 ml (4½ fl oz, ½ cup) lime juice. Pour the boiling milk on to this mixture, then return to the heat and bring to the boil, whisking all the time. Leave to cool.

Butter 4 ramekins liberally and coat with sugar. Add 2 egg yolks to the confectioner's custard (pastry cream). Stiffly whisk the whites of 6–8 eggs (depending on their size), blend in 75 g (3 oz, ⅓ cup) caster (superfine) sugar and fold the mixture into the confectioner's custard. Pour the mixture into the prepared moulds and place in a preheated oven at 200°C (400°F, gas 6). After 12 minutes, place a thin slice of lime on each soufflé, cover with a sheet of greaseproof (wax) paper and cook for a further 3 minutes. Serve immediately with a warm custard cream flavoured with blanched lime zest.

Mango dessert with passion fruit and rum

Remove the pulp from 500 g (18 oz) passion fruit and discard the seeds. Whisk the pulp together with an equal quantity of sugar syrup and freeze to make a sorbet.

Cut some Genoese sponge cake into 4 rounds, 10 cm (4 in) in diameter and 1 cm (½ in) thick, and scoop out a slight hollow in each. Cut the flesh of

4 well-ripened mangoes into slices. Fill the hollows in the sponge rounds with the passion fruit sorbet and arrange the slices of mango in the shape of a fan over the top. Place in the coldest part of the refrigerator.

Prepare a zabaglione mixture with rum: whisk 4 egg yolks with 7 tablespoons rum in a bain marie. When the mixture is light and fluffy, add 4 tablespoons whipped double (heavy) cream. Coat the slices of mango with the zabaglione, glaze for a short time under the grill (broiler), and decorate with Cape gooseberries.

Melon en surprise à la parisienne

Choose a good-quality ripe firm melon weighing about 2 kg (4½ lb). Remove a thick slice from the stalk end. Carefully remove the seeds and then scoop out the flesh without piercing the rind. Dice the flesh and place in the refrigerator to chill. Select some fruit in season, such as apricots, peaches and pears, and cut it into cubes. Add some grapes, stoned (pitted) plums, strawberries, raspberries and pineapple cubes. Mix this fruit with the melon, sprinkle with a little caster (superfine) sugar, and pour over some kirsch, Maraschino or other liqueur.

Sprinkle the inside of the rind with a little sugar, pour in a liqueur glass of the same liqueur, fill with the fruit, replace the top of the melon, and store in the refrigerator. Serve the melon in a dish containing crushed ice.

Alternatively, ripe small melons can be used. Cut them in half and prepare each half as above to serve as individual portions.

Meringues cuites

Put 8 egg whites and 500 g (18 oz, 4 cups) icing (confectioner's) sugar into a bowl resting on a pan of simmering water over a low heat and whisk the mixture until it is very stiff and holds its shape. Flavour with coffee essence, vanilla sugar or a little rum. Pipe the mixture into small mounds on a baking sheet either oiled or lined with non-stick baking parchment and bake in a very cool oven for about 2 hours.

Mirabelle custard pudding

Wash and stone (pit) 300 g (11 oz) mirabelle plums. Mix 4 eggs with 75 g (3 oz, 6 tablespoons) caster (superfine) sugar, add 400 ml (14 fl oz, 1¾ cups) milk and a generous pinch of salt. Gradually add 100 g (4 oz, 1 cup) plain (all-purpose) flour and whisk until smooth. Blend in 20 g (¾ oz, 4½ teaspoons) melted butter. Put the plums in a buttered ovenproof dish and cover with the mixture, tilting the dish so the mixture runs between the fruit. Bake in a preheated oven at 220°C (425°F, gas 7) for 35–40 minutes. Remove from the oven, sprinkle with caster sugar and serve hot, warm or cold.

Mont-blanc

A cold dessert made of vanilla-flavoured chestnut purée, topped with a dome of Chantilly cream and decorated. Alternatively, the cream may be surrounded by a border of sweetened chestnut purée and mounted on a base of sablé pastry or meringue.

Shell 1 kg (2¼ lb) chestnuts and simmer them until soft in 1 litre (1¾ pints, 4⅓ cups) milk with 150 g (5 oz, ⅔ cup) sugar, a pinch of salt and a vanilla pod (bean) split in two. Press the chestnuts through a potato ricer and pack the vermicelli-like chestnut purée into a buttered ring mould. Refrigerate for at least 30 minutes. Whisk together 400 ml (14 fl oz, 1¾ cups) double (heavy) cream, 1 teaspoon vanilla sugar and 25 g (1 oz, ¼ cup) icing (confectioner's) sugar to make Chantilly cream. Turn the chestnut ring out on to a dish and fill the centre with the Chantilly cream. Decorate with pieces of marrons glacés and crystallized (candied) violets. Refrigerate until served.

Mousseline of apples with walnuts

Peel and core 8 medium dessert (eating) apples, cut into slices, and make a compote by stewing them until soft with 2 knobs of butter, 3 tablespoons caster (superfine) sugar, 1 teaspoon vanilla-flavoured sugar and a small piece of finely chopped lemon zest.

Peel and core 3 more apples and cut each into 8 pieces. Poach these pieces of apple slowly in a syrup prepared with 350 ml (12 fl oz, 1½ cups) water, 125 g (4½ oz, scant ⅔ cup) sugar and a vanilla pod (bean): the fruit should be just softened. Remove 15 pieces of apple and complete the cooking of the other 9. Drain the fruit and put the syrup to one side.

As soon as the compote is cooked, mash it with a fork and reduce it over a high heat, turning it over with a spatula until a thick fruit paste is obtained. Remove from the heat and cool. Thicken with 120 ml (4½ fl oz, ½ cup) whipped double (heavy) cream, 3 beaten eggs and 3 yolks. Add 2 tablespoons crushed walnuts and the half-poached apple pieces.

Butter a charlotte mould and pour the mixture into it. Pile it up slightly and cook in a bain marie in a preheated oven at 190°C (375°F, gas 5) for about 40 minutes. Remove from the oven and turn after 15 minutes on to a hot dish.

Prepare a sauce by reducing the syrup in which the apples were cooked to 120 ml (4½ fl oz, ½ cup), remove it from the heat, and add 50 g (2 oz, ¼ cup) butter and then 250 ml (8 fl oz, 1 cup) whipped double (heavy) cream. Flavour with Noyau liqueur. Coat the mousseline with this sauce and decorate with the 9 fully cooked pieces of apple. Serve some langues-de-chat biscuits (cookies) separately.

Nanette fritters

Cut a stale brioche into round slices. Prepare a confectioner's custard (pastry cream) and add to it some chopped crystallized (candied) fruit which has been macerated in kirsch or rum. Spread a little of this mixture on each slice of brioche and sandwich together in pairs. Moisten with a little sugar syrup flavoured with kirsch or rum. Remove the fritters and drain. Dust with caster (superfine) sugar and serve. Fritters may also be served dusted with icing (confectioner's) sugar and glazed in a hot oven or under a grill (broiler).

Nègre en chemise

Melt 250 g (9 oz, 9 squares) chocolate in a double saucepan (boiler) with 1 tablespoon milk. Soften 250 g (9 oz, generous 1 cup) butter with a spatula. Mix the melted chocolate with the butter, beat thoroughly, and then add 5 tablespoons sugar and 4 or 5 egg yolks. Whisk 5 egg whites until very stiff and fold them carefully into the mixture. Oil a bombe or charlotte mould, pour in the chocolate cream and refrigerate for at least 12 hours.

Just before serving, make some Chantilly cream by whisking 200 ml (7 fl oz, ¾ cup) double (heavy) cream and 5 tablespoons very cold fresh milk, adding 40 g (1½ oz, ⅓ cup) icing (confectioner's) sugar and either 1 teaspoon vanilla sugar or a few drops of vanilla essence (extract). Unmould the chocolate cream on to a serving dish, then pipe over Chantilly cream, taking care that the chocolate shows through in places.

Nesselrode pudding

Mix 1 litre (1¾ pints, 4⅓ cups) crème anglaise with 250 g (9 oz, 1 cup) chestnut purée. Macerate 125 g (4½ oz, ¾ cup) candied orange peel and diced crystallized (candied) cherries in Málaga, and soak some sultanas (golden) and currants in warm water. Add all the ingredients to the crème anglaise together with 1 litre (1¾ pints, 4⅓ cups) whipped cream flavoured with maraschino. Line the base and sides of a large charlotte mould with greaseproof (wax) paper and add the mixture. Cover the mould with a double thickness of foil and secure it with an elastic (rubber) band. Place the mould in the freezer. When the pudding is frozen, unmould it on to the serving dish, peel off the paper and surround the base with marrons glacés.

Omelette à la dijonnaise

Beat 8 eggs with 2 tablespoons sugar, 2 or 3 finely crushed macaroons and 1 tablespoon double (heavy) cream. Make 2 flat omelettes. Put one of them on to a round ovenproof dish and spread it with 3 tablespoons very thick confectioner's custard (pastry cream) mixed with 1 tablespoon ground almonds flavoured with Cassis. Place the second omelette on top and completely coat with egg whites whisked to stiff peaks. Sprinkle with icing (confectioner's) sugar and glaze quickly in a very hot oven. Serve the omelette surrounded by a ribbon of blackcurrant jam (preserve).

Omelette flambée

Beat the eggs with some sugar and a pinch of salt, then cook the omelette in butter, keeping it very creamy. Dredge with sugar, sprinkle with heated rum and set light to it immediately before serving. The rum can be replaced by Armagnac, Calvados, Cognac, whisky or a fruit-based spirit.

Omelette Reine Pédauque

Beat 8 eggs with 1 tablespoon caster (superfine) sugar, 1 tablespoon ground almonds, 1 tablespoon double (heavy) cream and a pinch of salt. Make 2 flat omelettes. Place one of the omelettes in a round ovenproof serving dish. Mix 6 tablespoons thick apple compote with 2 tablespoons double (heavy) cream and 1 tablespoon rum. Spread this mixture over the omelette, put the second omelette on top, sprinkle with icing (confectioner's) sugar and glaze quickly in the oven or under the grill (broiler).

Omelette with fruit compote

Prepare a compote of peaches, plums, apples or apricots: cook the fruit in vanilla-flavoured syrup, drain, bind with jam (preserve) made from the same type of fruit and flavour with liqueur. Beat 8 eggs with 1 tablespoon caster (superfine) sugar and a pinch of salt. Cook the omelette in butter. Just before folding, fill with 4 tablespoons fruit compote. Fold the omelette, slip it on to a round plate and sprinkle with caster sugar. Glaze under the grill (broiler).

Orange dessert

Make a sponge cake 24 cm (9½ in) in diameter with 4 eggs, 125 g (4½ oz, ⅔ cup) caster (superfine) sugar and 125 g (4½ oz, 1 cup) plain (all-purpose) flour. Bake and cool on a wire rack.

Make a syrup with 300 ml (½ pint, 1¼ cups) water and 200 g (7 oz, 1 cup) sugar. Wash 2 oranges. Cut in two and slice finely into even slices. Cook the orange slices in the syrup, drain and put them to one side. Remove the zest of 2 oranges, blanch it twice and cook for 10 minutes in the syrup.

Divide the remaining syrup into 3 amounts. Dilute one amount with 3½ tablespoons orange liqueur to moisten the sponge cake. Dilute the second amount with a little orange juice and add 100 g (4 oz, ⅓ cup) orange jelly to make the sauce accompanying the dessert, which is then strained through a fine chinois. Dilute the third amount with 100 g (4 oz, ⅓ cup) orange jelly and a little orange juice, adding 1 leaf of gelatine, dissolved, for the final glazing.

Make a custard with 500 ml (17 fl oz, 2¼ cups) milk, flavoured with ½ vanilla pod (bean), 4 egg yolks, 100 g (4 oz, ½ cup) caster sugar and 60 g (2¼ oz, ½ cup) plain (all-purpose) flour. Add 2 sheets of dissolved leaf gelatine and cool it quickly. Whisk until smooth. Add 3½ tablespoons orange liqueur, 150 g (5 oz, 1 cup) candied orange zest, diced very small, and then gently fold in 300 ml (½ pint, 1¼ cups) double (heavy) cream, lightly whipped. Cut the sponge cake horizontally into 3 layers. Line the sides of a ring mould 24 cm (9½ in) in diameter, placed on iced (frosted) cardboard, with the half slices of candied orange, slightly overlapping. Place a layer of sponge cake at the bottom of the ring. Soak it with syrup and cover with half the cream. Put the second layer of sponge cake on top, soak it again and cover with the remaining cream. Put the last layer of sponge cake on top, with the golden side facing upward. Press gently and soak with the rest of the syrup. Put in the refrigerator for a few hours. Glaze with the jelly and put it back in the refrigerator to set. Carefully remove from the ring. Pour a fine ribbon of sauce around and decorate with candied orange zest and sprigs of mint.

Pannequets à la cévenole

Pannequets are sweet or savoury pancakes filled with chopped ingredients, a purée or a cream.

Make a batter with 250 g (9 oz, 2¼ cups) plain (all-purpose) flour, a pinch of salt, 3 beaten eggs, 1 tablespoon caster (superfine) sugar, 250 ml (8 fl oz, 1 cup) milk, 250 ml (8 fl oz, 1 cup) water and 1 tablespoon melted butter.

Mix 250 ml (8 fl oz, 1 cup) sweetened chestnut purée flavoured with kirsch with 3 tablespoons crème fraîche and 3 tablespoons fragments of marrons glacés. Spread the pancakes with the mixture and roll up. Arrange in a buttered ovenproof dish, dust generously with icing (confectioner's) sugar, and place in a preheated oven at 230°C (450°F, gas 8) for 8–10 minutes.

Pannequets à la créole

Prepare 8 sweet pancakes (see pannequets à la cévenole). Mix 300 ml (½ pint, 1¼ cups) confectioner's custard (pastry cream) flavoured with rum with 4 slices of canned pineapple cut into a salpicon. Spread the pannequets with this mixture and finish as for pannequets à la cévenole.

Pannequets with crystallized fruit

Prepare 8 sweet pancakes (see pannequets à la cévenole). Cut 250 g (9 oz, 1½ cups) crystallized (candied) fruit into small dice and macerate them in 100 ml (4 fl oz, 7 tablespoons) brandy or rum. Mix 4 egg yolks with 125 g (4½ oz, ½ cup) caster (superfine) sugar, add 65 g (2½ oz, ½ cup) plain (all-purpose) flour, and mix well. Sprinkle with 500 ml (17 fl oz, 2 cups) boiling milk, whisking quickly. Pour into a saucepan and boil for 2 minutes, beating with a whisk. Combine the crystallized fruit and the macerating spirit with this mixture, then leave until lukewarm.

Spread each pannequet with a generous tablespoon of the fruit cream mixture, roll them up and arrange in a buttered ovenproof dish. Dust with 100 g (4 oz, ¾ cup) icing (confectioner's) sugar and caramelize in a preheated oven at 220°C (425°F, gas 7). Serve as soon as they are taken out of the oven. The pannequets may be flamed with rum just before serving.

Peach compote

Prepare a vanilla-flavoured syrup with 350 g (12 oz, 1½ cups) granulated sugar to 600 ml (1 pint, 2½ cups) water. Plunge the peaches for about 30 seconds in boiling water and cool them under cold running water. It should then be easy to peel them. Either leave them whole or cut them in half and remove the stones (pits). Poach them in boiling syrup for 13 minutes if cut in half, or 18 minutes if they are whole.

Peaches à la bordelaise

Plunge 4 peaches into boiling water for 30 seconds. Drain, peel and remove the stones (pits). Sprinkle the fruit with sugar and leave to steep for 1 hour. Boil 300 ml (½ pint, 1¼ cups) Bordeaux wine with 8 lumps of sugar and a small piece of cinnamon stick. Place the peach halves in this syrup to poach for 10–12 minutes. When the fruit is cooked, drain, slice and place in a dish. Boil the syrup to reduce it, pour over the peaches and leave to cool. Serve with vanilla ice cream, decorated with wild strawberries and mint.

Peaches dame blanche

Macerate 4 slices pineapple in 1 tablespoon each of kirsch and Maraschino. Make a syrup using 250 ml (8 fl oz, 1 cup) water, 250 g (9 oz, 1 cup) caster (superfine) sugar and half a vanilla pod (bean), split in two. Peel 2 large peaches and poach gently in the syrup for about 10 minutes, turning them frequently, then remove from the heat.

Prepare some Chantilly cream by whipping 150 ml (¼ pint, ⅔ cup) double (heavy) cream with 1 tablespoon milk, 1 tablespoon caster (superfine) sugar and a little vanilla sugar or essence (extract) to taste; chill. Drain the peaches, halve them and remove the stones (pits). Divide 500 ml (17 fl oz, 2 cups) vanilla ice cream between 4 sundae glasses, add a slice of pineapple and a peach half to each, and decorate with a 'turban' of Chantilly cream using a piping (pastry) bag fitted with a fluted nozzle. Serve immediately.

Peaches Pénélope

Prepare a strawberry mousse as follows. Wash and hull 1 kg (2¼ lb) ripe strawberries and purée them in a blender. Add 300 g (11 oz, 1½ cups) caster (superfine) sugar, the juice of 1 lemon and 1 teaspoon vanilla sugar. Stir to dissolve. Prepare some Italian meringue with 100 g (4 oz, ½ cup) caster sugar and 2 egg whites and set aside to cool completely. Whip 250 ml (8 fl oz, 1 cup) double (heavy) cream with 150 ml (¼ pint, ⅔ cup) very cold milk. Add the Italian meringue to the strawberry purée, then carefully fold in the whipped cream. Put the mousse into individual 10 cm (4 in) soufflé moulds and place in the refrigerator to set.

In the meantime, poach some peaches in a vanilla-flavoured syrup for 15 minutes, then drain. Allow the peaches to cool, then place in the refrigerator. To serve, turn out the mousses into sundae dishes, place either a half peach or slices of peach on each mousse and decorate with fresh raspberries. Sprinkle with a little icing (confectioner's) sugar and serve with zabaglione flavoured with Parfait Amour liqueur.

Peaches with raspberries

Poach some peaches in a vanilla-flavoured sugar syrup, leave to cool completely, then chill. When ready to serve, drain and arrange them in a glass dish. Prepare a fresh raspberry purée, add a little of the reduced sugar syrup and flavour with a few drops of raspberry liqueur. Cover the peaches with the purée and decorate with fresh raspberries.

Pear and apple caramel compote

Prepare two batches of syrup as for pear compote and place in separate pans. Peel and quarter some apples and remove the pips (seeds) and cover with lemon juice. Prepare some pears as for pear compote. Boil the syrups, add the fruit and cook until the apples are tender and the pears translucent. Drain them and arrange them in layers in a fruit bowl. Place the bowl in the refrigerator. Mix the two lots of syrup together and reduce until it begins to turn pale gold in colour. Pour this boiling syrup over the cold fruit and set aside to cool. Do not refrigerate.

Pear and caramel-cream coupes

Prepare the caramel cream: cook 100 g (4 oz, 8 tablespoons) caster (superfine) sugar in 50 ml (2 fl oz, 3½ tablespoons) water to obtain a golden caramel. Pour 120 ml (4 fl oz, ½ cup) double (heavy) cream into a large basin, sprinkle it with the caramel, and whisk. Then transfer the mixture to a saucepan and cook over a gentle heat. Meanwhile work 100 g (4 oz, ½ cup) butter with a spatula in the deep basin until soft. Test a drop of the caramel cream in a bowl of cold water: if it forms a firm ball, the cream is cooked. Then pour it over the butter, whipping briskly. Set aside in a cool place until used. Divide 500 ml (17 fl oz, 2 cups) almond milk jelly or blancmange among 8 sundae dishes and place in the refrigerator. Divide 16 diced canned pear halves among the dishes, cover with caramel cream and put into a cool place. A few moments before serving, decorate with piped rosettes of whipped cream.

Pear and peach salad with raspberries

Peel 4 pears and 4 peaches, dice the flesh and put in a bowl with the juice of a lemon; sprinkle with 3 tablespoons sugar. Clean 200 g (7 oz, 1½ cups) raspberries, add them to the bowl and chill for at least 3 hours. Just before serving, mix very gently.

Pear charlotte

Peel 1 kg (2¼ lb) Williams pears and poach them in a syrup prepared with 250 ml (8 fl oz, 1 cup) water and 500 g (18 oz, generous 2 cups) granulated sugar. Cut them into medium-sized slices and set aside in the syrup.

Soften 8 sheets leaf gelatine or sponge 20 g (¾ oz, 3 envelopes) powdered gelatine in cold water. Then drain and dissolve the leaf gelatine in a little water or dissolve the sponged gelatine. Prepare a custard with 500 ml (17 fl oz, 2 cups) milk, 250 g (9 oz, generous 1 cup) caster (superfine) sugar, 8 egg yolks, and 1 vanilla pod (bean). Remove from the heat and add the gelatine. When the custard is cold, blend in 120 ml (4½ fl oz, ½ cup) juice extracted from Williams pears and 750 ml (1¼ pints, 3¼ cups) Chantilly cream.

Line a charlotte mould with sponge fingers (ladyfingers) and then fill it with alternate layers of cream and drained slices of pear. Place in the refrigerator for at least 4 hours or until set. Prepare a raspberry sauce by puréeing 300 g (11 oz, 2 cups) fruit, 125 g (4½ oz, 1 cup) icing (confectioner's) sugar and the juice of 1 lemon. Invert the charlotte and serve it with the sauce.

Pear charlotte (using canned fruit)

Put 15 g (½ oz, 2 envelopes) gelatine to soften in 5 tablespoons cold water. Press 350 g (12 oz) drained canned pears through a sieve and warm the pulp gently in a saucepan. Add the softened gelatine to the pear purée and stir to dissolve. Cut 350 g (12 oz) drained canned pears into 1 cm (½ in) cubes. Whip 250 ml (8 fl oz, 1 cup) whipping cream with 3 tablespoons icing (confectioner's) sugar. Whisk 2 egg whites with 50 g (2 oz, ¼ cup) caster (superfine) sugar until they form stiff peaks.

Line a charlotte mould with a ring of greaseproof (wax) paper. Line the bottom and the sides with sponge fingers (ladyfingers) trimmed at the ends to the height of the mould. Pour the pear and gelatine mixture into a large bowl, add the diced pears and 1½ tablespoons pear brandy, then incorporate the cream and the egg whites, using a spatula. Pour this mixture into the charlotte mould and chill in the refrigerator for about 10 hours until set.

Turn out the charlotte on to a serving dish and surround it with a ring of raspberry sauce. Serve the remainder of the sauce in a sauceboat.

Pear compote

Peel the pears, cut them into quarters and remove the cores. (If the pears are small, leave them whole.) Cook them in boiling vanilla-flavoured syrup, prepared with 350 g (12 oz, 1½ cups) granulated sugar to 600 ml (1 pint, 2½ cups) water, until they become translucent. Remove and place in a bowl.

Reduce the syrup and pour it over the pears. Cool before serving. Some pear brandy may be added to the cold syrup if desired.

Pears in wine

Peel 8 fine Williams' Bon Chrétien or Passe Crassane pears, but leave the stalk on and brush them with lemon juice. Put the pear peelings in a large saucepan and add 1 litre (1¾ pints, 4⅓ cups) red wine (Côtes du Rhône or Madiran), 100 g (4 oz, ⅓ cup) honey, 150 g (5 oz, ¾ cup, firmly packed) soft brown sugar, the zest of 1 lemon (previously blanched), a little white pepper, a few coriander seeds, a pinch of grated nutmeg and 3 vanilla pods (beans), slit in two. Bring to the boil and simmer. After 10 minutes, add the pears, stalks upright. Cover the pan and cook slowly for 20 minutes. Leave to cool before putting in the refrigerator for 24 hours. Serve coated with the gelled juice.

Pears Joinville

Line a 23 cm (9 in) savarin mould with caramel. Boil 1 litre (1¾ pints, 4⅓ cups) milk with half a vanilla pod (bean). Beat 12 eggs with 200 g (7 oz, ¾ cup) caster (superfine) sugar until thick and pale. Add the boiling milk gradually, whisking all the time, then strain the mixture through a fine sieve and pour it into the caramel-lined mould. Put the mould into a baking dish filled with enough water to reach halfway up the sides. Cook in a preheated oven at 200°C (400°F, gas 6) for 20 minutes or until the custard has set. Remove from the oven and allow to cool completely before turning out.

Drain the contents of a large can of pears. Melt 200 g (7 oz, ⅔ cup) apricot jam (preserve) over a gentle heat and flavour with 100 ml (4 fl oz, 7 tablespoons) kirsch or pear brandy. Make a Chantilly cream by whipping together 200 ml (7 fl oz, ¾ cup) double (heavy) cream, 5 tablespoons iced milk, 50 g (2 oz, ½ cup) icing (confectioner's) sugar and 1 teaspoon vanilla sugar. Cut the pears into thin slices and arrange them in the centre of the caramel mould. Put the Chantilly cream in a piping (pastry) bag fitted with a fluted nozzle and decorate the pears. Serve with the warm apricot sauce.

Pears Wanamaker

Cut 6 madeleines in half and arrange them on a buttered dish, spacing them out slightly. Soak with kirsch and coat with a thick, sweetened, pear purée mixed with a little redcurrant jelly. Poach 6 peeled pears in vanilla-flavoured syrup, cut in half, remove the cores and place a pear half on each half-madeleine. Prepare a vanilla soufflé mixture and cover the pears with it. Brown in the oven. If desired, serve with a kirsch zabaglione.

Pineapple compote

Remove the skin and core of a pineapple. Slice the fruit and cook in some vanilla-flavoured syrup for about 15–20 minutes. Arrange the pineapple slices in a dish, reduce the syrup and pour it over the pineapple. Cool completely, and keep in the refrigerator until ready to serve.

Pineapple coupes

Cut some fresh or canned pineapple into dice and diamond shapes and macerate them for 1 hour in white rum. Place 2 tablespoons diced pineapple in each dish, cover with vanilla ice cream and smooth out the surface. Decorate each dish with the pineapple diamonds and sprinkle with a few drops of the white rum.

Pineapple en surprise

Cut the top off a choice pineapple close to the leaves and hollow it out carefully, without splitting the skin. Cut the pulp into dice and macerate it with 100 g (4 oz, ½ cup) caster (superfine) sugar and 2 tablespoons rum for about 2 hours. Boil 600 ml (1 pint, 2½ cups) milk in a saucepan with a vanilla pod (bean) split in two. In a mixing bowl, beat 1 whole egg with 3 yolks and 100 g (4 oz, ½ cup) caster sugar; when the mixture is white and thick, blend in 50 g (2 oz, ½ cup) plain (all-purpose) flour to obtain a very smooth paste. Pour the boiling milk over the paste fairly slowly to avoid cooking the yolks, whisking rapidly all the time. Return the mixture to the pan, place over a gentle heat and stir until the cream has thickened. Then remove from the heat and add the juice in which the pineapple has been macerated.

Cool this cream in the refrigerator, then mix it gently with the diced pineapple, 3 egg whites whisked to very stiff peaks, and 100 ml (4 fl oz, 7 tablespoons) crème fraîche. Fill the pineapple with this preparation, replace its top and refrigerate until ready to serve.

Pineapple fritters

Slice a peeled fresh pineapple (alternatively, use canned pineapple). Sprinkle the slices with caster (superfine) sugar and kirsch or rum and macerate for 30 minutes. Drain thoroughly, dip in sweetened or unsweetened batter and deep-fry in hot oil. Remove the fritters from the oil and drain. Dust with caster (superfine) sugar and arrange on a napkin. Fritters may also be served dusted with icing (confectioner's) sugar and glazed in a hot oven or under a grill (broiler).

Pineapple surprise

Cut a pineapple in half lengthways through the whole fruit, including the leaves, and scoop out the flesh carefully, making sure you do not damage the skin. Cut the flesh into small, equal-sized cubes and macerate in 100 g (4 oz, ½ cup) caster (superfine) sugar and 3 tablespoons light rum for 2 hours.

Bring 600 ml (1 pint, 2½ cups) milk to the boil with a vanilla pod (bean), cut in half. Beat 1 whole egg and 3 egg yolks with 100 g (4 oz, ½ cup) caster sugar. When the mixture is white and foamy, add 65 g (2½ oz, ½ cup) plain (all-purpose) flour and stir to obtain a very smooth mixture. Pour the hot milk on to this mixture, very slowly so as not to cook the yolks and make the mixture curdle. Return to a low heat and whisk briskly until the custard has thickened. Remove from the heat. Drain the pineapple and add the rum-flavoured syrup to the crème pâtissière. Chill the mixture in the refrigerator. Reserve a few pieces of pineapple for decoration, then add the rest to the crème pâtissière. Fold in 3 very stiffly whisked egg whites and 100 ml (4 fl oz, 7 tablespoons) crème fraîche. Fill the pineapple halves with this mixture. Decorate with the reserved pinepple and a few wild strawberries. Add a little finely pared lime rind if liked. When they are available, small pineapples can be used, allowing ½ per portion.

Plombières cream

Place 8 egg yolks and 1 tablespoon rice flour in a saucepan and mix well. Add 500 ml (17 fl oz, 2 cups) milk, which is almost boiling. Place the saucepan over a moderate heat, stirring continuously with a wooden spoon. When the mixture begins to thicken, remove it from the heat and stir thoroughly until it is perfectly smooth. Then cook it over the heat for a further few minutes. This cream must have the same consistency as a confectioner's custard (pastry cream). Then add 175 g (6 oz, ¾ cup) caster (superfine) sugar and a minute pinch of salt.

Pour the mixture into another pan and set it on ice, stirring from time to time: it will thicken as it cools. When it is completely cold, just before serving, mix in 4 tablespoons of a liqueur (kirsch or rum, for example) and then a small quantity of whipped cream; the finished product should be light, velvety and perfectly smooth. Serve in a silver dish, in small pots, in a pastry case, a biscuit (cookie) crumb case or a dish-shaped base of almond paste.

Plum compote

Stone (pit) the plums carefully without splitting them in two. Poach them in boiling syrup, prepared with 350 g (12 oz, 1½ cups) granulated sugar to 600 ml (1 pint, 2½ cups) water, for 10–12 minutes. Serve well chilled, with or without cream.

This recipe can also be prepared using mirabelle plums.

Plum pudding

Put the following ingredients in a large mixing bowl: 125 g (4½ oz, 1 cup) suet, 175 g (6 oz, 1½ cups) chopped blanched almonds, 250 g (9 oz, 1½ cups) each of raisins and currants, 100 g (4 oz, 1 cup) sifted plain (all-purpose) flour, a generous pinch of salt, 250 g (9 oz, 1 cup) caster (superfine) sugar, 125 g (4½ oz, 1 cup) fairly dry white breadcrumbs, 250 g (9 oz, 1½ cups) chopped candied peel, the grated zest of ½ lemon and ½ teaspoon each mixed spice, ground cinnamon and grated nutmeg.

Beat 4 eggs with 4 tablespoons milk and the same quantity of rum. Add to the mixing bowl.

Boil 150 g (5 oz, ⅔ cup) granulated sugar with 4 tablespoons cold water until golden brown, then stir in 250 ml (8 fl oz, 1 cup) boiling water. Add this caramel to the ingredients in the mixing bowl. Stir the mixture thoroughly for 15 minutes.

Butter a large pudding basin (mould) and place a circle of greaseproof (wax) paper at the bottom. Place 125 g (4½ oz, ¾ cup) stoned (pitted) prunes (previously soaked in cold tea or water, then drained) in the basin and pour the pudding mixture on top. Cover with a circle of greaseproof paper, then with a pudding cloth or double thickness foil. Place the basin in the basket of a pressure cooker and add enough water to reach halfway up the basin. Cook for 1½ hours, beginning the timing from the moment that steam begins to escape. Alternatively, cook for 4 hours in a steamer or on an old saucer in a saucepan with enough boiling water to reach halfway up the basin (topping up with boiling water as necessary). Remove the basin, wrap in foil and store in a cool place.

Steam for 1 hour more in a pressure cooker, or 2 hours in a steamer or saucepan, before serving. Then turn the pudding out on to a serving dish and sprinkle with 3 tablespoons sugar. Pour 4 tablespoons warm rum over the pudding and set it alight. The pudding can also be served cold.

Poirissimo

This dessert consists of pear compote, pear conserve, pears in wine, pear tart and pear granita, a small portion of each being carefully arranged on individual plates. For all the recipes, the pears must be peeled quickly just before they are required, to prevent discoloration.

To make the compote, peel the pears, cut them into quarters and cook them for 10 minutes over a brisk heat in a covered saucepan with sugar, lemon juice and a little water.

For the conserve, allow 800 g (1¾ lb, 3½ cups) sugar and 100 ml (4 fl oz, 7 tablespoons) water per 1 kg (2¼ lb) fruit. Boil the sugar and water until the syrup coats the back of a spoon. Add the sliced pears to the syrup, together with vanilla extract to taste, and cook until the fruit is tender.

The syrup for the pears in wine is made by boiling a mixture of wine and honey, reducing it by half. Peel some small ripe pears without removing the stalks and cook them in the honey-and-wine mixture for 15 minutes. Cool and add some cassis (blackcurrant liqueur).

Roll out some shortcrust pastry (basic pie dough) into a circle and cover with slices of pear sprinkled with lemon juice. Sprinkle with sugar and bake for 20 minutes in a preheated oven at 220°C (425°F, gas 7). Serve warm.

Prepare the granita the day before. Make a purée with some very ripe pears and a little lemon juice and place it in the freezer. When it begins to solidify, purée in a blender, adding sugar, lemon juice and a little pear liqueur to taste. Return to the freezer and repeat the operation once. The resulting granita must have the colour and consistency of snow.

Praline pannequets

Pannequets are sweet or savoury pancakes filled with chopped ingredients, a purée or a cream.

Make a batter with 250 g (9 oz, 2¼ cups) plain (all-purpose) flour, a pinch of salt, 3 beaten eggs mixed with 1 tablespoon caster (superfine) sugar, 250 ml (8 fl oz, 1 cup) milk, 250 ml (8 fl oz, 1 cup) water and 1 tablespoon melted butter. Cook 8 fairly thick pancakes.

Prepare 300 ml (½ pint, 1¼ cups) confectioner's custard (pastry cream) flavoured with liqueur (Cointreau or Grand Marnier) or with Armagnac and mix with 100 g (4 oz, ½ cup) crushed praline. Spread the pancakes with this mixture and roll up. Arrange in a buttered ovenproof dish and sprinkle with 8 finely crushed macaroons. Place in a preheated oven at 230°C (450°F, gas 8) for a few minutes to heat through.

Prunes in Rasteau with fresh cream

Soak 36 prunes overnight in 500 ml (17 fl oz, 2 cups) light red Bordeaux wine and the same amount of Rasteau (a sweet wine of the Rhône Valley). The following day cook them in the wine together with a lemon and an orange cut into thick slices: bring to the boil, reduce the heat and simmer for 15 minutes.

Leave to cool, then cover and chill for 3 days in the cooking liquid. Remove the slices of fruit and serve the prunes coated with double (heavy) cream.

Quince compote

Peel the quinces, cut them into quarters and remove the seeds. Cut each quarter into two and blanch the pieces. Cool them under cold running water and pat dry. Cook until tender in a vanilla-flavoured syrup made with 350 g (12 oz, 1½ cups) granulated sugar to 600 ml (1 pint, 2½ cups) water. Arrange in a dish and pour the syrup over.

Raspberry charlotte (1)

Make a syrup with 300 g (11 oz, 1⅓ cups) granulated sugar and 250 ml (8 fl oz, 1 cup) water. Add 500 g (18 oz, 3¼ cups) raspberries and cook for 30 minutes. Dissolve 15 g (½ oz, 2 envelopes) powdered gelatine in 2 tablespoons hot water over a pan of simmering water and mix with the raspberries. Allow to cool. Soak some sponge fingers (ladyfingers) in kirsch and use them to line a charlotte mould. Whip 250 ml (8 fl oz, 1 cup) double (heavy) cream and mix it with the raspberries. Fill the lined mould with the mixture and leave to set in the refrigerator for at least 3 hours. Serve with custard.

Raspberry charlotte (2)

Line a charlotte mould with sponge fingers (ladyfingers) soaked in raspberry-flavoured syrup. Whip some fresh cream with caster (superfine) sugar and vanilla sugar. Add an equal quantity of raspberry purée made with either fresh or frozen raspberries. Fill the lined mould with the mixture and cover with a layer of sponge fingers, also soaked in raspberry syrup. Press the sponge fingers down, put a plate over the mould and chill for at least 3 hours. Invert on to a plate just before serving.

Raspberry compote

Wash, hull, dry, but do not cook the raspberries. Arrange them in a heatproof dish. Prepare boiling syrup with 350 g (12 oz, 1½ cups) granulated sugar to 600 ml (1 pint, 2½ cups) water. Pour the syrup over the fruit and leave to cool. Serve warm or chilled.

Redcurrant compote

Pull the fruit very carefully from the stalks with a fork and place in a saucepan. Cover with boiling syrup, prepared with 350 g (12 oz, 1½ cups) granulated sugar to 600 ml (1 pint, 2½ cups) water. Bring back to the boil, then pour both the fruit and the syrup into a dish. Cool, then place in the refrigerator. (Raw strawberries or raspberries can be added if desired.)

Rhubarb compote

Use only fresh sticks of rhubarb and carefully remove the strings. Cut the sticks into pieces 6–7.5 cm (2½–3 in) long. Blanch them in boiling water for 3 minutes, drain and cool. Place them in a preserving pan. Cover with a syrup prepared with 350 g (12 oz, 1½ cups) granulated sugar to 600 ml (1 pint, 2½ cups) water. Cover and cook without stirring. Serve either warm or cold. This compote can be used as a filling for tarts.

Rhubarb compote with strawberries

Peel 1 kg (2¼ lb) rhubarb, carefully removing all the stringy parts, and cut into even-shaped chunks 4–5 cm (1½–2 in) long. Place in a large bowl and sprinkle generously with vanilla sugar. Leave the chunks to soak for 3 hours, stirring occasionally to redistribute the sugar. Put the rhubarb in a saucepan and cook for 15 minutes over moderate heat. Wash, hull and quarter 300 g (11 oz, 2 cups) ripe strawberries. Add to the rhubarb and cook for another

5 minutes. Transfer the rhubarb to a fruit bowl and allow to cool. Serve in bowls, on its own or with vanilla ice cream and small warm madeleines.

Rice à l'impératrice

Soak 15 g (½ oz, 2 envelopes) gelatine in 3 tablespoons warm water. Soak 125 g (4½ oz, ¾ cup) crystallized (candied) fruit in 3 tablespoons rum. Add 250 g (9 oz, 1⅓ cups) short-grain rice to 1 litre (1¾ pints, 4⅓ cups) boiling water and boil for 2 minutes. Drain, and then add the rice to 1 litre (1¾ pints, 4⅓ cups) boiling milk containing 1 vanilla pod (bean), a pinch of salt and 15 g (½ oz, 1 tablespoon) butter. Cook gently for about 20 minutes until the rice is just beginning to soften. Now add 200 g (7 oz, scant 1 cup) caster (superfine) sugar and cook for a further 5 minutes. Remove from the heat and add the crystallized fruit with the rum.

While the rice is cooking, prepare a custard with 250 ml (8 fl oz, 1 cup) milk, half a vanilla pod, 4 eggs, 5 tablespoons caster sugar and a tiny pinch of salt. While the custard is still hot, add the soaked gelatine and stir until dissolved. Then rub the custard through a fine sieve and flavour with 1 tablespoon rum if desired. Leave the rice and the custard to cool.

Whip 250 ml (8 fl oz, 1 cup) double (heavy) cream with 3–4 tablespoons very cold milk until thick, then add 1 teaspoon vanilla sugar and 3 table-spoons caster sugar. Mix the custard into the chilled rice, then very carefully fold in the cream. Pour into a savarin mould or a deep sandwich tin (layer cake pan) and keep in the refrigerator until required. Unmould on to a serving dish and decorate with crystallized fruit or fruit in syrup.

Rice cakes Pompadour

Prepare 175 g (6 oz, ¾ cup) short-grain rice, cooking it until all the milk has been absorbed and the grains begin to burst; allow to cool slightly. Butter a baking sheet and spread the warm rice to a thickness of about 1 cm (½ in). Dot the surface with butter and allow to cool completely.

Prepare 200 ml (7 fl oz, ¾ cup) thick confectioner's custard (pastry cream) flavoured with rum. Chop 150 g (5 oz, 1 cup) crystallized (candied) fruits into small pieces. Cut the rice into 5 cm (2 in) squares. Mix the custard and crystallized fruits and coat the undersides of the squares with this mixture; stick the squares together in pairs. Coat twice with breadcrumbs and deep-fry in hot oil at 180°C (350°F). Drain the cakes on paper towels and serve with hot apricot sauce.

Rice cooked in milk

Cook 200 g (7 oz, 1 cup) washed round-grain rice for 2 minutes in boiling salted water. Drain and pour it into 900 ml (1½ pints, 1 quart) boiling milk. Add 75 g (3 oz, 6 tablespoons) caster (superfine) sugar, a pinch of salt and either a pinch of ground cinnamon or a vanilla pod (bean). Cover the pan and cook over a very low heat for 30–40 minutes. Add 50 g (2 oz, ¼ cup) butter, and, if desired, 2 or 3 egg yolks. Serve either warm or chilled.

Rice cooked in milk for ring moulds and cakes

Blanch 200 g (7 oz, 1 cup) round-grain rice in boiling water for 2 minutes. Drain, refresh under cold running water and drain again. Bring 900 ml (1½ pints, 1 quart) milk to the boil, add ½ teaspoon salt and a vanilla pod (bean), then add the rice, together with 75 g (3 oz, 6 tablespoons) caster (superfine) or granulated sugar and 25 g (1 oz, 2 tablespoons) butter. Cook either over a very low heat in a covered pan for 30 minutes without stirring, or in a preheated oven at 200°C (400°F, gas 6) for 35 minutes. Remove the vanilla pod. Mix 4–6 egg yolks with a little of the rice, then pour it into the pan and stir well. If liked, 4 egg whites, whisked until stiff, may be added.

Rice fritters

Prepare a thick rice pudding. Spread in a layer 1.5 cm (½–¾ in) thick and allow to cool completely. Cut into small squares, rectangles or lozenges. Dip in batter and deep-fry in hot oil. Remove the fritters and drain. Dust with caster (superfine) sugar and arrange on a napkin.

Rice fritters may also be made of two rounds of the chilled pudding mixture spread with confectioner's custard (pastry cream) and sandwiched tightly together.

Rice gâteau with caramel

Prepare some plain rice cooked in milk. Remove the vanilla pod (bean), if one has been used, and add 175–200 g (6–7 oz, 1–1¼ cups) caster (superfine) sugar and 3 egg yolks. Gently mix, then add the 3 egg whites whisked to stiff peaks. Place 100 g (4 oz, ½ cup) granulated sugar, the juice of ½ a lemon and 1 tablespoon water in a saucepan, then cook until the mixture turns brown. Pour it immediately into a charlotte mould with a diameter at the top of 20 cm (8 in). Tilt the mould to line the bottom and sides with caramel. Pour the rice mixture into the mould, press it down and place the mould in a bain marie. Bring to the boil, then bake in a preheated oven at 200°C (400°F, gas 6) for about 45 minutes. Leave to cool, then turn out on to a serving dish.

Heat a little hot water in the mould to dissolve the remaining caramel and pour it over the gâteau. Serve with crème anglaise or a purée of red fruits. Crystallized (candied) fruit and raisins, soaked for 2 hours in a small glass of rum, can be added to the rice before the whisked egg whites.

Rice pudding

Wash 250 g (9 oz, 1½ cups) round-grain rice and blanch it in boiling water. Drain it and place in a flameproof casserole, then add 1 litre (1¾ pints,

4⅓ cups) milk boiled with 150 g (5 oz, ⅔ cup) caster (superfine) sugar, half a vanilla pod (bean) and a pinch of salt. Add 50 g (2 oz, ¼ cup) butter, stir and bring slowly to the boil. Then cover the casserole and finish cooking in a preheated oven at 220°C (425°F, gas 7) for 25–30 minutes.

Remove from the oven and beat in 8 egg yolks, mixing carefully. Then fold in 7–8 egg whites whisked into very stiff peaks. Use this mixture to fill about 10 small moulds which have been buttered and sprinkled with fine breadcrumbs. Cook in the oven in a bain marie for 30–35 minutes. Turn out and serve with a rum-flavoured zabaglione, a custard cream or a fruit sauce flavoured with liqueur.

The mixture may be flavoured with 50 g (2 oz, ½ cup) cocoa per 500 g (18 oz, 3 cups) cooked rice.

Rice ring à la créole

Butter a ring or savarin mould. Fill with thick rice pudding, press down, heat through in the oven, then turn out on to a serving dish. Poach 16 half slices of pineapple in vanilla-flavoured syrup and fill the centre of the ring with them. Decorate with cherries and angelica. Serve either slightly warmed, or very cold, with apricot sauce flavoured with rum.

Rice ring à la montmorency

Prepare a rice ring as in the previous recipe. Separately, prepare some confectioner's custard (pastry cream) flavoured with kirsch, and also some stoned (pitted) cherries poached in syrup. Fill the centre of the ring with alternate layers of confectioner's custard and poached cherries, then sprinkle with crushed macaroons and melted butter and place in a preheated oven at 240°C (475°F, gas 9) for a few minutes to heat through. Serve with cherry sauce flavoured with kirsch.

Rice with almond milk and citrus fruit jelly

Cook 75 g (3 oz, ½ cup) round-grain Camargue rice in 250 ml (8 fl oz, 1 cup) milk and 25 g (1 oz, 2 tablespoons) sugar. Incorporate a mixture of 200 ml (7 fl oz, ¾ cup) double (heavy) cream, 1 egg, 1 egg yolk and 1 teaspoon almond milk. Place in 4 ovenproof dishes and cook for 15 minutes in a pre-heated oven at 120°C (250°F, gas ½). Place in a cool place. Peel 4 oranges and 3 pink grapefruit, then quarter lengthways and cut the segments across into slices. Collect the fruit juice, warm slightly and add 2 sheets of soaked and drained gelatine, heat gently, stirring until the gelatine has dissolved. Put in a cool place. Decorate each dessert with the slices of orange and grapefruit and cooked shreds of finely pared zest. Pour the syrupy jelly on top.

Roast figs with a coulis of red fruits

Melt 50 g (2 oz, ¼ cup) butter in a frying pan. Add 16 fresh ripe figs and 3 tablespoons icing (confectioner's) sugar. Fry until lightly golden, then cook in a preheated oven at 200°C (400°F, gas 6) for 8–10 minutes. Remove from the oven and, using scissors, cut the figs open to look like flowers. Fill the figs with 200 g (7 oz) fresh raspberries. Pour 300 ml (½ pint, 1¼ cups) raspberry or strawberry coulis on 4 plates and decorate with the figs. Place 1 scoop of vanilla ice cream in the centre of each plate. Serve immediately.

Rum zabaglione with marrons glacés

Beat 10 egg yolks and 200 g (7 oz, 1 cup) granulated sugar with a whisk in a bain marie, until the mixture becomes pale and thick. Mix in 3 wine glasses white wine and 3 tablespoons white rum, beating all the time, until the mixture becomes thick and frothy. Flavour lightly with a few drops of vanilla essence (extract). Arrange some marrons glacés in sundae dishes, cover with zabaglione and chill in the refrigerator until required.

Remove the ice cream from the freezer 30 minutes before serving. Keep in the refrigerator until ready to serve. Serve in bowls, decorated with the scoops of cream and slivers of pistachio nut.

Saffron rice à la néerlandaise

Wash about 175 g (6 oz, ¾ cup) short-grain rice. Blanch it for 2 minutes in boiling water. Drain, rinse in cold water and drain again. Boil 1 litre (1¾ pints, 4⅓ cups) milk with ½ teaspoon salt and 1 generous tablespoon soft light brown sugar. Add the rice and cook for 35–40 minutes until very soft. Then add 1 tablespoon lemon juice and a generous pinch of powdered saffron and mix well. Pour the rice into individual sundae dishes and leave to cool completely. Serve as a cold dessert, sprinkled with brown sugar, accompanied by cinnamon or ginger biscuits (cookies).

Salad of Maltese oranges with candied zest

Prepare a syrup with 250 g (9 oz, 1 cup) sugar, 200 ml (7 fl oz, ¾ cup) grenadine syrup, 250 ml (8 fl oz, 1 cup) water and the juice of 1 lemon. Thoroughly wash 3 kg (6½ lb) Maltese oranges. Peel, without removing the white pith from the fruit. Cut the zest into very fine strips. Cook these strips for 1 hour in the syrup which should bubble only very lightly. Allow the candied zest to cool in the syrup and set aside in a cool place. Then remove and discard the white pith from the oranges. Place the orange segments in a salad bowl and pour the syrup on top. Decorate the orange salad with the candied zest and serve immediately.

Scotch pudding

Place 500 g (18 oz, 9 cups) fresh breadcrumbs in a large bowl and moisten with a little boiled milk. Add 100 g (4 oz, ½ cup) sugar, 100 g (4 oz, ¾ cup) currants, 100 g (4 oz, ¾ cup) sultanas (golden raisins), 100 g 4 oz, ¾ cup) raisins, 175 g (6 oz, 1 cup) chopped crystallized (candied) fruit, 4 beaten eggs and 4 tablespoons rum. Pour the mixture into a smooth buttered mould, filling it up to 1 cm (½ in) from the brim. Place in a bain marie and cook in a preheated oven at 200°C (400°F, gas 6) for 1 hour. Serve with a rum-flavoured zabaglione or a Madeira-flavoured custard cream.

Semolina fritters

Add some small raisins that have been soaked in rum to thick semolina pudding. Spread in a layer 1.5 cm (½–¾ in) thick and allow to cool completely. Cut into small squares, rectangles or lozenges. Dip in batter and deep-fry in hot oil. Remove the fritters and drain. Dust with caster (superfine) sugar and arrange on a napkin.

Semolina fritters may also be made of two rounds of the chilled mixture sandwiched tightly together with confectioner's sugar (pastry cream) .

Semolina pudding (rich)

Sprinkle 250 g (9 oz, 1¾ cups) semolina into 1 litre (1¾ pints, 4⅓ cups) boiling milk in which has been dissolved 125 g (4½ oz, ½ cup) caster (superfine) sugar, a generous pinch of salt and 100 g (4 oz, ½ cup) butter. Mix and cook over a very gentle heat for 25 minutes. Leave to cool slightly, then add 6 egg yolks and 1 small liqueur glass of orange-flavoured liqueur. Using a metal spoon, gently stir into the mixture 4 egg whites whisked into very stiff peaks. Pour this mixture into a savarin mould, buttered and dusted with semolina. Place in a bain marie and cook in a preheated oven at 200°C (400°F, gas 6) until the mixture is slightly springy to the touch. Leave the pudding to stand for 30 minutes before turning it out. Serve with either custard or an orange sauce.

Semolina pudding (simple baked)

Bring to the boil in a flameproof casserole 1 litre (1¾ pints, 4⅓ cups) milk containing 150 g (5 oz, ⅔ cup) caster (superfine) sugar, a pinch of salt and a vanilla pod (bean) split in half. Mix in 250 g (9 oz, 1½ cups) semolina and 75–100 g (3–4 oz, 6–8 tablespoons) butter, then cover the pan and cook in a preheated oven at 200°C (400°F, gas 6) for 25–30 minutes.

Semolina ring with fruit

Butter a ring or savarin mould and fill with a stiff, cooked semolina pudding mixed with finely diced crystallized (candied) fruit. Place in a preheated oven at 160°C (325°F, gas 3) for a few minutes, until set. Turn out on to a serving dish. Fill the centre with whole, halved or cubed fruit, poached in vanilla-flavoured syrup. Heat again for a few minutes in the oven. Just before serving, sprinkle the ring with a very hot fruit sauce flavoured with rum or kirsch.

Semolina subrics

Make a simple baked semolina pudding, remove from the oven and mix in 6 egg yolks. Leave to cool a little, then spread it in a layer 2 cm (¾ in) thick over a buttered baking sheet. Brush the surface with melted butter to prevent a crust from forming and leave to cool completely. Cut out rounds using a 6 cm (2½ in) pastry (cookie) cutter and brown them in a frying pan in clarified butter. Arrange them in a ring in a round dish and fill the centre with redcurrant jelly or with another red jelly or jam (preserve).

Soufflé Ambassadrice

Make a confectioner's custard (pastry cream) with 1 litre (1¾ pints, 4⅓ cups) milk, 8 egg yolks, a pinch of salt, 100 g (4 oz, 1 cup) plain (all-purpose) flour (or 4 tablespoons cornflour (cornstarch) or potato flour) and 300 g (11 oz,

1⅓ cups) granulated sugar. Add 1 teaspoon vanilla essence (extract), 8 crushed macaroons and 50 g (2 oz, ½ cup) shredded (slivered) almonds soaked in rum. Fold in 12 stiffly whisked egg whites, turn into a soufflé dish and cook in a preheated oven at 200°C (400°F, gas 6) for 30–35 minutes.

Soufflé lapérouse

Prepare a confectioner's custard (pastry cream) using 250 ml (8 fl oz, 1 cup) milk. Add 65 g (2½ oz) praline, 100 ml (4 fl oz, 7 tablespoons) rum and 50 g (2 oz, ⅓ cup) crystallized (candied) fruit. Stiffly whisk the whites of 5 eggs (whose yolks have been used for the custard) and fold them into the mixture. Butter a 20 cm (8 in) soufflé mould, then coat with caster (superfine) sugar. Pour in the mixture. Place in a preheated oven at 180°C (350°F, gas 4) and bake for 15 minutes. Sprinkle with icing (confectioner's) sugar and allow to cook for a further 5 minutes, so that the top of the soufflé is caramelized.

Soufflé omelette

Mix together in a bowl 250 g (9 oz, generous 1 cup) caster (superfine) sugar, 6 egg yolks and 1 teaspoon vanilla sugar or 1 tablespoon grated orange or lemon zest. Beat until the mixture turns white and thick. Whisk 8 egg whites to stiff peaks and fold carefully into the yolk mixture.

Butter a long ovenproof dish and sprinkle it with caster sugar. Pour in three-quarters of the omelette mixture and smooth it into a low mound with the blade of a knife. Put the rest of the mixture into a piping (pastry) bag with a plain round nozzle and pipe an interlaced decoration on top of the omelette. Sprinkle with caster sugar. Cook in a preheated oven at 200°C (400°F, gas 6) for about 20 minutes. Dredge with icing (confectioner's) sugar and glaze under the grill (broiler). The omelette can also be flavoured with chocolate, coffee or a liqueur.

Soufflé omelette with wild strawberries

Clean, wash and drain some wild strawberries. Leave them to macerate in a few spoonfuls of Alsace framboise (raspberry-flavoured spirit) with a pinch of vanilla sugar. Whisk 4 egg whites to stiff peaks and separately beat the yolks with a little sugar. Mix the two carefully, then pour into a heavy frying pan containing very hot butter. When the eggs begin to set, add the strawberries, fold the omelette over and continue to cook over a low heat. Dredge very lightly with sugar and serve. A little fresh strawberry purée can be poured over the omelette.

Soufflé Rothschild

Cut 150 g (5 oz, 1 cup) crystallized (candied) fruit into small pieces and macerate in 100 ml (4 fl oz, 7 tablespoons) Danziger Goldwasser for at least 30 minutes to soften.

Whisk together 200 g (7 oz, 1 cup) caster (superfine) sugar and 4 egg yolks until the mixture turns white and thick. Then mix in 75 g (3 oz, ¾ cup) plain (all-purpose) flour and 500 ml (17 fl oz, 2 cups) boiling milk. Pour into a saucepan and bring to the boil, stirring constantly, then cook for 1–2 minutes. Pour this confectioner's custard (pastry cream) into a bowl and add 2 egg yolks and the pieces of fruit with their macerating liquid. Whisk 6 egg whites to stiff peaks with a pinch of salt and fold them carefully into the custard mixture.

Butter 2 soufflé dishes (for 4 servings each) and sprinkle the insides with 1½ tablespoons caster sugar. Divide the mixture between the 2 dishes and bake in a preheated oven at 200°C (400°F, gas 6).

After 25 minutes, sprinkle the tops of the soufflés with icing (confectioner's) sugar, taking care to leave the oven door open for the shortest possible time, then continue to cook for another 5 minutes.

Soufflé Simone

Generously butter a 20 cm (8 in) soufflé mould. Melt 100 g (4 oz, 4 squares) cooking (semisweet) chocolate in 2½ tablespoons milk. Add 2 tablespoons confectioner's custard (pastry cream) and 50 g (2 oz, ¼ cup) caster (superfine) sugar and bring to the boil. Remove from the heat and mix in 2 egg yolks. Stiffly whisk the whites of 5 eggs and sweeten very slightly. Lightly sprinkle the buttered mould with 2 tablespoons caster sugar. Fold the egg whites into the chocolate mixture and pour into the mould. Bake in a preheated oven at 200°C (400°F, gas 6) for about 25 minutes. Serve with lightly whipped cream.

Spiced gingerbread fruit charlotte

Heat 200 ml (7 fl oz, ¾ cup) milk. Stir 50 g (2 oz, 3 tablespoons) clear honey into the milk. Add 2 tablespoons very finely chopped candied orange peel and the same of candied lemon peel, with 1 teaspoon powdered cinnamon, 1 powdered clove and a pinch of grated nutmeg. Allow to infuse off the heat.

Beat 4 egg yolks and 25 g (1 oz, 2 tablespoons) caster (superfine) sugar until the mixture has thickened and doubled in volume. Stir this mixture into the flavoured milk and cook gently over a low heat, stirring all the time without boiling until the mixture thickens. Remove from the heat.

Roast 40 g (1½ oz, ¼ cup) chopped almonds and hazelnuts under the grill (broiler) until golden. Soak and dissolve 3 sheets of leaf gelatine or 7 g (¼ oz, 1 envelope) powdered gelatine in a little cold water. Stir the dissolved gelatine into the fruit custard. Add 250 ml (9 fl oz, 1 cup) very cold whipped cream, then the almonds and nuts. Flavour with 2 teaspoons kirsch. Refrigerate.

Mix 250 ml (8 fl oz, 1 cup) sugar syrup and 4 teaspoons kirsch. Dip 12 slices of gingerbread in this syrup and line the bottom and sides of a charlotte mould, overlapping them. Fill with the cooled cream, smooth the top and cover with gingerbread. Leave in the refrigerator for at least 6 hours.

Soak mixed dried fruits (prunes, apricots, figs and raisins) and fresh raisins in warm Gewürztraminer and place in a dish. Unmould the charlotte on a dish, sprinkle with crushed praline and serve with the dried fruit.

• *Individual charlottes* Instead of making a large charlotte, ramekins or individual soufflé dishes can be used to make individual charlottes. Line the bases only – not the sides of the dishes – and top the mixture with gingerbread. Chill any leftover cream, then scoop it into neat ovals (as for quenelles) and serve with the charlottes. The charlottes may be served on plates flooded with crème anglaise, feathered with chocolate custard, and the dried fruit can be spooned into tuile or brandy snap cups.

Strawberries à la maltaise

Cut some oranges in half and scoop out the flesh. Trim the bases of the orange halves so that they can stand upright. Place them in the refrigerator. Squeeze the pulp and sieve it to obtain the juice. Wash, wipe and hull some small strawberries. Add some sugar and a little Curaçao or Cointreau to the orange juice, and pour the mixture over the strawberries. Store in the refrigerator. To serve, fill the orange halves with the strawberries and arrange them in a dish on a bed of crushed ice.

Strawberries cardinal

Arrange some chilled strawberries in glass goblets. Cover with fresh raspberry purée and sprinkle with flaked almonds.

Strawberries Condé

Bind some rice cooked in milk, flavoured with sugar and vanilla, with egg yolk, and fill a ring mould. Cook in a bain marie for 30 minutes in a preheated oven at 200°C (400°F, gas 6), then leave to cool and turn out of the mould on to a serving dish. Wash some large strawberries, drain, hull and divide into 2 equal quantities. Sprinkle half with sugar and brandy and leave in a cool place to macerate for at least 1 hour. Press the other half of the strawberries through a sieve, together with some raspberries (a quarter of the weight of strawberries); add some lemon juice – 1 tablespoon per 500 g (18 oz) strawberries – and just enough caster (superfine) sugar for the purée not to taste sour. Drain the whole strawberries and arrange in the middle of the rice. Serve the fruit purée with the rice ring.

Strawberry charlotte

First prepare some sponge fingers (ladyfingers). Beat together 6 egg yolks and 150 g (5 oz, ⅔ cup) caster (superfine) sugar until pale and creamy; whisk 7 egg whites until they form stiff peaks. Combine a quarter of the beaten egg whites with the yolk-sugar mixture, then add the rest of the egg whites together with 150 g (5 oz, 1¼ cups) plain (all-purpose) flour. Butter and flour 4 baking sheets. Mark a 23 cm (9 in) diameter circle on 3 of the sheets; pipe the mixture through a piping (pastry) bag in a circular pattern within the circles on these sheets. Pipe the remaining mixture in diagonal lines to cover the fourth sheet. Bake in a preheated oven at 240°C (475°F, gas 9) for 10–12 minutes.

Now prepare a strawberry Bavarian cream. Reduce 1 kg (2¼ lb, 8 cups) strawberries to a purée and press through a sieve. Heat 450 ml (¾ pint, 2 cups) of this purée with 25 g (1 oz, 2 tablespoons) sugar until it boils. Soak and dissolve 3 sheets leaf gelatine or 7 g (¼ oz, 1 envelope) powdered gelatine in a little cold water and add to the strawberry pulp. Set aside to cool. When the mixture is cold, mix in 450 ml (¾ pint, 2 cups) whipped cream.

Line the sides of a 23 cm (9 in) deep round cake tin (pan) with strips cut from the diagonally piped sponge mixture. Place a sponge round in the base.

Fill with the Bavarian cream (inserting the second round of sponge in the centre). Cover with the last sponge and refrigerate for 4 hours. Unmould the charlotte and dust with icing (confectioner's) sugar. Prepare a sauce by mixing the remaining strawberry purée with the juice of ½ a lemon and 125 g (4½ oz, ½ cup) caster sugar. Dip a large strawberry in this sauce and place in the centre of the charlotte; serve the rest of the sauce in a sauceboat.

Strawberry compote

Wash, hull, dry, but do not cook the strawberries. Arrange them in a heatproof dish. Prepare boiling syrup with 350 g (12 oz, 1½ cups) granulated sugar to 600 ml (1 pint, 2½ cups) water and pour this over the fruit. The syrup may be flavoured with orange or other flavourings.

Strawberry mousse

Put 400 g (14 oz, 3 cups) strawberries through a blender or food processor and sweeten the purée with 150 g (5 oz, ⅔ cup) caster (superfine) sugar. Flavour with a small amount of strawberry liqueur and leave to stand. Stiffly whisk 4 egg whites and add 15 g (½ oz, 1 tablespoon) sugar. Carefully fold the whisked egg whites into the strawberry purée. Place the mixture in individual glass dishes and refrigerate. Serve with a strawberry sauce made by adding a little lemon juice to about 150 g (5 oz, ⅔ cup) strawberry purée.

Strawberry or raspberry soufflé

Prepare a confectioner's custard (pastry cream) using 1 litre (1¾ pints, 4⅓ cups) milk, 8 egg yolks, a generous pinch of salt, 100 g (4 oz, 1 cup) plain (all-purpose) flour (or 4 tablespoons cornflour (cornstarch) or potato flour) and 300 g (11 oz, 1⅓ cups) granulated sugar. Add 300 g (11 oz, 2–3 cups) puréed wild strawberries, large strawberries soaked in sugar or raspberries. Fold in

12–14 very stiffly whisked egg whites with a metal spoon. Pour the mixture into a well-buttered large soufflé mould coated with sugar. Bake in a pre-heated oven at 190°C (375°F, gas 5) for 20–25 minutes.

Striped chocolate and vanilla Bavarian cream

This consists of creams of different colours and flavours placed in alternating layers in the mould. Striped Bavarian cream can also be made directly in crystal or glass bowls: preparation is quicker and the cream more delicate because the amount of gelatine used can be significantly reduced as the bavarois will not be turned out.

Soak 15–20 g (½–¾ oz, 2–3 envelopes) gelatine in 3 tablespoons cold water. Heat 500 ml (17 fl oz, 2 cups) milk with a vanilla pod (bean). Put 225 g (8 oz, 1 cup) caster (superfine) sugar, a pinch of salt and 8 egg yolks in a saucepan and stir together. Add the vanilla-flavoured milk (without the vanilla pod) and the dissolved gelatine and mix. Warm this cream over a gentle heat, stirring constantly. As soon as it coats the back of a spoon, remove from the heat. Strain or sieve and then divide into two portions. Melt 50 g (2 oz, 2 squares) plain (bittersweet) chocolate and add to half the Bavarian cream mixture.

Complete each half of the cream separately and add to each, as soon as they start to thicken, half the prepared whipped-cream mixture made from 350 ml (12 fl oz, 1½ cups) chilled double (heavy) cream and 60 ml (2 fl oz, ¼ cup) cold milk. Brush the inside of a mould with oil. Fill with alternate layers of the two creams, taking care not to pour in the next layer before the previous one has set. Chill until completely set, then turn out.

All kinds of flavourings and combinations may be used, such as vanilla and strawberry, vanilla and coffee, chocolate and coffee, pistachio and strawberry and vanilla with praline.

Summer pudding

Cook some redcurrants and blackcurrants with sugar until their juice runs and they are just tender. Then add a mixture of strawberries (halving or quartering any that are large) and raspberries; blackberries can be added for an autumn pudding, when they are available. Taste the fruit mixture and mix in sufficient caster (superfine) sugar to sweeten it and create a generous amount of syrup.

Line a deep basin (bowl) with medium-thick slices of bread, trimmed of crusts, overlapping them evenly. Place a neat slice in the bottom of the bowl first, so that it will look neat when the pudding is turned out. Fill with the fruit mixture, pressing it down well, then cover with bread slices. Stand the basin in a shallow dish and cover the top with a saucer or plate. Place a heavy weight on top to press the pudding and chill overnight. (The shallow dish will catch any juice that seeps from the pudding.) Reserve any leftover fruit juices to spoon over the pudding before it is served.

Ease a knife between the pudding and the basin before inverting it on to a serving dish. Spoon any reserved juices over the top of the pudding, especially if there are any white patches of bread visible, and serve at once, with clotted or whipped cream.

Sweet omelette à la normande

Peel, core and slice 3 dessert (eating) apples. Cook them in 50 g (2 oz, ¼ cup) butter and some caster (superfine) sugar. Add 200 ml (7 fl oz, ¾ cup) double (heavy) cream and reduce to a creamy consistency, then flavour with 2–3 tablespoons Calvados.

Beat 10 eggs with a pinch of salt, sugar and 2 tablespoons double cream. Cook the omelette, fill it with the apple mixture, then place under a hot grill (broiler) to glaze.

Swiss meringues

Work 500 g (18 oz, 4 cups) icing (confectioner's) sugar with 2 egg whites, 3 drops of white vinegar, 1 teaspoon vanilla sugar and a pinch of salt. When the mixture is white and smooth, add 4 stiffly whisked egg whites. Mix well and pipe the mixture on to a buttered and floured baking sheet. Dry the meringues in a preheated oven on the lowest possible setting for 12 hours; if possible, prop the oven door slightly ajar to maintain a low temperature for drying out, rather than cooking, the meringues.

Tapioca dessert

Boil 500 ml (17 fl oz, 2 cups) milk with a pinch of salt, 25 g (1 oz, 2 table-spoons) sugar and 1 teaspoon vanilla sugar. Sprinkle in 75 g (3 oz, ⅔ cup) tapioca, stir, then add 2 beaten egg yolks. Continue mixing, then blend in 3 egg whites whisked to stiff peaks with 75 g (3 oz, ⅔ cup) icing (confectioner's) sugar. Serve thoroughly chilled.

Tapioca with milk

Boil 1 litre (1¾ pints, 4⅓ cups) milk with a pinch of salt, 2 tablespoons sugar and, as desired, either a vanilla pod (bean) or ½ teaspoon orange-flower water. Sprinkle in 75–100 g (3–4 oz, ⅔–¾ cup) tapioca, mix, then cook for 10 minutes, stirring regularly. Remove the vanilla pod.

Terrine of fruit with honey jelly

You will need 2 rectangular terrines for this recipe. Add 2 tablespoons honey, 500 g (18 oz, 2¼ cups), caster (superfine) sugar, some orange and lemon peel and a few leaves of lemon-balm to 1.5 litres (2¾ pints, 6½ cups) water in a pan. Boil for 30 minutes, then strain through coarse muslin (cheesecloth). Soak 75 g (3 oz, 12 envelopes) powdered gelatine in a little cold water, add to the strained liquid, then chill. Meanwhile, clean some strawberries, raspberries and alpine strawberries, cut some peeled pears into quarters, seed some grapes and dice some candied orange and lemon peel. Pour the half-set jelly on to the fruit and gently mix together. Put into the terrine and leave to set in a cool place for at least 2 hours. Serve with raspberry purée decorated with a band of honey.

Turban of croûtes à la Beauvilliers

Cut from a stale brioche 12 rectangular slices, 6 cm (2½ in) long and slightly wider than a banana. Arrange these slices on a baking sheet, dust with caster (superfine) sugar and glaze in a preheated oven at 230°C (450°F, gas 8). Peel 6 bananas and cut them in half lengthways. Lay these banana halves on a buttered baking sheet, sprinkle them with caster sugar and cook them for 5 minutes in the preheated oven at 230°C (450°F, gas 8).

Make a turban shape on a round ovenproof dish, alternating the bananas and the slices of brioche. Cook some semolina in sweetened vanilla-flavoured milk, bind with egg yolks, and add a salpicon of crystallized (candied) fruit, macerated in a fruit liqueur. Fill the centre of the turban with this mixture. Sprinkle the whole preparation with finely crumbled macaroons, moisten with melted butter and brown in the preheated oven. Just before serving, surround the turban with a thin ribbon of apricot sauce flavoured with rum or with a fruit liqueur.

Two-fruit charlotte

Cut thin slices of stale bread into strips and trim them to a suitable length to line a charlotte mould. Butter the mould and line the bottom and sides with the strips of bread. Mix some apple purée with some apricot purée and reduce – 100 ml (4 fl oz, 7 tablespoons) of the mixture are required. Peel and core some apples, cut them into pieces and sprinkle with a little lemon juice, sugar and vanilla-flavoured sugar. Fill the mould with alternate layers of purée and pieces of raw apple. Cover the top with breadcrumbs and press down firmly. Cook the charlotte in a preheated oven at 200°C (400°F, gas 6) for about 40 minutes.

Vanilla meringues with exotic fruit

Whip 200 ml (7 fl oz, ¾ cup) whipping cream with 2 tablespoons caster (superfine) sugar and put in the refrigerator. Peel and dice 1 mango, 2 kiwis and 1 pineapple. Coat the fruit with 200 g (7 oz) confectioner's custard (pastry cream). Add to this mixture the pulp of 8 passion fruit, the seeds of a vanilla pod (bean) and the seeds of a pomegranate. Fold in the whipped cream. Spoon the mixture into individual flameproof bowls. Place a layer of thin slices of exotic fruit on top of the creamy mixture. Whisk 2 egg whites until they form stiff peaks and fold in 2 tablespoons caster sugar. Cover the fruit with the meringue, smooth the surface with a spatula, brown under the grill (broiler) and serve dusted with icing (confectioner's) sugar. The meringue can be piped on top of the fruit, if preferred.

Vanilla soufflé

Pour 250 ml (8 fl oz, 1 cup) milk into a saucepan and add a vanilla pod (bean). Heat gently until boiling, stirring occasionally, then cover and remove from the heat. Leave to infuse until completely cold, or for at least 30 minutes. Remove the vanilla pod.

Mix 4 egg yolks with 3 tablespoons caster (superfine) sugar and 25 g (1 oz, ¼ cup) plain (all-purpose) flour. Gradually stir in a little of the vanilla-flavoured milk to make a smooth paste. Then stir in the remaining milk and pour the mixture into the saucepan. Bring to the boil, stirring continuously, until smooth and thick. Remove from the heat and cover the surface of this confectioner's custard (pastry cream) with wet greaseproof (wax) paper or cling film (plastic wrap) and leave to cool.

Butter a 20 cm (8 in) soufflé dish and sprinkle it with caster sugar. Whisk 6 egg whites until stiff, but not dry, then beat a spoonful of them into the confectioner's custard to soften it slightly. Fold in the remaining whites and turn the mixture into the dish. Run your fingertip or end of a mixing spoon around the inside of the rim to make a shallow channel in the mixture, then bake the soufflé in a preheated oven at 190°C (375°F, gas 5) for 20 minutes. Working quickly, dust the surface soufflé with icing (confectioner's) sugar and cook for a further 5 minutes to glaze the surface. Serve at once.

Vatrouchka

This Russian cheesecake consists of a sablé base, covered with a mixture of eggs, sugar, crystallized (candied) or sometimes dried fruits and curd cheese, usually topped with a lattice of pastry and dusted with sugar after cooking.

Macerate 200 g (7 oz, 1 generous cup) diced crystallized (candied) fruits in 2 tablespoons Cognac, Armagnac or rum.

To prepare the pastry, beat together in a bowl 3 egg yolks and 1 egg white with 200 g (7 oz, 1 cup) caster (superfine) sugar until the mixture is thick and creamy. Whisk in 125 g (4½ oz, ½ cup) softened butter, then sprinkle with 350 g (12 oz, 3 cups) sifted plain (all-purpose) flour. Form the pastry into a ball and chill for about 1 hour. Cut the pastry in half. Use one portion to line a 25 cm (10 in) round, fairly deep, loose-bottomed flan tin (pan). Prick the pastry with a fork and bake blind in a preheated oven at 200°C (400°F, gas 6) for 12–15 minutes, then leave to cool.

Meanwhile prepare the filling: combine 4 whole eggs and 5 yolks with 400 g (14 oz, 1¾ cups) caster sugar in a bowl until the mixture is thick and creamy; add the crystallized fruits with the alcohol in which they have been macerating and 1 kg (2¼ lb, 4½ cups) curd cheese; mix well together.

Pour the filling into the cooled pastry and smooth the surface. Roll out the reserved pastry into a rectangle and cut it into narrow strips. Arrange these in a lattice on top of the filling sealing the ends on the sides of the pastry case. Glaze the filling and the strips with beaten egg and bake in a preheated oven at 180°C (350°F, gas 4) for 40–50 minutes. Take out the *vatrouchka*, dust with icing (confectioner's) sugar and leave until completely cold before serving.

Waffles

In a large earthenware bowl sift 500 g (18 oz, 4½ cups) plain (all-purpose) flour with 2 teaspoons bicarbonate of soda (baking soda), 4 teaspoons baking powder and 2 teaspoons salt. Add 30–40 g (1–1½ oz, 2–3 tablespoons) caster (superfine) sugar, 150 g (5 oz, ⅔ cup) melted butter, 5 beaten eggs and 750 ml (1¼ pints, 3¼ cups) milk (or more, if very light waffles are preferred). Mix well until the batter is runny and completely smooth.

Heat and, if necessary, grease a waffle iron. Pour a small ladle of batter in one half of the open waffle iron. Close the iron and turn it over so that the batter is distributed equally in both halves. Leave to cook. Open the waffle iron, take out the waffle, sprinkle with icing (confectioner's) sugar and serve.

Waffles with praline butter cream

Mix 15 g (½ oz, 1 cake) fresh (compressed) yeast or 1½ teaspoons dried yeast with 300 ml (½ pint, 1¼ cups) tepid water. Blend in 500 g (18 oz, 4½ cups) strong plain (bread) flour, then add 125 g (4½ oz, generous ½ cup) butter, 40 g (1½ oz, 3 tablespoons) caster (superfine) sugar and 2 teaspoons salt. Knead to obtain a smooth dough. Leave to rise under a cloth overnight, then shape it into little balls and leave to rise on a floured board for 1–2 hours.

When the balls have doubled in size, heat a waffle iron, grease it if necessary, place a ball of dough in it, close it and leave to cook. As soon as the waffle has browned, take it out, slice it in two horizontally and leave to cool completely. Do the same with the remaining dough.

In a warm basin, cream 250 g (9 oz, generous 1 cup) butter, 200 g (7 oz, 1½ cups) icing (confectioner's) sugar and 200 g (7 oz) as the filling.

Zabaglione

Put 5 egg yolks into a basin and add the grated zest of ½ a lemon, a pinch of powdered vanilla or a few drops of vanilla essence (extract) and 180 g (6½ oz, ¾ cup) granulated sugar. Whisk the mixture until it is thick and pale, then place the basin over a bain marie and continue whisking, adding 200 ml (7 fl oz, ¾ cup) white wine and 100 ml (4 fl oz, 7 tablespoons) Marsala a little at a time. When the zabaglione is thick and frothy, take the basin out of the bain marie. Frost the rim of 6–8 sundae dishes with lemon juice and granulated sugar. Divide the zabaglione among these dishes and serve immediately with plain petits fours.

Iced desserts

Apricot coupes

Soak some diced fresh or canned apricots and some apricot halves in brandy. Divide the diced fruit among some sundae dishes (2 tablespoons per dish). Cover with a layer of apricot water ice, smooth and top with an apricot half and some fresh split almonds. Sprinkle with a few drops of brandy or kirsch.

Apricot water ice

Cook some stoned (pitted) apricots with a little water until soft. Drain and press the fruit through a sieve (or purée in a blender), adding sufficient cooking juice to make a purée of pouring consistency. Prepare a sugar syrup by heating 225 g (8 oz, 1 cup) sugar with 600 ml (1 pint, 2½ cups) water. Stir from time to time until the sugar has completely dissolved. This yields 750 ml (1¼ pints, 3¼ cups) syrup. Combine equal quantities of apricot purée and sugar syrup, and flavour to taste with lemon juice – 1 lemon to each 600 ml (1 pint, 2½ cups) mixture. Either pour the cooked mixture into a prepared ice-cream maker, or freeze until slushy in a freezer, then beat thoroughly before refreezing until firm.

Baked Alaska

First prepare some vanilla ice cream: make a custard using 7–8 egg yolks, 200 g (7 oz, 1 cup) caster (superfine) sugar, 750 ml (1¼ pints, 3 cups) single (light) cream and a vanilla pod (bean) or 1 teaspoon vanilla sugar. Freeze in an ice-cream churn. When the ice cream is fairly hard, pack it into a square cake tin (pan) and leave it in the freezer for 1 hour.

Meanwhile, make a sponge by beating 125 g (4 oz, ½ cup) caster sugar with 4 egg yolks until the mixture turns thick and white. Sprinkle with 150 g (5 oz, 1¼ cups) sifted plain (all-purpose) flour, then add 40 g (1½ oz, 3 tablespoons) melted butter and fold in 4 egg whites whisked to stiff peaks with a pinch of salt. Pour the batter into a greased square cake tin and bake in a preheated oven at 200°C (400°F, gas 6) for 35 minutes. Turn the sponge out and leave it to cool.

Immediately before serving make a meringue mixture whisking 4 egg whites, a pinch of salt and 6 tablespoons caster sugar and put the mixture into a large piping (pastry) bag. Split the sponge in two through the middle and trim the edges neatly, if necessary, then arrange the pieces side by side on a baking sheet. Sprinkle with 3 tablespoons sugar flavoured with Cointreau or Grand Marnier. Unmould the ice cream and place on the sponge. Mask the sponge and ice cream entirely with half of the meringue, smoothing it with a metal spatula. Use the rest of the meringue to decorate the top with swirls. Dredge with icing (confectioner's) sugar and place in a preheated oven at 250°C (475°F, gas 9) until the meringue is coloured. Serve immediately.

Baked Alaska can be flamed when it is taken out of the oven, using the same liqueur that was used to flavour the sponge.

Banana ice cream

Peel firm, ripe bananas and purée in a food processor or blender with lemon juice (use 1 lemon for 6 bananas). Mix with an equal volume of sugar syrup. Flavour with rum and freeze in the usual way.

Blackcurrant sorbet

Place 250 g (9 oz, 1¼ cups) sugar and 400 ml (14 fl oz, 1¾ cups) water in a saucepan. Heat to dissolve the sugar. (The density should be 1.14; if it is less than this, add a little more sugar.) Warm the syrup, then add 350 ml (12 fl oz, 1½ cups) blackcurrant juice and the juice of ½ lemon. Mix well and pour into an ice-cream machine or freeze, beating at intervals. 'Real' sorbet is made by adding a quarter of the volume of Italian meringue to the ingredients.

Bombe glacée

A frozen dessert made from a bombe mixture, often enriched with various ingredients, and frozen in a mould. The dessert was named after the spherical mould in which it used to be made. Nowadays, cylindrical moulds with rounded tops are used.

Traditionally, bombe moulds are filled with two different mixtures. The bottom and sides of the mould are lined with a layer of plain ice cream, a fruit ice or a sorbet; the inside is filled with the chosen bombe mixture. The mould is then hermetically sealed, clamped and frozen. To serve, the bombe is turned out on to a folded napkin placed on the serving dish. The bombe may be decorated in a number of ways depending on its ingredients: crystallized (candied) fruit or violets, marrons glacés, pistachios, fruit macerated in liqueur or whipped cream.

Chill the mould in the refrigerator for about 20 minutes. At the same time soften the ice cream or water ice chosen to line the mould. Spread it roughly on the bottom and sides of the mould with a plastic or stainless steel spatula. Place the mould in the freezer for about 15 minutes to harden and then smooth the ice with the spatula. Replace the mould in the freezer for a further hour before filling with the bombe mixture, unless the mixture is a parfait, in which case pour it down the sides of the lined mould until filled and place in the freezer for 5–6 hours.

In traditional cuisine, the mixture is made with 32 egg yolks per 1 litre (1¾ pints, 4⅓ cups) syrup (density: 1.285). Pour the syrup and egg yolks into a saucepan and place the pan in a bain marie over a moderate heat. Whisk vigorously until the mixture is thick and creamy, then press it through a very fine sieve. Whisk again, away from the heat, until completely cold: by this stage it should be light, fluffy and white. Finally add an equal volume of whipped cream and the chosen flavouring.

Bombes are often made with a far lighter mixture. For example, a 1 litre (1¾ pint, 4⅓ cup) bombe Hawaii can be made using 500 ml (17 fl oz, 2 cups) pineapple sorbet to line the bombe mould and 500 ml (17 fl oz, 2 cups) kirsch parfait made with 2 egg yolks, about 60 ml (2 fl oz, ¼ cup) syrup (density: 1.2407) and about 250 ml (8 fl oz, 1 cup) whipped cream together with 1½ teaspoons kirsch.

- *bombe Aïda:* line the mould with tangerine ice cream and fill with vanilla bombe mixture flavoured with kirsch.
- *bombe Alhambra:* line the mould with vanilla ice cream and fill with strawberry bombe mixture (a combination of strawberry purée, Italian meringue and whipped cream). Turn out the bombe and surround with large strawberries macerated in kirsch.
- *bombe archiduc:* line the mould with strawberry ice cream and fill with praline bombe mixture.
- *bombe bourdaloue:* line a mould with vanilla ice cream. Fill with an anisette-flavoured bombe mixture and freeze the ice cream until set. Turn out and decorate with candied violets.
- *bombe cardinal:* line a conical ice mould with a layer of strawberry or raspberry ice cream and fill the inside with vanilla mousse mixture flavoured with praline.
- *bombe chateaubriand:* line the mould with apricot ice cream and fill with vanilla bombe mixture mixed with crystallized (candied) apricots macerated in kirsch.

- *bombe diplomate*: line the mould with vanilla ice cream and fill with maraschino bombe mixture mixed with diced crystallized (candied) fruit macerated in maraschino.
- *bombe Doria*: coat a bombe mould with pistachio ice cream. Macerate some pieces of marrons glacés in Curaçao, then add them to a vanilla-flavoured bombe mixture. Fill the mould with this mixture and place in the refrigerator to set.
- *bombe duchesse*: line the mould with pineapple ice cream and fill with pear bombe mixture.
- *bombe glacée Montmorency*: coat a bombe mould with a layer of kirsch ice cream. Prepare a bombe mixture flavoured with cherry brandy and add cherries macerated in kirsch. Fill the mould with this. Finish as usual .
- *bombe Grimaldi*: line the mould with vanilla ice cream and fill with kümmel-flavoured bombe mixture. Decorate with crystallized (candied) violets and halved pistachio nuts.
- *bombe Monselet*: line the mould with tangerine ice cream and fill with port-flavoured bombe mixture mixed with chopped crystallized (candied) orange peel that has been macerated in brandy.

Capucine iced pudding

Prepare a Genoese sponge and cook it in a charlotte mould. Leave it to cool completely, then slice a thin layer of sponge from the top (to serve as a lid). Scoop out the rest of the sponge, leaving a lining crust and fill it with alternate layers of tangerine-flavoured iced mousse and Kümmel-flavoured iced mousse. Cover with the sponge lid and put in the freezer for 6 hours. Just before serving, decorate with Chantilly cream, using a piping (pastry) bag. Traditionally, this iced pudding is set on a base of nougatine and decorated with flowers and ribbons made of sugar.

Caramel ice cream

Whisk together 9 egg yolks and 300 g (11 oz, 1⅓ cups) caster (superfine) sugar until the mixture becomes white and foamy. Make caramel without water: warm 100 g (4 oz, ½ cup) sugar in a heavy based saucepan over a gentle heat, stirring with a wooden spoon. As soon as the sugar has melted and turned into a smooth mass, add 100 g (4 oz, ½ cup) sugar, melt, then blend in another 100 g (4 oz, ½ cup) sugar. Continue to stir until the caramel turns brown. Add 1 teaspoon lemon juice or vinegar, and remove from heat.

Boil 1 litre (1¾ pints, 4⅓ cups) milk. Mix with the hot caramel over a gentle heat, stirring with a wooden spoon. Pour this boiling mixture over the sugar and egg yolk mixture, whisking vigorously, then stir the mixture into the saucepan, over a low heat. When the mixture begins to coat the spoon, remove the saucepan from the heat and immerse the base in cold water. Continue to stir until the mixture is cold. Freeze in an ice-cream maker.

Cherry water ice

Purée some stoned (pitted) cherries in a blender. Add a sugar syrup flavoured with kirsch, using 200 ml (7 fl oz, ¾ cup) water and 400 g (14 oz, 1¾ cups) sugar to 1 litre (1¾ pints, 4⅓ cups) purée and thoroughly mix together. Set in an ice cream freezer, then turn out and serve with a cherry sauce.

Chestnut plombières ice cream

Pound thoroughly in a mortar (or use a blender or processor) 300 g (11 oz, 2 cups) blanched fresh almonds and (if desired) 15 g (½ oz, 1½ tablespoons) ground bitter almonds, gradually adding 4 tablespoons milk. Then add 1.5 litres (2¾ pints, 6½ cups) scalded single (light) cream and mix thoroughly. Press through a fine sieve. Place 300 g (11 oz, 1½ cups) caster (superfine) sugar and 12 egg yolks in a large bowl and beat until the mixture

123

becomes white and thick. Bring the almond milk to the boil and pour it on to the egg and sugar mixture, whisking continuously. Place over the heat and stir gently until the cream coats the back of the spoon. Then immerse the base of the saucepan in cold water to stop the cooking process and continue to whisk until the cream has cooled. Place in an ice-cream freezer.

When the mixture is partially frozen, mix in 250 g (9 oz, 1 cup) sweetened chestnut purée, obtained by cooking the chestnuts in vanilla-flavoured sweetened milk (alternatively, use a can of sweetened chestnut purée), 400 ml (14 fl oz, 1¾ cups) whipped double (heavy) cream and 150 ml (¼ pint, ⅔ cup) milk, both very cold. Place in an ice-cream mould and freeze.

Chocolate ice cream

Beat 8 egg yolks and 200 g (7 oz, ¾ cup) caster (superfine) sugar together until pale and thick. Melt 250 g (9 oz, 1½ cups) grated bitter (bittersweet) chocolate in a covered pan with 200 ml (7 fl oz, ¾ cup) water. Add 1 litre (1¾ pints, 4⅓ cups) boiling milk to the chocolate and stir until the mixture is completely smooth. Pour the boiling chocolate mixture over the egg yolk mixture and cook over a very gentle heat until the custard coats the spoon. Immediately dip the saucepan in cold water to prevent further cooking and continue to beat until the cream is lukewarm. Stir it occasionally until it is completely cold. Complete the ice cream in the usual way, using an ice-cream churn or mould and whisking the part-frozen mixture until smooth.

For a richer ice cream, replace 200 ml (7 fl oz, ¾ cup) of the milk with the same volume of double (heavy) cream, and use 10 egg yolks instead of 8.

Coffee and brandy bombe

Chill a 1 litre (1¾ pint, 1 quart) bombe mould in the freezer. Make a custard with 500 ml (17 fl oz, 2 cups) milk, 6 egg yolks and 125 g (4½ oz, ½ cup) caster (superfine) sugar, then add 1 tablespoon instant coffee. Continue to stir until the mixture is completely cold. Freeze in an ice-cream maker.

Bring to the boil a syrup made with 200 ml (7 fl oz, ¾ cup) water and 250 g (9 oz, 1 heaped cup) caster sugar. While still boiling, pour the syrup over 8 egg yolks and beat with an electric mixer until cool. Whip 6 tablespoons milk with 250 ml (8 fl oz, 1 cup) very cold double (heavy) cream. Blend the cream with the egg yolk mixture, flavour it with 3 tablespoons liqueur brandy and chill.

Line the mould with coffee ice cream. Fill with the brandy-flavoured cream, then freeze. Remove from the mould and decorate with coffee beans soaked in liqueur.

Coffee ice cream

Blend together 6 eggs, 200 g (7 oz, ¾ cup) caster (superfine) sugar and 3 tablespoons instant coffee to make a coffee-flavoured custard. Whip 200 ml (7 fl oz, ¾ cup) cold double (heavy) cream with a quarter of its own volume of very cold milk and 1 tablespoon vanilla-flavoured sugar. Fold the whipped cream gently into the cold custard until completely mixed and leave it to freeze in an ice-cream maker. The ice cream can be decorated with sugar coffee beans or coffee sugar crystals.

Coupes glacé à la cévenole with kirsch

The term *à la cévenole* is used for many savoury or sweet dishes containing chestnuts, in this case candied as marrons glacés. Prepare separately 500 ml (17 fl oz, 2 cups) vanilla ice cream and 300 ml (½ pint, 1¼ cups) Chantilly cream. Add 1 liqueur glass of kirsch to 250 g (9 oz, 1¼ cups) marron-glacé fragments and divide equally between 4 sundae glasses. Cover each with a layer of the vanilla ice cream and smooth the surface with a metal spoon or palette knife. Use a piping (pastry) bag with a fluted nozzle to decorate with Chantilly cream, then arrange marrons glacés and sugar violets on top.

Coupes glacé à la cévenole with rum

Prepare 500 ml (17 fl oz, 2 cups) vanilla ice cream for coupes. Macerate 300 g (11 oz, 1⅓ cups) split marrons glacés in 200 ml (7 fl oz, ¾ cup) rum for 1 hour. Chill 6 sundae dishes in the refrigerator. Fifteen minutes before serving, divide the marrons glacés among the sundae dishes and cover with the vanilla ice cream. Decorate the dishes with whipped cream using a piping (pastry) bag with a fluted nozzle. Each dish can then be topped with crystallized (candied) violets.

Coupes dame blanche

Prepare some Chantilly cream by mixing 200 g (7 oz) double (heavy) cream with 2 tablespoons milk, 25 g (1 oz, 2 tablespoons) caster (superfine) sugar, a little vanilla sugar or essence (extract) to taste and a crushed ice cube; whip until the cream forms peaks. Chill.

Melt 200 g (7 oz, 7 squares) dark chocolate in a bain marie with 2 tablespoons milk. Add 25 g (1 oz, 2 tablespoons) butter and mix well; then add 3 tablespoons single (light) cream. Keep the sauce hot in the bain marie.

Take 6 individual sundae glasses and put 2 scoops of vanilla ice cream into each. Using a piping (pastry) bag fitted with a fluted nozzle, pipe a dome of Chantilly cream into each glass. Serve the hot chocolate sauce separately in a sauceboat (gravy boat).

Coupes malmaison

Prepare 500 ml (17 fl oz, 2 cups) vanilla ice cream. Remove the seeds from 400 g (14 oz) Muscat grapes, plunge them into a saucepan of boiling water and then immediately into cold water, then drain and peel them. Boil together 3 tablespoons water with 150 g (5 oz, ⅔ cup) caster (superfine) sugar until the sugar just caramelizes. Divide the ice cream among 4 sundae dishes, cover with the grapes and top with the caramel.

Fruit sorbet

For soft fruit, prepare a syrup using 200 g (7 oz, 1 cup) granulated sugar and 150 ml (¼ pint, ⅔ cup) water per 500 g (18 oz) fruit. Poach the fruit in the syrup, then purée in a blender or food processor: the density of the mixture should be 1.1513. For citrus fruit use 100 g (4 oz, ½ cup) sugar and 150 ml (¼ pint, ⅔ cup) water for every 3–4 fruit. Finely grate the zest, then squeeze the juice from the fruit and mix with the syrup: the density of the mixture should be 1.1697. Correct the density by adding more sugar if it is too weak or more water if it is too strong. Pour into an ice-cream maker and allow to freeze. Halfway through the cycle some Italian meringue (one third of the volume of the sorbet) can be added.

Granita

A type of Italian sorbet popularized by Tortoni in Paris in the 19th century. It is a half-frozen preparation with a granular texture (hence its name), made of a lightly sweetened syrup or of a syrup flavoured with coffee or liqueur. Unlike sorbets, granita does not contain any Italian meringue. It is served in sundae dishes or a glass bowl, either between the courses of a meal or as a light refreshment.

Make a light syrup with fruit juice (such as lemon, orange, tangerine, passion fruit or mango) or very strong coffee. Cool the syrup, then pour it into an ice tray and freeze for 3–4 hours without stirring. The granita will then have a granular texture.

Honey ice cream

Infuse 10 g (⅓ oz) mixed ground spices (such as black pepper, juniper, cloves, cinnamon) in 1 litre (1¾ pints, 4⅓ cups) milk. Beat 10 egg yolks with 400 g (14 oz, 1¼ cups) dark Yonne honey until pale and creamy. Add the boiling milk and cook gently at 85°C (185°F) until slightly thickened. Allow to cool and strain through a chinois. Freeze in an ice-cream maker.

Honey sorbet with pine nuts

Mix 900 g (2 lb, 2½ cups) orange-blossom honey, the juice of 1 lemon, a few drops orange-flower water and 1 litre (1¾ pints, 4⅓ cups) water. After processing in an ice-cream maker, add some lightly toasted pine nuts, then pour into a mould and place in the freezer until required.

Iced charlotte with chestnuts

Line a charlotte mould with sponge fingers (ladyfingers). Prepare a syrup with 175 g (6 oz, ¾ cup) granulated sugar, 1 tablespoon lemon juice and 3 tablespoons water. Cook for 3–4 minutes. Gradually add the syrup to 500 g (18 oz, 2 cups) chestnut purée (fresh or canned). Prepare 1 litre (1¾ pints, 4⅓ cups) custard, using 9 or 10 egg yolks. Put half on one side. Flavour the other half with rum and add it to the chestnut purée. Pour a little of this mixture into the mould, cover with a layer of sponge fingers soaked in the syrup, then fill with the remainder. Cover with more sponge fingers. Place in the freezer for 30 minutes. Turn out and serve with the remaining custard.

Iced chestnut vacherin

A vacherin is a cold dessert, made of a ring of meringue or almond paste filled with ice cream or whipped cream (or both). It owes its name to its shape and colour, which resemble the cheese of the same name.

Whisk 8 egg whites to stiff peaks, then mix in 500 g (18 oz, 2¼ cups) caster (superfine) sugar with a spatula. Make a round layer of meringue by piping a flat spiral on greased greaseproof (wax) paper on a baking sheet. Pipe 2 rings of the same diameter on to baking sheets. Cook in a very low oven, then leave to cool. Cook 400 g (14 oz) peeled chestnuts in milk for 40 minutes, drain them and reduce to a purée. When the purée is cold, add 1 liqueur glass of rum, 3 stiffly whisked egg whites, 25 g (1 oz, 2 tablespoons) melted butter and 3 coarsely chopped marrons glacés. Freeze for 4 hours in the freezer. Place the rings of meringue on to the flat round to form a shell, then pile the ice cream into this meringue shell. Decorate with Chantilly cream and a few marrons glacés. Return to the freezer until ready to serve.

Iced cream mousse

Prepare a custard cream with 500 ml (17 fl oz, 2 cups) milk, 350 g (11 oz, 1¾ cups) sugar, and some egg yolks (8 for a liqueur mousse; up to 16 for a fruit mousse). Leave to cool completely. Then add the chosen flavouring – vanilla, orange or lemon zest, liqueur, or 500 ml (17 fl oz, 2 cups) fruit purée – and 500 ml (17 fl oz, 2 cups) double (heavy) cream. Place the mixing bowl in a basin containing crushed ice and whisk the preparation well. Pour into a mould and put in the freezer for at least 4 hours to set.

Iced fruit mousse

Prepare an Italian meringue with 300 g (11 oz, 1⅓ cups) sugar, 6 tablespoons water and 4 egg whites and put it in the refrigerator. Prepare a fruit purée – with 375 g (13 oz, 2½ cups) strawberries, for example. Whip 500 ml (17 fl oz, 2 cups) very cold double (heavy) cream with 150 ml (¼ pint, ⅔ cup) very cold milk until stiff. Mix the meringue and the fruit purée and then add the cream. Pour into a mould and put in the freezer for at least 4 hours to set.

Iced fruit soufflé

Cook 300 g (11 oz, 1⅓ cups) caster (superfine) sugar in 100 ml (4 fl oz, 7 tablespoons) water to the large pearl or soufflé stage (113–115°C (235–239°F). Pour this syrup over 5 very stiffly whisked egg whites, whisking until completely cold. Purée 350 g (12 oz, about 2 cups) fresh strawberries or raspberries, or apricots, peaches or pears cooked in sugar. Fold the purée into the egg white and sugar mixture together with 500 ml (17 fl oz, 2 cups) stiffly whipped cream.

Cut a strip of greaseproof (wax) paper or foil 23 cm (9 in) wide and longer than the circumference of the soufflé mould. Fold in half to reduce its width to 11.5 cm (4½ in). Surround the mould with this double strip so that it comes well above the edge and keep it in place with an elastic band or adhesive tape. Pour the soufflé mixture into the mould until it reaches the top of the paper, smooth over the surface and freeze until firm (about 4 hours). Remove the paper to serve.

Iced liqueur mousse

Make a syrup with 4 tablespoons water and 200 g (7 oz, 1 cup) sugar; while still very hot, pour it in a thin trickle over 7 egg yolks, whisking until the mixture has cooled. Then add 3 tablespoons liqueur, followed by 500 ml (17 fl oz, 2 cups) very cold double (heavy) cream, whisked with 150 ml (¼ pint, ⅔ cup) cold milk. Pour into a mould and put into the freezer for at least 4 hours to set.

Iced parfait

A parfait is an iced dessert made with fresh cream, which gives it smoothness and allows it to be sliced. Mix 4 tablespoons water with 200 g (7 oz, ¾ cup) caster (superfine) sugar and cook to the fine thread stage (110°C, 230°F).

Place 8 egg yolks in a bowl and pour the boiling syrup over them, little by little, whisking all the time. Continue to whisk until the mixture has cooled. Then add the chosen flavouring from the suggestions below.

Whip 200 ml (7 fl oz, ¾ cup) double (heavy) cream with 100 ml (4 fl oz, 7 tablespoons) milk (both chilled) until very firm. Blend the whipped cream with the cooled mixture of egg yolks and syrup and pour into a parfait mould. Place in the freezer and leave to set for at least 6 hours.

- *suggested flavourings:* add 3–4 tablespoons brandy or liqueur; 4–5 tablespoons coffee essence (extract); 200 g (7 oz, 7 squares) melted plain (dark) chocolate; 150 g (5 oz, ⅔ cup) powdered almond praline; or about 10 drops of vanilla extract.

Iced persimmon à la créole

Persimmons can only be eaten when their flesh becomes transparent: this indicates that they are ripe. Cut a hole in each persimmon around the stalk and scoop out the pulp with a teaspoon, taking care not to break the skin. Sprinkle a little marc brandy or liqueur into each fruit and leave to macerate for 1 hour. Mix the fruit pulp with some pineapple ice (1 tablespoon pulp to 3–4 tablespoons pineapple ice). Press the mixture through a fine sieve and fill the fruit shells with the cream. Freeze for about 1 hour before serving.

Iced pineapple à la bavaroise

Choose a large, well-shaped pineapple with a good cluster of fresh leaves. Cut off the top 1 cm (½ in) below the crown and set aside. Scoop out the flesh, leaving an even 1 cm (½ in) thickness around the outside. Fill the inside with a mixture of pineapple Bavarian cream and a salpicon of finely diced pineapple soaked in white rum. Leave to set in a cool place or on ice. Replace the top of the pineapple before serving.

Iced pineapple à la bourbonnaise

Prepare a large pineapple, scooping out the flesh as for iced pineapple *à la bavaroise*. Soak the chopped flesh in rum. Sprinkle the inside of the pineapple case with 2 tablespoons white rum and leave in a cool place for about 2 hours. Just before serving, fill the pineapple case with alternate layers of rum ice cream and the soaked flesh. Replace the top and arrange the pineapple on a napkin or in a fruit bowl, surrounded with crushed ice.

Iced pineapple à la Chantilly

This is prepared as for iced pineapple *à la bourbonnaise*, but the rum ice cream is replaced with a mixture of vanilla ice cream and whipped cream.

Iced pineapple à la créole

The term *à la créole* is given to numerous sweet and savoury preparations inspired by West Indian cookery. Sweet dishes *à la créole* contain rum, pineapple, vanilla or banana. Slice the top off a pineapple and keep it in a cool place, wrapping the leaves so that they do not wilt. Carefully scoop out the flesh of the pineapple and discard the core.

Make a pineapple water ice with the pulp. Soak some finely chopped crystallized (candied) fruit in a little rum. When the pineapple ice is frozen, fill the pineapple by placing the crystallized fruits between two layers of pineapple ice. Replace the top of the pineapple and keep it in the freezer until ready to serve. Serve on a bed of crushed ice.

Iced pineapple à la parisienne

This dish is prepared in the same way as iced pineapple *à la bourbonnaise*, but with banana ice cream. Each layer of ice cream is scattered with blanched sliced almonds.

Iced raspberry soufflé

Sort and clean 400 g (14 oz, 2¾ cups) raspberries. Put the best 20 to one side; crush the others and press through a sieve. Mix with an equal amount of caster (superfine) sugar and add 500 ml (17 fl oz, 2 cups) Chantilly cream. Whisk 2 egg whites very stiffly, whisking in 50 g (2 oz, ¼ cup) caster (superfine) sugar. Fold lightly into the purée and cream mixture, then pour into a 15 cm (6 in) soufflé mould, around which has been wrapped a band of oiled greaseproof (wax) paper 6 cm (2½ in) higher than the mould. Freeze for at least 8 hours. When the soufflé is firm, remove the paper. Decorate with the reserved raspberries and serve immediately, with a lightly sweetened purée of fresh raspberries and almond tuiles. Serve with a dry champagne.

Iced strawberry mousse

Dissolve 900 g (2 lb, 4 cups) granulated sugar in 500 ml (17 fl oz, 2 cups) water and boil until a thick syrup is obtained (104.5°C, 220°F). Add 900 g (2 lb, 4 cups) sieved freshly prepared strawberry purée, then fold in 1 litre (1¾ pints, 4⅓ cups) very stiffly whipped cream. Freeze in the usual way. (Iced raspberry mousse can be prepared in the same way.)

Iced turban

Pour into a ring mould some vanilla ice cream mixed with diced crystallized (candied) fruits steeped in rum. Freeze until set. Turn out on to a layer of nougatine and fill the centre with some vanilla-flavoured Chantilly cream.

Iced vacherin

Prepare 3 layers of meringue: draw 3 circles on sheets of greaseproof (wax) paper, marking their centres. Grease the paper on the side on which the circles have been drawn, then place the ungreased side on baking sheets. Whisk 8 egg whites to very stiff peaks with a pinch of salt; towards the end of this operation scatter in 500 g (18 oz, 2¼ cups) caster (superfine) sugar (the mixture will be pearly). Fill a large piping (pastry) bag fitted with a large, smooth nozzle with this meringue mixture, then, starting from the centre of the circles, cover these with meringue, forming a flat spiral. Place the baking sheets in a preheated oven at 110°C (225°F, gas ¼), or at the coolest setting, close the door, turn off the oven and cook for 1½–2 hours as it cools. Allow the meringues to become completely cold.

Prepare some vanilla ice cream: make a light custard cream with 5 egg yolks, 150 g (5 oz, ⅔ cup) sugar, 100 ml (4 fl oz, 7 tablespoons) milk, a vanilla pod (bean) and 400 ml (14 fl oz, 1¾ cups) double (heavy) cream. Freeze this cream in an ice-cream maker, making sure that it remains soft. Prepare 500 ml (17 fl oz, 2 cups) soft strawberry ice cream in the same way.

To assemble the vacherin, remove the greaseproof paper from the meringue layers with the point of a knife. Place a ball of vanilla ice cream in the centre of one layer, then place the second layer on top, pressing sufficiently to allow the ice cream to come to the edges of the layer. Replace in the freezer to harden the ice cream, then remove and repeat the process with the strawberry ice cream between the second and third layers. Replace the vacherin in the freezer and prepare the decoration.

Heat 100 g (4 oz, ½ cup) sugar with 400 ml (14 fl oz, 1¾ cups) water and boil for 1 minute. Whisk 2 egg whites to very stiff peaks, pour the boiling syrup over them and whisk until the mixture is cold. Add 500 ml (17 fl oz, 2 cups) double (heavy) cream and whisk until the mixture has set. Chill in the refrigerator then, using a piping bag with a fluted nozzle, pipe it decoratively on the top of the cake. Alternatively, simply apply a smooth covering over the top and sides of the vacherin, giving it the appearance of a cheese. The vacherin may also be decorated with crystallized (candied) fruits or violets.

Jamaican coupes

Prepare 500 ml (17 fl oz, 2 cups) coffee ice cream. Chill 6 sundae dishes in the refrigerator. Clean 165 g (5½ oz, 1 cup) currants and macerate them in 100 ml (4 fl oz, 7 tablespoons) rum for 1 hour. Peel a pineapple and cut the flesh into small dice. Divide the diced pineapple among the sundae dishes and cover with coffee ice cream. Sprinkle the drained currants over the top.

Lemon sorbet

Cut away the zest from 3 lemons, chop it and add it to 500 ml (17 fl oz, 2 cups) cold light syrup with a density of 1.2850. Leave to infuse for 2 hours. Add the juice of 4 lemons, then strain. (The density should be between 1.1699 and 1.1799.) Freeze by the usual method.

Mango sorbet

Choose ripe mangoes, peel them, and rub the flesh through a fine sieve. Add an equal volume of sugar syrup and some lemon juice – the juice of 2 lemons is needed per 1 litre (1¾ pints, 4⅓ cups) sorbet. Add a little extra lemon juice if the syrup is too heavy or some sugar if it is too light. Freeze and finish the sorbet in the usual way.

Mocha vacherin

Place a 20 cm (8 in) flan ring, 5 cm (2 in) deep, on a cardboard base. Put a baked succès base in the ring and place it in the freezer for 20 minutes; this is the mould to be filled.

Prepare a mocha ice cream: coarsely grind 50 g (2 oz) good-quality coffee beans and add to 500 ml (17 fl oz, 2 cups) milk sweetened with 100 g (4 oz, ½ cup) caster (superfine) sugar. Bring to the boil, then cover and leave to infuse, away from the heat, for 10 minutes. Pour the milk through a fine strainer to remove the coffee grounds and replace it in the pan over a gentle heat. Whisk 6 egg yolks in a bowl with 100 g (4 oz, ½ cup) caster sugar. When the mixture is white and thick, add a little of the hot coffee-flavoured milk, whisking, then pour the contents of the bowl into the milk saucepan. Heat gently, stirring constantly with a wooden spoon. When the custard mixture coats the spoon at 83°C (180°F) withdraw the pan from the heat and stir occasionally until it is cold. Then mix in 250 ml (8 fl oz, 1 cup) double (heavy) cream and freeze in an ice-cream maker.

Fill the mould with this ice cream, gently mixing into it 20 coffee beans that have been steeped in liqueur. Smooth the surface with a palette knife, put the mould back in the freezer and leave to freeze for 3 hours. Place a serving dish in the refrigerator for 30 minutes, then carefully remove the flan ring and place the vacherin on the plate.

To make the decoration, prepare coffee-flavoured Chantilly cream, made with 200 ml (7 fl oz, ¾ cup) double (heavy) cream, 60 ml (2 fl oz, ¼ cup) milk, 3 tablespoons icing (confectioner's) sugar and 1 teaspoon instant coffee powder. Place this mixture in a piping (pastry) bag; first decorate the sides of the vacherin with vertical bands of cream, then decorate the top, piping 8 spirals around it to indicate the portion for each guest. Finish with a rosette in the centre. Place 1 liqueur-soaked coffee bean in each whirl. Replace in the freezer until ready to serve.

Orange sorbet

Select 10 very large juicy oranges and remove the peel and pith. Put the pulp through a juice extractor to obtain the maximum amount of juice. Measure the juice and add 300 g (11 oz, 1⅓ cups) sugar per 1 litre (1¾ pints, 4⅓ cups) (more if the juice is very sour). Pour the juice into an ice-cream maker and freeze until set.

Passion fruit sorbet

Halve some ripe passion fruit, strain the pulp through a vegetable mill, then through a fine sieve. Measure the pulp and add an equal volume of cold syrup made from 500 ml (17 fl oz, 2 cups) mineral water and 675 g (1½ lb, 3 cups) caster (superfine) sugar. The density of the mixture should be 1.135; add a little lemon juice, the density then being 1.075. Pour the mixture into an ice-cream maker and freeze until set. It is also possible – and easier – to add caster sugar to the pulp and enough water to obtain a density of 1.075, then strain the mixture through a fine sieve before putting it in the ice-cream maker. Serve scoops of sorbet with a fan of mango slices and a passion fruit pulp.

Peach Melba

Prepare 500 ml (17 fl oz, 2 cups) vanilla ice cream and 300 ml (½ pint, 1¼ cups) raspberry purée. Plunge 8 peaches into boiling water for 30 seconds, then drain, cool and peel them. Make a syrup with 1 litre (1¾ pints, 4⅓ cups) water, 500 g (18 oz, 2½ cups) sugar and 1 vanilla pod (bean). Boil for 5 minutes, then add the peaches and poach them in the syrup for 7–8 minutes on each side. Drain and cool completely.

Cut the peaches in half and remove the stones (pits). Either line a large fruit bowl with the vanilla ice cream, lay the peaches on top, and coat them with the raspberry purée or spoon the ice cream into individual glasses, top with the peaches and the Melba sauce, and serve scattered with flaked (slivered) almonds.

Peach sorbet

Prepare a sugar syrup with 350 g (12 oz, 1½ cups) sugar and 300 ml (½ pint, 1¼ cups) of water. Bring to the boil, simmer for 3 minutes and cool. Plunge 1 kg (2¼ lb) ripe peaches into boiling water for 30 seconds. Drain, peel and remove the stones (pits). Reduce the fruit to a purée in a blender and add the juice of 1 lemon. Mix the cold sugar syrup and the peach purée together, pour into an ice-cream maker and freeze.

Peach sorbet with champagne

Prepare a syrup by boiling 100 ml (4 fl oz, 7 tablespoons) water with 300 g (11 oz, 1⅓ cups) granulated sugar and allow to cool. Peel 1 kg (2¼ lb) white peaches, cut into quarters and purée in a blender or food processor. Add the juice of 1 large lemon and mix the purée with the cold syrup. Pour into an ice-cream maker and set in operation for 1 hour. When the sorbet has frozen, switch off the machine and put the container in the freezer, together with 4 sorbet glasses, for about 1 hour. To serve, place 2 balls of sorbet in each glass and pour over some well-chilled champagne (½ bottle for the 4 glasses).

Peach sundaes

Prepare 500 ml (17 fl oz, 2 cups) vanilla ice cream. Plunge some peaches in boiling water for 30 seconds (allow 6 peaches for 4 sundaes). Drain, peel and remove the stones (pits). Reserve a few slices of peach for decoration, setting them aside to soak in a little liqueur. Chop the remainder. Sprinkle with 1 tablespoon lemon juice and 2 tablespoons fruit liqueur (preferably straw-berry). Whip 200 ml (7 fl oz, ¾ cup) double (heavy) cream. Chill 4 sundae glasses, divide the peaches among them, cover with a layer of ice cream and pipe whipped cream on top, using a piping (pastry) bag fitted with a star (fluted) nozzle. Decorate with a thin slices of raw peach soaked in liqueur.

Pear sorbet

Peel 4 juicy pears and cut them into quarters. Remove the pips (seeds) and dice the flesh. Sprinkle this with the juice of 1 lemon. Reduce to a fine purée, with 300 g (11 oz, 1⅓ cups) granulated sugar, in a blender or food processor. Pour the resulting purée into an ice-cream maker and operate for 1½ hours, or until the sorbet has frozen. Put the container into the freezer until required or serve immediately.

Pineapple ice

Add the crushed flesh of ½ a fresh pineapple to 500 ml (17 fl oz, 2 cups) sugar syrup and leave to soak for at least 2 hours. Reduce to a purée in a blender and flavour with rum. Measure the density with a syrup hydrometer and adjust the sugar content as necessary to achieve a density of 1.609. Freeze in an ice-cream maker.

Plombières ice cream

Pound thoroughly in a mortar (or use a blender or processor) 300 g (11 oz, 2 cups) blanched fresh almonds and (if desired) 15 g (½ oz, 1½ tablespoons) ground bitter almonds, gradually adding 4 tablespoons milk. Then add 1.5 litres (2¾ pints, 6½ cups) scalded single (light) cream and mix thoroughly. Press through a fine sieve. Place 300 g (11 oz, 1½ cups) caster (superfine) sugar and 12 egg yolks in a large bowl and beat until the mixture becomes white and thick. Bring the almond milk to the boil and pour it on to the egg and sugar mixture, whisking continuously. Place over the heat and stir gently until the cream coats the back of the spoon. Then immerse the base of the saucepan in cold water to stop the cooking process and continue to whisk until the cream has cooled. Place in an ice-cream freezer.

When the mixture is partially frozen, mix in 200 g (7 oz, 1 cup) finely chopped crystallized (candied) fruit soaked in kirsch or rum, 400 ml (14 fl oz, 1¾ cups) whipped double (heavy) cream and 150 ml (¼ pint, ⅔ cup) milk, both very cold. Then place in an ice-cream mould and freeze.

Raspberry sorbet

Prepare a syrup by boiling 250 g (9 oz, 1 cup) granulated sugar and 400 ml (14 fl oz, 1¾ cups) water. Allow to cool. Pour in 400 g (14 oz, 2¾ cups) raspberries and the juice of ½ a lemon. Purée in a blender or food processor and then rub through a sieve if wished. Pour the mixture into an ice-cream maker and set in operation for about 1 hour. When the sorbet begins to freeze, pour into a mould and place in the freezer until required.

Redcurrant sorbet

Slowly dissolve 175 g (6 oz, ¾ cup) granulated sugar in 450 ml (¾ pint, 2 cups) water. Bring the syrup to the boil and boil steadily for 10 minutes. Cool. Mix 500 ml (17 fl oz, 2 cups) filtered redcurrant juice with 500 ml (17 fl oz, 2 cups) sugar syrup. Add a few drops of lemon juice and mix well. Then freeze the sorbet in the usual way.

Saffron ice cream with rose water

Whip 150 ml (¼ pint, ⅔ cup) milk with 150 ml (¼ pint, ⅔ cup) double (heavy) cream. Place in the freezer to harden.

Beat 3 egg yolks in a bowl with 75 g (3 oz, 2 cup) caster (superfine) sugar until the mixture foams. In a saucepan, bring to the boil 450 ml (¾ pint, 2 cups) milk, 150 g (5 oz, generous ⅔ cup) crème fraîche and ½ teaspoon vanilla essence (extract). Reduce the heat so that the mixture does not simmer. Slowly incorporate the egg yolk mixture, stirring all the time. Remove from the heat. Pound ½ teaspoon saffron, then stir in a little hot water and pour into the saucepan with 1 tablespoon rose water. Stir and leave to cool , stirring occasionally. Chill well, then transfer to an ice-cream maker and freeze until firm. Remove the frozen whipped cream from the freezer and scoop it into small pieces using 2 teaspoons. Return to the freezer.

Remove the ice cream from the freezer 30 minutes before serving. Keep in the refrigerator until ready to serve. Serve in bowls, decorated with the scoops of cream and slivers of pistachio nut.

Saffron rice à la néerlandaise

Wash about 175 g (6 oz, ¾ cup) short-grain rice. Blanch it for 2 minutes in boiling water. Drain, rinse in cold water and drain again. Boil 1 litre (1¾ pints, 4⅓ cups) milk with ½ teaspoon salt and 1 generous tablespoon soft light brown sugar. Add the rice and cook for 35–40 minutes until very soft. Then add 1 tablespoon lemon juice and a generous pinch of powdered saffron and mix well. Pour the rice into individual sundae dishes and leave to cool completely. Serve as a cold dessert, sprinkled with brown sugar, accompanied by cinnamon or ginger biscuits (cookies).

Sorbet

For soft fruit, prepare a syrup using 200 g (7 oz, 1 cup) granulated sugar and 150 ml (¼ pint, ⅔ cup) water per 500 g (18 oz) fruit. Poach the fruit in the syrup, then purée in a blender or food processor: the density of the mixture should be 1.1513. For citrus fruit use 100 g (4 oz, ½ cup) sugar and 150 ml (¼ pint, ⅔ cup) water for every 3–4 fruit. Finely grate the zest, then squeeze the juice from the fruit and mix with the syrup: the density of the mixture should be 1.1697. Add more sugar if it is too weak or more water if it is too strong. Pour into an ice-cream maker to freeze. Halfway through the cycle some Italian meringue (one third of the volume of the sorbet) can be added.

Sorbet in frosted grapefruit

Cut the tops off some grapefruit, hollow them out with a grapefruit knife without piercing the rind and separate the segments. Press the segments (or blend, then strain them) to obtain the juice and use this to prepare a grapefruit ice in the same way as for sorbet in frosted oranges. Put the grapefruit skins in the freezer. When the ice has just started to freeze, fill the grapefruit skins with it. Place the caps on the fruits and return to the freezer until the ice has frozen. Transfer to the refrigerator 40 minutes before serving.

Sorbet in frosted lemons

Cut the stalk ends off some large thick-skinned lemons and reserve. Using a spoon with a cutting edge, remove all the pulp from the lemon without piercing the peel. Then chill the peel in the refrigerator. Press the pulp, strain the juice and use it to prepare a lemon sorbet. When the sorbet is set, fill the chilled peel with it and cover with the section that was removed. Freeze until time to serve. Decorate with leaves of marzipan (almond paste).

Sorbet in frosted oranges

Choose some unblemished thick-skinned oranges. Cut off the top of each orange at the stalk end. Using a sharp-edged spoon, scrape out all the pulp, taking care not to pierce the skin. Cut a small hole at the top of the orange caps, where the stalk was attached. Put the orange shells and the caps into the freezer. Make an orange sorbet with the pulp. When it begins to set, put it into the orange shells, smoothing the top into a dome shape. Replace the caps and insert a long lozenge-shaped piece of candied angelica into the hole, to resemble a leaf. Put back in the freezer until ready to serve.

Sorbet in frosted tangerines

Choose fine even-sized tangerines with thick skins. Cut off the tops and remove the segments without breaking the peel. Place the empty shells and tops in the freezer. Squeeze the pulp, strain the juice and add 300 g (11 oz, 1⅓ cups) caster (superfine) sugar for every 500 ml (17 fl oz, 2 cups) juice. Dissolve the sugar completely in the juice. Add a little more juice if too thick or a little more sugar if too thin. Place in an ice-cream maker, but stop the process before the ice sets. Fill the frosted shells with the iced pulp and cover each with its top. Return to the freezer to allow the ice to set.

Sorbet in iced melon

Choose a large melon weighing about 2 kg (4½ lb) and cut a fairly large slice from the stalk end. Carefully remove the seeds and then scoop out the flesh without piercing the skin. Make a sorbet with the flesh. Put the empty melon shell and the top into the freezer. When the sorbet has set, but is still a little mushy, fill the empty case, pressing down well. Replace the top of the melon and store in the freezer until ready to serve. Serve the melon standing on a dish of crushed ice.

Sorbet of exotic fruits

Peel 1 very ripe pineapple, cut it into 4, remove the centre and dice the pulp, retaining the juice. Cut 2 mangoes in half, remove the stones (pits) and scoop out the flesh with a spoon. Peel and slice 1 banana. Put the fruit into a blender or food processor with the juice of 1 lemon and purée it. Measure the juice obtained. Add 75 g (3 oz, ⅓ cup) caster (superfine) sugar per 250 ml (8 fl oz, 1 cup) juice. Mix with a fork and add 1 teaspoon vanilla sugar and a pinch of cinnamon. Pour into an ice-cream maker and set in operation for 1½ hours. When the sorbet begins to freeze, place in the freezer until required.

Sorbet with Calvados

Dissolve 200 g (7 oz, 1 cup) caster (superfine) sugar in 325 ml (11 fl oz, 1⅓ cups) water. Add a vanilla pod (bean) cut in half. Bring to the boil to obtain a light syrup. Remove from the heat and discard the vanilla pod. Add the juice of 1 lemon and a pinch of cinnamon. Mix well. Whisk 3 egg whites to stiff peaks and mix them gently into the syrup. Pour into an ice-cream maker. When the sorbet begins to freeze, add 4–5 liqueur glasses aged Calvados. Beat for a few moments, turn into a mould and freeze.

Strawberry cassata

Prepare 500 ml (17 fl oz, 2 cups) strawberry ice cream, the same quantity of vanilla ice cream, and 400 ml (14 fl oz, 1¾ cups) whipped cream mixed with crystallized (candied) fruits that have been steeped in brandy or a liqueur. Spread the vanilla ice cream in a rectangular mould, cover with the whipped cream and fruits, and place in the freezer until the cream just hardens. Cover with the strawberry ice cream, press down firmly, smooth the surface and leave to set.

Strawberry gratin with lemon zabaglione

Cut 24 large strawberries in half and arrange them on the bottom of a gratin dish, with the cut sides down. Make a lemon zabaglione: put 4 whole eggs, the grated zest and juice of 4 lemons, 100 g (4 oz, ½ cup) granulated sugar and 100 g (4 oz, ½ cup) butter into a saucepan (preferably copper-bottomed). Beat the mixture with a whisk, in a bain marie, until it becomes very frothy. Cover the strawberries with this mixture and brown under the grill (broiler).

Strawberry ice cream

Make a custard with 500 ml (17 fl oz, 2 cups) milk, 6 egg yolks, 125 g (4½ oz, ½ cup) caster (superfine) sugar and little natural vanilla extract (essence). Cool, stirring. Purée 450 g (1 lb) strawberries with 4 tablespoons icing (confectioner's) sugar and stir into the custard. Freeze in an ice-cream maker.

Strawberry sorbet

Wash and hull 1 kg (2¼ lb, 8 cups) strawberries and purée in a blender or food processor. Add 300 g (11 oz, 1⅓ cups) caster (superfine) sugar. Mix well to dissolve, then add the juice of ½ a lemon and 1 orange. Pour into an ice-cream maker. Set in operation for about 1 hour. Pour the sorbet into a mould and place in the freezer for a further 1½–2 hours to allow to freeze completely.

Tangerines en surprise

Prepare some frosted tangerines, but do not fill completely with the sorbet mixture and do not cover. When they are completely frozen, top up with a tangerine-flavoured soufflé, sprinkle with icing (confectioner's) sugar and brown quickly in a preheated oven at 220°C (425°F, gas 7).

Tea sorbet

Prepare quite a strong infusion of tea according to taste. Add sugar in the proportion of 300 g (11 oz, 1⅓ cups) per 1 litre (1¾ pints, 4⅓ cups) and freeze in an ice-cream churn. Prunes cut up into tiny pieces may be added to the sorbet. Green tea flavoured with jasmine gives excellent results.

Truffle ice cream

Boil 3 large well-scrubbed truffles in 1 litre (1¾ pints, 4⅓ cups) milk for about 1 hour. In the meantime, whisk 8 egg yolks with 250 g (9 oz, 1 cup) sugar. Drain, dry and trim the truffles. Pour the milk over the sugar and egg mixture to make a custard; cook until it forms ribbons when the spoon is lifted, then add the chopped truffle trimmings. Cool, then leave to set in an ice-cream maker. Cut the truffles into julienne strips. Fill tulip glasses with alternate layers of ice cream and truffle, finishing with a decoration of julienne strips of truffle.

Tutti-frutti bombe

Line a bombe mould with 1 litre (1¾ pints, 4⅛ cups) pineapple ice and harden in the freezer. Then make a sugar syrup using 250 g (9 oz, 1 cup) sugar and 100 ml (4 fl oz, 7 tablespoons) water, pour into a saucepan in a bain marie and blend in 8 egg yolks. Whisk on the hob (stove top) until thick and frothy. Strain, then whisk again in a basin. Blend in 400 ml (14 fl oz, 1¾ cups) Chantilly cream. Flavour with 1 tablespoon kirsch and add 400 g (14 oz, 3 cups) finely diced crystallized (candied) fruits steeped in kirsch, together with 100 g (4 oz, ⅔ cup) raisins soaked in rum and drained. Pour the mixture into the mould and freeze for 4 hours. Turn out and decorate with glacé (candied) cherries, candied angelica and shredded (slivered) almonds.

Vanilla ice cream

Prepare a crème anglaise with 100 ml (4 fl oz, 7 tablespoons) milk and a vanilla pod (bean) cut in two, 5 or 6 egg yolks, 150 g (5 oz, ⅔ cup) caster (superfine) sugar and 400 ml (14 fl oz, 1¾ cups) double (heavy) cream. Pour the custard cream into an ice-cream maker and allow to set in the freezer for 4 hours. Pile up the mixture in a mould and replace in the freezer to complete the setting of the ice cream.

It may be unmoulded on to a serving dish and decorated with crystallized (candied) fruit or fruit poached in syrup, or coated with cold fruit purée (strawberry, peach or mango, for example). Alternatively it may be used in balls in sundaes or to fill profiteroles.

Vanilla ice cream charlotte

Line a charlotte mould with sponge fingers (ladyfingers). When ready to serve, fill the inside of the mould with vanilla ice cream, vanilla-flavoured bombe mixture, or plombières ice cream.

Vanilla ice cream for coupes

For about 500 ml (17 fl oz, 2 cups) ice cream, use 4 egg yolks, 250 ml (8 fl oz, 1 cup) milk, 1 vanilla pod (bean), 125 g (4½ oz, ½ cup) caster (superfine) sugar, and 2 tablespoons double (heavy) cream. Split the vanilla pod in two, add it to the milk, and bring to the boil. Work the egg yolks into the sugar with a wooden spoon. When the mixture lightens in colour, remove the vanilla pod, and add the boiling milk, little by little, whisking constantly. Heat the mixture, add the cream and continue to heat until the mixture coats the spoon. Strain the mixture into a bowl and allow to cool, stirring continuously. Pour into an ice-cream churn and operate until the ice cream is frozen.

Water ices

The density of the light sugar syrup in these recipes can be measured with a saccharometer or syrup hydrometer. As a guide, a translucent coating syrup boils at 100°C (212°F) or very slightly above – 100.5°C (213°F) – and has a density of 1.2407. To make a light syrup of this type, use 10% sugar to water: 100 g (4 oz, ½ cup) sugar to 1 litre (1¾ pints, 4⅓ cups) water.

- *Grand Marnier ice:* make 1 litre (1¾ pints, 4⅓ cups) clear, coating syrup (density 1.2407). Whisk in the juice of ½ a lemon and 6 tablespoons Grand Marnier. Freeze in an ice-cream maker.
- *liqueur ice:* mix cold, clear sugar syrup (density 1.1407) with the chosen liqueur, generally 6 tablespoons liqueur to 1 litre (1¾ pints, 4⅓ cups) syrup. Add a little lemon juice. (The density of the mixture must be between 1.1425 and 1.1799.) Freeze in an ice-cream maker.
- *mango ice:* use very ripe mangoes. Halve, peel and stone them. Blend the pulp with the juice of ½ a lemon or lime. For 500 ml (17 fl oz, 2 cups) puréed pulp, use 400 ml (14 fl oz, 1¾ cups) clear, coating syrup (density 1.2407). Whisk the syrup and pulp together. Freeze in an ice-cream maker.

BISCUITS, CAKES, PASTRIES & SWEET BREADS

Biscuits (cookies)

Almond bâtonnets

Pound 225 g (8 oz, 1⅔ cups) blanched almonds with 225 g (8 oz, 1 cup) caster (superfine) sugar, or combine in a blender. Bind to a thick paste with 2–3 egg whites and then add 7 tablespoons white rum. Roll out thinly on a floured marble slab or work surface. Cut into strips 8 cm (3½ in) wide and cut these into sticks 2 cm (¾ in) wide. Lightly beat 2 egg whites. Dip the sticks in the egg whites, then in sugar. Arrange on a buttered and floured baking sheet and bake in a preheated oven at about 170°C (325°F, gas 3) until the sugar crisps.

Almond croquets

A dry petit four in the shape of a small stick, generally made of almonds, sugar and egg white.

Soften 50 g (2 oz, ¼ cup) butter with a palette knife (spatula); coarsely chop 75 g (3 oz, ¾ cup) unskinned almonds. In a basin, mix 200 g (7 oz, 1¾ cups) plain (all-purpose) flour with ½ teaspoon baking powder, 75 g (3 oz, ⅓ cup) caster (superfine) sugar, 1 egg and the butter; add the chopped almonds and knead the paste to make it smooth. Shape the paste into a sausage 20 cm (8 in) long and flatten it into a rectangle 10 cm (4 in) wide. Place on a buttered baking sheet and leave to stand for 15 minutes.

Prepare a caramel with 1 tablespoon sugar and the same amount of water, leave until lukewarm, then add 1 egg and beat all together with a fork. Brush the rectangle with this mixture and use a fork to score the surface. Cook in a preheated oven at 200°C (400°F, gas 6) for 10 minutes, remove from the oven and immediately cut into rectangles about 2 × 5cm (¾ × 2 in).

Aniseed biscuits

Whisk together 500 g (18 oz, 2¼ cups) caster (superfine) sugar and 12 eggs in a basin, as for a sponge cake. When pale and light, add 500 g (18 oz, 4½ cups) plain (all-purpose) flour, 200 g (7 oz, ¾ cup) cornflour (cornstarch) and 50 g (2 oz, ¼ cup) aniseed. Mix well. Drop tablespoons of the mixture on to a wet baking sheet. Place in a warm place to dry. When the biscuits (cookies) begin to rise , bake in a preheated oven at 160°C (325°F, gas 3) for about 15 minutes.

Bar-sur-Aube croquets

Mix together in a basin 500 g (18 oz, 2¼ cups) caster (superfine) sugar and 250 g (9 oz, 2 cups) ground almonds, then work in 8 egg whites, one by one. Carefully blend in 275 g (10 oz, 2½ cups) plain (all-purpose) flour and 1 teaspoon vanilla sugar. Turn this paste out on to the worktop, cut it into small tongue shapes and place these on an oiled baking sheet. Bake in a preheated oven at 180°C (350°F, gas 4). When ready, cool the croquets on a marble slab and store them in a dry place, in a jar or airtight tin.

Bâtons with vanilla icing

In a processor combine 225 g (8 oz, 1⅔ cups) ground almonds and 225 g (8 oz, 1 cup) caster (superfine) sugar to a firm paste with 2–3 egg whites.

Flavour with 2 teaspoons natural vanilla essence (extract). Roll out the paste to a thickness of 1 cm (½ in). Cover with vanilla-flavoured royal icing (frosting). Cut into strips 2 cm (¾ in) wide by 10 cm (4 in) long. Place the sticks on a buttered and floured baking sheet and bake in a preheated oven at about 160°C (325°F, gas 3) for about 10 minutes or until the icing turns white.

Bordeaux croquets

Finely pound 300 g (11 oz, 2¾ cups) skinned almonds in a mortar with 150 g (5 oz, 1⅓ cups) unskinned almonds, 300 g (11 oz, 1⅓ cups) sugar, 125 g (4½ oz, ½ cup) butter, 2 eggs, the grated zest of a lemon or an orange, 3 teaspoons dried (active dry) yeast and a pinch of salt. Chop this mixture coarsely with a knife, then roll it up into a large sausage shape, slightly flattened at the edges. Place on a buttered baking sheet, glaze with egg yolk and score the surface. Bake in a preheated oven at 180°C (350°F, gas 4) for 15 minutes. Cut up into even-sized slices.

Brandy snaps

Melt 100 g (4 oz, ½ cup) butter with 100 g (4 oz, ½ cup) sugar. Stir in 100 g (4 oz, ¼ cup) golden (light corn) syrup, 100 g (4 oz, 1 cup) plain (all-purpose) flour and 1 teaspoon ground ginger. Mix well. Ladle the mixture in small heaps, very well spaced, on to a baking sheet. Place in a preheated oven at 180°C (350°F, gas 4) and bake for 7–8 minutes. To roll the brandy snaps, wrap each one round a wooden spoon handle, pressing them together where they join so that they do not unroll.

Broyé poitevin

This is a large biscuit (cookie) made of shortbread-type dough. Place 250 g (9 oz, 1 cup) caster (superfine) sugar and a pinch of salt in an earthenware dish;

make a well and drop 1 egg and 250 g (9 oz, 1 cup) butter, cut into pieces, into the centre. Knead by hand. Add 500 g (18 oz, 4 cups) plain (all-purpose) flour, a spoonful at a time, then 1 tablespoon rum or brandy and knead until the dough no longer sticks to the fingers (it should be fairly soft). Butter a pie dish 25 cm (10 in) in diameter and spread the dough in the dish, smoothing it with the palm of the hand. Brush the surface with 1 egg yolk mixed with 2 teaspoons black coffee. Draw a crisscross pattern or geometric designs with a fork. Bake in a preheated oven at 180°C (350°F, gas 4) for 30 minutes. Allow to cool before turning out of the mould dish as the cake is crumbly.

Bugnes

Put in a food processor 250 g (9 oz, 2¼ cups) plain (all-purpose) flour, 50 g (2 oz, ¼ cup) softened butter, 2 tablespoons caster (superfine) sugar, a large pinch of salt, 2 large beaten eggs and 1½ tablespoons rum, brandy or orange-flower water. Process thoroughly, then shape into a ball and allow to rest for 5–6 hours in a cool place. Roll the dough out to a thickness of 5 mm (¼ in). Cut the dough into strips about 10 cm (4 in) long and 4 cm (1½ in) wide. Make a slit in the middle 5 cm (2 in) long. Thread one end of the dough through the slit; this makes a kind of knot. Fry the *bugnes* in hot oil, turning once. Drain on paper towels, and sprinkle with icing (confectioner's) sugar.

Chocolate bâtonnets

Pound 225 g (8 oz, 1⅔ cups) blanched almonds with 225 g (8 oz, 1 cup) caster (superfine) sugar, 200 g (7 oz, 1½ cups) cocoa powder (unsweetened cocoa) and 2 tablespoons vanilla-flavoured sugar, or combine in a blender. Bind to a thick paste with 3 egg whites and then add 7 tablespoons white rum. Roll out thinly on a floured marble slab or work surface. Cut into strips 8 cm (3½ in) wide and cut these into sticks 2 cm (¾ in) wide. Lightly beat 2 egg whites. Dip the sticks in the egg whites, then in sugar. Arrange on a buttered and floured baking sheet and bake in a preheated oven at about 170°C (325°F, gas 3) until the sugar crisps.

Chocolate soufflé biscuits

Melt 300 g (11 oz, 11 squares) plain (semisweet) chocolate and stir in 2 egg yolks. Beat 500 g (18 oz, 2¼ cups) caster (superfine) sugar with 10 egg whites in a small saucepan over a very low heat or in a bain marie. When the meringue mixture is fairly firm, add the chocolate mixture. Grease and flour a baking sheet and pipe the biscuit (cookie) mixture on to it, in the shape of macaroons or sponge fingers (ladyfingers). Bake in a preheated oven at 180°C (350°F, gas 4) for about 10 minutes.

Cigarettes russes

Butter a baking sheet. Melt 100 g (4 oz, ½ cup) butter in a bain marie. Whisk 4 egg whites into very stiff peaks, adding a pinch of salt. In a mixing bowl, blend 90 g (3½ oz, 1 cup less 2 tablespoons) plain (all-purpose) flour, 165 g (5½ oz, ¾ cup less 1 tablespoon) caster (superfine) sugar, 1 tablespoon vanilla-flavoured sugar and the melted butter. Carefully add the egg whites. Spread this mixture on the baking sheet, making very thin discs about 7.5 cm (3 in) in diameter; bake only 3 or 4 at a time. Place them in a preheated oven at 180°C (350°F, gas 4) and cook for 10 minutes or until the biscuits (cookies) turn golden. Loosen them and roll each around the handle of a wooden spoon while still hot. Leave them to cool completely.

Craquelins

Knead 250 g (9 oz, 2¼ cups) plain (all-purpose) flour with 125 g (4½ oz, ½ cup) butter, 2 egg yolks, 3 tablespoons cold milk, 25 g (1 oz, 2 tablespoons) caster (superfine) sugar and a generous pinch of salt. Leave the dough to rest for 2 hours, then roll it out to a thickness of 1.5 cm (⅝ in). Cut it into 5 cm (2 in) squares, arrange the squares on a baking sheet, glaze them with egg and bake in a preheated oven 240°C (475°F, gas 9) until golden brown. Sprinkle with vanilla-flavoured sugar when cooked.

Langues-de-chat (1)

A small, dry, finger-shaped biscuit (cookie), whose name (meaning 'cat's tongue') is probably derived from its shape. Langues-de-chat are thin and fragile, but they keep well and are usually served with iced desserts, creams, fruit salad, champagne and dessert wines.

Cut 125 g (4½ oz, heaping ½ cup) butter into pieces and beat with a wooden spatula until smooth. Add 1 tablespoon vanilla sugar and 75–100 g (3–4 oz, ⅓–½ cup) caster (superfine) sugar; work for about 5 minutes with a wooden spatula. Blend in 2 eggs, one at a time. Finally, add 125 g (4½ oz, 1 generous cup) sifted self-raising flour a little at a time, mixing it in with a whisk. Lightly grease a baking sheet. Using a piping (pastry) bag with a round nozzle, pipe the mixture into strips 5 cm (2 in) long, leaving a space of about 2.5 cm (1 in) between them. Bake in a preheated oven at 220°C (425°F, gas 7) for about 8 minutes: remove as soon as the langues-de-chat have begun to turn golden.

Langues-de-chat (2)

Work together in a mixing bowl 250 g (9 oz, 1 generous cup) caster (superfine) sugar, 200 g (7 oz, 1¾ cups) plain (all-purpose) flour and 1 tablespoon vanilla sugar. Gently fold in 3 stiffly whisked egg whites. Pipe the mixture and bake as described in the previous recipe. When the langues-de-chat are cooked, turn off the heat and leave them to cool in the oven.

Leckerli

Also known as *lecrelet*. A spiced biscuit (cookie) with a distinctive flavour, sometimes coated with icing (frosting). It is a Swiss speciality from Basle. The name is an abbreviation of *leckerli kuchen*, meaning 'tempting cake'.

Sift 500 g (18 oz, 4½ cups) plain (all-purpose) flour into a bowl, add 350 g (12 oz, 1 cup) liquid honey and beat with a spoon. Add 75 g (3 oz, ½ cup) candied orange peel, 40 g (1½ oz, ⅓ cup) flaked (slivered) almonds, 20 g (¾ oz, ¼ cup) spices (half mixed spice, half ground ginger), and 1 teaspoon bicarbonate of soda (baking soda). (The candied peel and flaked almonds can be replaced with chopped hazelnuts and cinnamon.) Mix well until blended. Butter some square baking sheets and spread the mixture in them to a depth of 2.5 cm (1 in). Bake in a preheated oven at 180°C (350°F, gas 4), for about 20 minutes, or until well browned. When done, brush with milk and cut into even rectangles.

Lemon cigarettes

Butter a baking sheet. Melt 100 g (4 oz, ½ cup) butter in a bain marie. Whisk 4 egg whites into very stiff peaks, adding a pinch of salt. In a mixing bowl, blend 90 g (3½ oz, 1 cup less 2 tablespoons) plain (all-purpose) flour, 165 g (5½ oz, ¾ cup less 1 tablespoon) caster (superfine) sugar, 1 tablespoon vanilla-flavoured sugar, the melted butter and 100 g (4 oz, ⅔ cup) finely chopped candied lemon peel. Carefully add the egg whites. Spread this mixture on the baking sheet, making very thin discs about 7.5 cm (3 in) in diameter; bake only 3 or 4 at a time. Place them in a preheated oven at 180°C (350°F, gas 4) and cook for 10 minutes or until the biscuits (cookies) turn golden. Loosen them and roll each around the handle of a wooden spoon while still hot. Leave them to cool completely. Once the cigarettes have cooled, fill both ends with lemon-flavoured butter cream using a piping (pastry) bag.

Milanais sablés

Using the fingers only, blend 250 g (9 oz, 2¼ cups) plain (all-purpose) flour with 125 g (4½ oz, ⅔ cup) softened butter. Add 1 egg, 125 g (4½ oz, ⅔ cup) sugar and ½ teaspoon vanilla essence (extract) or 1 teaspoon vanilla sugar. Knead the dough quickly, shape it into a ball, put it into a floured bowl, and place in the refrigerator for 1 hour.

Roll out the dough to a thickness of 5 mm (¼ in) and cut it with a 6 cm (2½ in) oval biscuit (cookie) cutter into an even number of sablés. Using a small round cutter about 1 cm (½ in) in diameter, cut out 2 circles of dough, one towards either end from half of the sablés (these pieces will form the tops). Place the sablés on a buttered baking sheet and bake in a preheated oven at 180°C (350°F, gas 4) for about 12 minutes: they should be just golden. Allow them to cool completely.

Sprinkle the pieces from which holes have been cut out with icing (confectioner's) sugar and spread the others with a layer of redcurrant jelly. Lightly press the tops and bottoms together.

Milan sablés

Place 250 g (9 oz, 2¼ cups) plain (all-purpose) flour in a bowl. Add the grated zest of 1 lemon, 125 g (4½ oz, ½ cup) softened butter cut into small pieces, 125 g (4½ oz, ½ cup) sugar, 4 egg yolks, a pinch of salt and 1 teaspoon brandy or rum. Knead these ingredients together quickly, roll the dough into a ball and chill for 30 minutes. Then roll out the dough to a thickness of 5 mm (¼ in) and cut out the sablés with a round or oval pastry (cookie) cutter. Arrange the sablés on a greased baking sheet, brush them with beaten egg and score the surfaces lightly with a fork. Bake in a preheated oven at 200°C (400°F, gas 6) for 15 minutes, when the sablés should be scarcely golden. Allow to cool.

Napolitain biscuits

Rub 250 g (9 oz, generous 1 cup) chilled butter into 250 g (9 oz, 2¼ cups) plain (all-purpose) flour until the mixture resembles breadcrumbs. Add 250 g (9 oz, generous 1 cup) caster (superfine) sugar, 250 g (9 oz, 2¼ cups) ground almonds and 2 or 3 egg yolks. Mix quickly without kneading and roll out to a thickness of 1 cm (½ in). Cut out rounds with a pastry (cookie) cutter and bake in a preheated oven at 200°C (400°F, gas 6) for 10 minutes. Decorate the biscuits (cookies) with butter cream or jam (preserve) when cold.

Orange gimblettes

A speciality of Albi, gimblettes are small ring biscuits (cookies) arranged in the shape of a crown.

Grate the rind (zest) of ½ an orange on a lump of sugar; crush the sugar to a fine powder and mix it with caster (superfine) sugar so that the whole amount measures 175 g (6 oz, ¾ cup). Pound thoroughly 100 g (4 oz, ⅔ cup) fresh almonds. Place 225 g (8 oz, 2 cups) sifted plain (all-purpose) flour in a circle around this mixture, and in the centre put 15 g (½ oz, 1 cake) fresh yeast dissolved in 70 ml (2½ fl oz, ¼ cup) milk. Add 50 g (2 oz, 4 tablespoons) butter, 2 egg yolks, a pinch of salt, the almonds and the orange-flavoured sugar. Knead all these ingredients and leave the dough in a warm place for 5–6 hours to allow the yeast to ferment.

Knock back the dough and divide it into 5–6 strips, each the width of a little finger. Cut the strips diagonally into pieces 13 cm (5 in) long. Make these into little rings so that the joins are invisible. Drop the rings into a large saucepan of boiling water. Stir very gently with a spatula for a few minutes to prevent the rings from sticking and to bring them to the surface. Drain them and drop them into cool water. When they are cold, drain again, then toss them to dry them.

Dip each ring in a little beaten egg (2 eggs should be used in all) 2–3 times. Leave them to drain for a few minutes. Arrange them carefully on 3 lightly greased baking sheets and bake them in a preheated oven at 200°C (400°F, gas 6) for 20–30 minutes, until they are a good colour.

Little plaited biscuits (cookies) or little rolls about as long as a thumb can also be made this way. These gimblettes may also be flavoured with the rind (zest) of lemon, citron or Seville (bitter) orange, or with aniseed, vanilla or orange-flower water.

Oublies à la parisienne

A small flat or cornet-shaped wafer, widely enjoyed in France in the Middle Ages, but whose origins go even further back in time. Oublies, which were perhaps the first cakes in the history of cooking, are the ancestors of waffles. They were usually made from a rather thick waffle batter and were cooked in flat, round, finely patterned iron moulds.

Put 250 g (9 oz, 2¼ cups) sifted plain (all-purpose) flour, 150 g (5 oz, ⅔ cup) sugar, 2 eggs and a little orange-flower water or lemon juice into a bowl. Work together until everything is well mixed, then gradually add 575 ml (19 fl oz, 2⅓ cups) milk, 65 g (2½ oz, 5 tablespoons) melted butter and the grated zest of 1 lemon. Heat an oublie or waffle iron and grease it evenly; pour in 1 tablespoon batter and cook over a high heat, turning the iron over halfway through. Peel the wafer off the iron and either roll it into a cornet round a wooden cone or leave it flat.

Petits fours Souvarov

Make a pâte sablé using 675 g (1½ lb, 6 cups) plain (all-purpose) flour, 400 g (14 oz, 1¾ cups) butter, 200 g (7 oz, 1 cup) caster (superfine) sugar, and 1 tablespoon double (heavy) cream. Leave to stand for 1 hour in a cool place.

Roll out the dough to a thickness of 5 mm (¼ in) and cut out shapes using a round or fluted oval pastry (cookie) cutter. Place on a baking sheet and cook in a preheated oven at 200°C (400°F, gas 6) for 15 minutes. Leave to cool, then spread the sablés with thick sieved apricot jam (preserve), sandwich together in pairs and sprinkle with icing (confectioner's) sugar.

Pine-nut crescents

Boil 4 tablespoons water with an equal quantity of sugar in a small saucepan, then remove the syrup from the heat. In a mixing bowl blend 50 g (2 oz, ½ cup) plain (all-purpose) flour with 150 g (5 oz, 1¼ cups) ground almonds, 200 g (7 oz, ¾ cup) caster (superfine) sugar and 3 egg whites. When the dough is quite smooth, divide it into 30 pieces and shape into small crescents. Cover a baking sheet with lightly oiled greaseproof (wax) paper. Dip the crescents in beaten egg, then roll them in 200 g (7 oz, 2 cups) pine nuts. Arrange the crescents on the baking sheet and bake in a preheated oven at 200°C (400°F, gas 6) for 8–10 minutes. Remove from the oven and brush the crescents with the sugar syrup. Transfer to a wire rack to cool.

Redcurrants in a tulip

Using a spatula, spread 250 g (9 oz) tuile mixture in circles 12 cm (4¾ in) in diameter. Cook in a preheated oven at 230°C (450°F, gas 8) until lightly coloured, then shape by pressing on to an upturned bowl. Leave to cool. Soak 1½ sheets of gelatine in cold water. Finely chop ¼ bunch of basil. Heat 300 g (11 oz, 1¾ cups) strawberries with 40 g (1½ oz, 3 tablespoons) sugar and bring to the boil. Simmer for 8–10 minutes, crushing the fruit coarsely with a fork. Incorporate half the basil and put in a cool place. Whip 300 ml (½ pint, 1¼ cups) whipping cream to make a Chantilly, adding 25 g (1 oz, 2 tablespoons) caster (superfine) sugar. Then, very delicately, add 300 g (11 oz, 1½ cups) redcurrants and the rest of the basil. Pour a little basil-flavoured strawberry coulis on to each plate and garnish with a tulip filled with redcurrant cream. Decorate with peaks of crème fraîche and a few redcurrants.

Reims biscuits

Whisk 300 g (11 oz, 1⅓ cups) caster (superfine) sugar, 10 egg yolks and 12 egg whites together in a double or heatproof bowl over a pan of hot water until pale and thick. Fold in 175 g (6 oz, 1½ cups) sifted plain (all-purpose) flour and 1 tablespoon vanilla sugar. Using a plain piping (pastry) nozzle, pipe the mixture on to buttered greaseproof (wax) paper into finger shapes, well separated from each other. Bake in a preheated oven at 180°C (350°F, gas 4) for about 10 minutes.

Shortbread

Cream 175 g (6 oz, ¾ cup) butter with 75 g (3 oz, ⅓ cup) caster (superfine) sugar until very soft and pale. Gradually work in 250 g (9 oz, 2¼ cups) plain (all-purpose) flour to make a firm dough. Divide among two 15 cm (6 in) round greased sandwich tins (layer cake pans), pressing the dough out evenly, and chill well. Mark into wedges and bake in a preheated oven at 160°C (325°F, gas 3) for 50–60 minutes, until pale golden. Dust with caster sugar and cut the wedges, but leave in the tins for 15 minutes, until set, then transfer to a wire rack to cool.

Spéculos

Also known as *speculaas*, this is a Dutch and Belgian speciality consisting of small, flat, spicy, ginger biscuits (cookies) made in the shapes of legendary and traditional characters. Spéculos are traditionally made in carved wooden moulds and sold at Flemish fairs.

Put 500 g (18 oz, 4½ cups) sifted plain (all-purpose) flour in a pile on the worktop. Make a well in the centre and add a pinch of salt, 1 teaspoon bicarbonate of soda, 1½ teaspoons ground cinnamon, 3 eggs, 4 finely crushed (or ½ teaspoon ground) cloves, 300 g (11 oz, 1¾ cups) brown sugar and 200 g (7 oz, 1 cup) softened butter. Mix these ingredients thoroughly, gradually incorporating the flour. Roll the dough into a ball and leave in a cool place overnight. Divide into several pieces and roll them out. Mould them in spéculos moulds coated with flour. Turn out on to a lightly buttered baking sheet and bake in a preheated oven at 190°C (375°F, gas 5) until the biscuits (cookies) have browned (about 20 minutes).

Sponge biscuits

Make a basic sponge cake mixture. Flavour with Curaçao and add chopped candied orange peel. Using a piping (pastry) bag with a smooth nozzle, pipe the mixture on to a sheet of greaseproof (wax) paper in figures of 8. Dust with icing (confectioner's) sugar. Bake in a preheated oven at 180°C (350°F, gas 4) for about 10 minutes. Remove the biscuits (cookies) from the paper while still warm and cool completely before storing them in an airtight container.

Tuiles

A tuile is a crisp thin biscuit (cookie), so named as it was considered to resemble the shape of a curved tile. The basic mixture consists of sugar, shredded (slivered) or ground almonds, eggs and flour, sometimes with added butter and flavoured with vanilla and orange. This is spread on to a baking sheet. The tuile acquires its characteristic shape by being laid over a rolling pin while still hot, then left to set until cool and crisp. Flat round tuiles (called *mignons*) can be stuck together in pairs with meringue, then dried off in the oven.

Whisk together 100 g (4 oz, ½ cup) caster (superfine) sugar, 1 teaspoon vanilla sugar, 75 g (3 oz, ¾ cup) plain (all-purpose) flour, 2 eggs and a small pinch of salt. Blend in 25 g (1 oz, 2 tablespoons) melted butter and 75 g (3 oz, ¾ cup) shredded (slivered) almonds (optional). Using a teaspoon, place small quantities of the mixture, well apart from one another, on a buttered baking sheet. Spread them out slightly with the back of a fork dipped in cold water. Bake in a preheated oven at 240°C (475°F, gas 9) for about 4 minutes – the edges of the tuiles should be golden brown, the centres remaining white. Take out of the oven, remove from the baking sheet and bend them, while still hot, over a rolling pin or a very clean bottle; leave to cool.

Vanilla and cinnamon sablés

Mix 250 g (9 oz, 2¼ cups) sifted plain (all-purpose) flour with 125 g (4½ oz, ½ cup) butter until crumbly. Add 125 g (4½ oz, ½ cup) caster (superfine) sugar and 1 egg. Work together quickly, roll the mixture into a ball, then chill for 1 hour. Cut the dough in half; sprinkle one half with 1 teaspoon ground cinnamon and the other with 1 teaspoon vanilla sugar. Knead each half until the flavourings are well blended, then roll each out into a rectangle, 5 mm (¼ in) thick. Brush the vanilla dough with water and lay the cinnamon dough on top. Roll up the 2 layers as for a Swiss roll into a sausage shape. Brush with water, sprinkle with 3 tablespoons sugar and cut into slices 5 mm (¼ in) thick. Arrange on a greased baking sheet and bake in a preheated oven at 200°C (400°F, gas 6) for about 15 minutes. Allow the sablés to cool completely, then store in an airtight container.

Cakes & gâteaux

Almond financiers

Financiers is the term for cake made from a sponge mixture using ground almonds and whisked egg whites. Small financiers are oval or rectangular in shape; they may be used as a base for iced petits fours.

Large cakes made with the same mixture are decorated with shredded almonds and crystallized (candied) fruits. These large financiers may be cooked in cake tins (pans) of decreasing size and then built up in layers to form a large gâteau.

Butter 16 tins (pans), each 10 × 5 cm (4 × 2 in). Put 100 g (4 oz, 1 cup) plain (all-purpose) flour into a mixing bowl. Add 100 g (4 oz, 1 cup) ground almonds, 300 g (11 oz, 1⅓ cups) caster (superfine) sugar, 2–3 tablespoons vanilla sugar and a pinch of salt. Mix everything thoroughly. Add a pinch of salt to 8 egg whites and whisk them into very stiff peaks. Fold them carefully into the cake mixture. Quickly fold in 150 g (5 oz, ⅔ cup) melted unsalted butter. Divide the mixture between the tins and bake in a preheated oven at 200°C (400°F, gas 6) for 15–20 minutes until the financiers are golden brown, then turn them out and cool on a wire rack. They may be coated with kirsch- or chocolate-flavoured fondant icing (frosting).

Almond sandwich cake

Prepare a sponge cake mixture using 500 g (18 oz, 2¼ cups) caster (superfine) sugar, 1 tablespoon vanilla sugar, 12 egg yolks, 175 g (6 oz, 1½ cups) sifted plain (all-purpose) flour and an equal quantity of cornflour (cornstarch). When the egg and sugar mixture is very pale, and thick enough to form a ribbon trail, add the flour and cornflour, then 200 g (7 oz, 1¾ cups) blanched almonds (with 4 or 5 bitter almonds if desired), which have been pounded to a paste with 2 egg whites and a few drops of orange-flower water. Whisk 10 egg whites until stiff and fold into the mixture. Butter a very large round cake tin (pan) and dust the inside with caster sugar. Pour in the mixture, which should fill only two-thirds of the tin. Bake in a preheated oven at 160°C (325°F, gas 3) until risen and springy to the touch – about 1–1¼ hours depending on the size of the tin. Turn the cake out on to a cooling rack and, when cool, slice horizontally into 3 equal layers. Spread the bottom round with apricot jam (preserve) and the middle round with raspberry jelly. Reassemble the cake and coat the top and sides with apricot glaze. It may be iced (frosted) with vanilla fondant icing (frosting) and decorated with chopped almonds on the top and sides, if desired.

Apricot bouchées

Petit fours made from sponge-cake shapes, hollowed out and filled or sandwiched together in layers with a filling, are known as *bouchées sucrées* in French, or sweet bouchées. Place 250 g (9 oz, 1 cup) caster (superfine) sugar and 8 eggs in a bowl and whisk together over a pan of hot water. When the mixture is thick and fluffy, fold in alternately 200 g (7 oz, 1¾ cups) sifted plain (all-purpose) flour and 200 g (7 oz, ¾ cup) melted butter mixed with a small glass of rum. Three-quarters fill some small round moulds with the mixture and bake in a preheated oven at 180°C (350°F, gas 4) for about 20 minutes. Turn out on to a rack and cool. Cut in two, spread the bottom half with apricot jam (preserve) flavoured with rum and sandwich the two halves together. Reduce some apricot jam, flavour with rum and brush it on the top and sides of the bouchées. Decorate with blanched toasted almonds and a glacé (candied) cherry.

Apricot Genoese sponge

Bake a Genoese sponge cake. When completely cold, slice it horizontally into 3 layers of equal thickness. Cover each with apricot jam (preserve) rubbed through a fine sieve, flavoured with a little rum and warmed over a gentle heat. Reassemble the cake. Ice with fondant icing (frosting) and decorate with toasted almonds and crystallized (candied) fruits.

Bacchus

Two days in advance, prepare some macerated raisins: wash 75 g (3 oz, ⅔ cup) Californian raisins or sultanas (golden raisins) in lukewarm water, changing the water several times. Soak for 4 minutes, then drain and place in a non-stick saucepan. Cook gently, stirring, until the raisins are hot. Add a small liqueur glass of rum and flambé while rotating the saucepan. When the raisins have coloured slightly, remove from the heat, then transfer to a dish. Cover and leave to macerate for 2 days.

Make two meringue bases using 6 egg whites and 100 g (4 oz, ¾ cup) icing (confectioner's) sugar, whisked into a soft meringue. Fold in 100 g (4 oz, 1 cup) ground almonds and bake the mixture in a Swiss roll tin (jelly roll pan). Leave to cool in the tin.

Make a chocolate sponge cake base and a whipped chocolate ganache. Prepare a syrup with equal quantities of water and granulated sugar flavoured with a little rum. Saturate the chocolate sponge with this syrup. Add two-thirds of the raisins to the ganache.

Assemble the cake, starting with a layer of the almond base, then a layer of ganache with raisins, chocolate sponge, another layer of ganache and, finally a second layer of the almond base. Decorate the top with a few raisins. Glaze the whole cake with pouring (unwhipped) ganache. Place in the refrigerator until set. Serve with crème anglaise and any remaining macerated raisins.

Béarn pastis

While pastis is commonly known as the name of the aniseed-flavoured drink, in south-western France, the term *pastis* is used for various pastries.

Break 12 eggs into a mixing bowl and add 1 tablespoon orange-flower water, 3 tablespoons brandy, 400 g (14 oz, 1¾ cups) caster (superfine) sugar, a little milk and 100 g (4 oz, ½ cup) melted butter. Beat quickly, then beat in 25 g (1 oz) fresh yeast (2 cakes compressed yeast) dissolved in a little water and sufficient flour to make a soft dough. Gather the dough into a ball in the bowl, sprinkle with flour, cover with a cloth and leave it to rise in a warm place for 12 hours. Place the risen dough in a buttered mould and cook in a preheated oven at 220°C (425°F, gas 7) for about 45 minutes.

Blackcurrant ice cream cake

Trim some sponge-cake fingers to the height of a rectangular cake tin (pan). Prepare a sugar syrup flavoured with blackcurrant liqueur and allow to cool. Soak some whole sponge-cake fingers in the syrup and use to line the bottom of the tin. Repeat the process for the cut sponge-cake fingers and use these to line the sides.

To make about 675 g (1½ lb) filling, beat 6 egg yolks and 200 g (7 oz, ¾ cup) sugar until white and fluffy. Add 60 ml (2 fl oz, ¼ cup) blackcurrant liqueur and, if available, some blackcurrants macerated in sugar. Add 6 tablespoons cold milk to 400 ml (14 fl oz, 1¾ cups) very thick, cold double (heavy) cream and whip until the cream stands in peaks. Mix the whipped cream with the blackcurrant mixture and pour into the mould.

Place in the freezer until slightly set, then soak some more sponge-cake fingers in the syrup and cover the mixture with them. Leave in the freezer until set. Just before serving, turn out of the mould and pipe with whipped cream. This dish may be served with a hot or cold blackcurrant sauce.

Black Forest gâteau

Whisk 250 g (9 oz, 1 generous cup) caster (superfine) sugar with 6 eggs until pale, very thick and creamy. Then gently fold in 100 g (4 oz, 1 cup) plain (all-purpose) flour sifted with 50 g (2 oz, ½ cup) cocoa, and 150 g (5 oz, ⅔ cup) melted butter. Butter and flour 3 round 23 cm (9 in) cake tins (pans) and pour in the cake mixture. Bake in a preheated oven at 180°C (350°F, gas 4) for about 25 minutes. Turn the cakes out of the tins and allow to cool.

Make a syrup with 200 g (7 oz, ¾ cup) caster sugar and 350 ml (12 fl oz, 1½ cups) water. Flavour with kirsch. Grate 200–250 g (7–9 oz, 7–9 squares) bitter (semisweet) chocolate into thick shavings and put in the refrigerator. Soak the cooled layers of cake in the syrup.

Make some Chantilly cream by whipping together 750 ml (1¼ pints, 3¼ cups) chilled double (heavy) cream, 200 ml (7 fl oz, ¾ cup) very cold milk, 75 g (3 oz, ⅔ cup) icing (confectioner's) sugar and 2 teaspoons vanilla sugar. Cover each layer of cake with a quarter of the cream and a dozen brandy-flavoured cherries. Cover the sides of the cake with the remaining cream. Decorate the whole cake with chocolate shavings. Serve chilled.

Bordeaux Twelfth-Night cake

This is a traditional cake to be eaten on the day of Epiphany. A bean is inserted in the cake before cooking, and the person whose portion contains the bean is appointed 'king' or 'queen' for the occasion.

Make a well in 500 g (18 oz, 4½ cups) plain (all-purpose) flour and crumble in 20 g (¾ oz, 1½ cakes) fresh (compressed) yeast and 2 teaspoons salt. Work in 8 whole eggs, one by one, the zest of a grated lemon, 200 g (7 oz, 1 cup) caster (superfine) sugar in small quantities, and 200 g (7 oz, 1 cup) butter softened until creamy. Knead the dough well until evenly blended, then leave it to rise in a warm place for 10 hours.

Knock back the dough as for brioche dough and divide it into 4 equal parts. Shape each one into a crown and place these crowns, after inserting the bean on the underside of one of them, on a piece of buttered paper. Allow to rise in a very cool oven, then leave to cool. Brush the crowns with beaten egg. Decorate with thin slices of citron and crystallized (candied) sugar. Bake in a preheated oven at 200°C (400°F, gas 6) for about 40 minutes.

Traditionally, the 4 crowns are placed on top of each other.

Chestnut log

Line 2 shallow square cake tins (pans) measuring about 23 cm (9 in) square with squares of greaseproof (wax) paper. Prepare a Genoese cake mixture using 125 g (4½ oz, 1 cup) plain (all-purpose) flour, 4 eggs and 125 g (4½ oz, ½ cup) caster (superfine) sugar. Spread the mixture in the buttered lined tins with a moistened metal spatula, leaving a gap of 2 cm (¾ in) between the mixture and the top of the tin. Put straight into a preheated oven at about 180°C (350°F, gas 4) and bake for 25–30 minutes. Take the tins out of the oven, turn over on to a cloth and immediately remove the paper from the bottom of the cakes. Cover with another cloth and allow to cool.

Prepare 200 ml (7 fl oz, ¾ cup) sugar syrup by boiling 100 g (4 oz, ½ cup) granulated sugar with 100 ml (4 fl oz, 7 tablespoons) water and flavour it with rum or vanilla. To prepare the chestnut mixture, soften 225 g (8 oz, 1 cup) butter with a spatula and add 450 g (1 lb, 2 cups) chestnut cream and, if desired, 2 tablespoons rum. Beat the mixture for 6–8 minutes until light and fluffy, then divide into 2 portions. Soak the 2 squares of cake in the cooled sugar syrup and spread each with half the chestnut mixture. Place the 2 squares of cake facing each other and roll the first one up tightly, then wrap the second one over the first. Cut both ends off diagonally and stick these to the top of the log to represent knots in the wood. Place the cake in the refrigerator for 1 hour. Soften the remaining cream again and cover the entire log with it. Mark with the prongs of a fork to imitate the bark. Decorate with 8 marrons glacés, put back in the refrigerator and dust with icing (confectioner's) sugar just before serving.

Chocolate cake

Separate 3 eggs. Add 125 g (4½ oz, ½ cup) caster (superfine) sugar to the yolks and beat until the mixture is pale, thick and foamy.

Break 150 g (5 oz, 5 squares) bitter (bittersweet) chocolate into small pieces in a saucepan. Heat it gently with 4 tablespoons milk in a bain marie with the lid on. Blend 125 g (4½ oz, ½ cup) softened butter with the chocolate, stir until it has melted and become smooth and then pour this chocolate mixture into a warm mixing bowl. Immediately add the egg yolk mixture and stir briskly. In a clean bowl, whisk the egg whites until stiff. Add 125 g (4½ oz, 1 cup) plain (all-purpose) flour to the chocolate mixture and stir until combined. Then quickly fold in the whisked egg whites. Pour the mixture into a buttered manqué mould and bake in a preheated oven at 190°C (375°F, gas 5) for about 45 minutes.

Meanwhile, prepare a caramel with 2 tablespoons sugar, 1 tablespoon water and 1 tablespoon vinegar. Roll 10 walnuts in the caramel and set aside on an oiled plate. When the cake is cooked, leave it to cool in its mould and prepare a French chocolate icing (frosting). Turn out the cold cake on to a rack over a dish. Pour the icing over the cake and spread it over the top and sides with a palette knife (spatula). Decorate with the walnuts.

Chocolate gâteau with chestnuts

Cut a chocolate sponge cake horizontally into three equal layers. Bring to the boil 200 ml (7 fl oz, ¾ cup) water with 150 g (5 oz, ⅔ cup) sugar and cook for

3 minutes. Remove from the heat and add 1 tablespoon rum. Soak the three layers of the chocolate sponge with this syrup after it has cooled down.

Bring 3½ tablespoons milk to the boil. Add 250 g (9 oz, 9 squares) grated plain (dark) chocolate and stir until the mixture is smooth. Add 25 g (1 oz, 2 tablespoons) butter, then cool before adding 250 ml (8 fl oz, 1 cup) whipped Chantilly cream. Coat the first layer of chocolate sponge with this chocolate mousse.

Mix 200 g (7 oz, ¾ cup) chestnut purée with 50 g (2 oz, ¼ cup) soft butter. Beat vigorously and incorporate 1 tablespoon flamed rum, then 300 ml (½ pint, 1¼ cups) whipped Chantilly cream. Using a wide spatula, spread this chestnut mousse on the next chocolate sponge layer, arrange 75 g (3 oz, ½ cup) crumbled marrons glacés on the mousse and cover with the third layer. Put the cake in the refrigerator for 1 hour.

Bring 200 ml (7 fl oz, ¾ cup) milk to the boil and add 1½ teaspoons sugar. Now add 150 g (5 oz, 5 squares) grated plain chocolate, then 25 g (1 oz, 2 tablespoons) butter. Stir well and cool slightly. Coat the cake with this ganache, decorate with a few marrons glacés and store in a cool place until it is required.

Chocolate Genoese sponge

Melt 65 g (2½ oz, 5 tablespoons) butter in a bain marie and use part of it to butter a Genoese mould.

In a heatproof bowl, mix 75 g (3 oz, 6 tablespoons) caster (superfine) sugar with an equal quantity of cocoa and 4 eggs. Place over a saucepan of hot, not boiling, water or in a bain marie, and whisk until the mixture is greatly increased in volume and thick. Remove from the heat or bain marie and continue to whisk until completely cool (the mixture should run off the whisk in a ribbon).

Fold in 125 g (4½ oz, 1 cup) plain (all-purpose) flour and the remaining melted butter. Pour into the mould and cook in a preheated oven at 180°C (350°F, gas 4) for 25 minutes.

Turn the cake out on to a rack and leave it to cool. Cut the cake horizontally in half. Sandwich the layers of cake together with *crème au beurre* or whipped cream. The outside may be spread with cream and coated with toasted chopped almonds.

Chocolate log

Prepare Genoese cakes as for the chestnut log. To prepare the syrup, boil 100ml (4 fl oz, 7 tablespoons) water and 100 g (4 oz, ½ cup) granulated sugar in a small saucepan, allow to cool, then add 2 tablespoons rum. Finally, prepare a chocolate *crème au beurre* using 400 g (14 oz, 1¾ cups) butter. Using a pastry brush, cover the 2 cakes with rum syrup; coat with three-quarters of the cream and roll up. Completely cover the log with the remaining cream and make uneven furrows along it with a fork. Decorate with small sugar or meringue shapes and store in a cool place until required for serving (the *crème au beurre* may also be flavoured with coffee or vanilla).

Chocolate truffles with butter

Truffles are a type of confectionery made of chocolate, melted with butter or cream, sugar and sometimes eggs. The truffles are flavoured with brandy, rum, whisky, vanilla, cinnamon or coffee and shaped into balls, which are coated with chocolate or rolled in cocoa. They are a good accompaniment to coffee. *Muscadines* are long truffles, dipped in chocolate, then sprinkled with icing (confectioner's) sugar. Chambéry truffles, or *truffettes*, a speciality of the town, are made of praline mixed with chocolate, fondant icing (frosting) and butter, then coated with cocoa and sugar or rolled in grated chocolate.

To make 20 truffles, melt in a bain marie 250 g (9 oz, 9 squares) bitter (bittersweet) chocolate with 1 tablespoon milk. When the mixture is very smooth, add 100 g (4 oz, ½ cup) unsalted (sweet) butter cut into small pieces and mix well. Blend in 2 egg yolks, then 3 tablespoons double (heavy) cream and 125 g (4½ oz, 1 cup) icing (confectioner's) sugar. Leave in the refrigerator for 24 hours. Shape the truffles rapidly, spooning out the paste with a teaspoon and rolling it into walnut-sized balls on a marble surface with the palm of the hand. Drop them one by one into a bowl containing 50 g (2 oz, ½ cup) unsweetened cocoa, twisting the bowl to coat the truffles with cocoa. Store in a cool place.

Chocolate truffles with cream

Melt 300 g (11 oz, 11 squares) bitter (bittersweet) chocolate and 75 g (3 oz, ¾ cup) pure cocoa with 120 ml (4½ fl oz, ½ cup) strong coffee in a bain marie. Mix well. Heat 250 ml (8 fl oz, 1 cup) double (heavy) cream and, as soon as it starts to boil, mix with the chocolate paste. Remove from the heat and leave for a few hours in a cool place. Pipe into small balls on foil, leave in a cool place for 1½ hours, then roll in pure cocoa.

Coconut cake

Prepare a syrup using 200 g (7 oz, ¾ cup) caster (superfine) sugar and 200 ml (7 fl oz, ¾ cup) water. Whisk 4 egg yolks in a bowl over hot (but not boiling) water, then slowly pour in the sugar syrup, whisking constantly. When the yolks have almost doubled in volume, remove the bowl from the hot water and whisk until the mixture is cold. Make 250 ml (8 fl oz, 1 cup) fresh Chantilly cream, adding 1 teaspoon vanilla sugar and 2 tablespoons rum. Blend well, then add the egg-yolk mixture and 300 g (11 oz, 4 cups) fresh or desiccated (shredded) grated coconut. Pour into a deep sandwich tin (layer cake pan) and put in the freezer until the mixture is firm to the touch. Then remove the cake from the tin, cover with grated coconut and keep in the refrigerator until required.

Coconut pyramids

Open a coconut, extract the pulp and grate it. Add 75 g (3 oz, ¾ cup) ground almonds, 150 g (5 oz, ⅔ cup) sugar, 2 teaspoons vanilla sugar (or a few drops of vanilla extract) and 2 or 3 egg whites, depending on their size. Mix well together, then add another 3 egg whites, whisked to stiff peaks with a pinch of salt. Divide this mixture into portions about the size of tangerines, shape them into pyramids and arrange them on a buttered or oiled baking sheet. Bake in a preheated oven at 180°C (350°F, gas 4) for about 12 minutes.

Coffee progrès

Grease 3 baking sheets, dust with flour and trace a circle, about 23 cm (9 in) in diameter, on each with a spoon. In a bowl mix together 150 g (5 oz, ⅔ cup) granulated sugar, 250 g (9 oz, 2 cups) ground almonds and a pinch of salt. Whisk 8 egg whites until stiff with 100 g (4 oz, ½ cup) granulated sugar and gently fold into the first mixture with a wooden spoon. Put this mixture into a piping (pastry) bag with an 8 mm (⅜ in) nozzle and fill the 3 circles, piping in a spiral from the centre to the edge. Bake in a preheated oven at 180°C (350°F, gas 4) for 45 minutes. Ease the discs off the sheets to cool on a flat surface.

   While the oven is still hot, roast 150 g (5 oz, 1 cup) flaked (slivered) almonds for 5 minutes. Put 250 g (9 oz, 1¼ cups) granulated sugar in a saucepan with 3 tablespoons water and bring to the boil. Beat 6 egg yolks in a bowl, then gradually pour over the boiling syrup, beating hard until the mixture cools. Dissolve 2 tablespoons instant coffee in 1 tablespoon boiling water. Cream 350 g (12 oz, 1½ cups) butter and gradually beat in the egg–syrup mixture; then pour in the dissolved coffee and beat well. Reserve one-quarter of this butter cream; cover each disc with one-third of the remaining cream. Then put the discs one on top of the other and cover the sides with the reserved butter cream. Decorate the top with the flaked almonds. Place in the refrigerator for about 1 hour.

Cut out some strips of thick paper 1 cm (½ in) wide and 25 cm (10 in) long. Place them on top of the cake without pressing, leaving a gap of 2 cm (¾ in) between each, and dust the cake with sifted icing (confectioner's) sugar. Carefully remove the paper strips and put the *progrès* back in the refrigerator for at least 1 hour before serving.

Commercy madeleines

Cream 150 g (5 oz, ⅔ cup) butter with a wooden spoon. Add 200 g (7 oz, scant 1 cup) caster (superfine) sugar and mix well. Add 6 eggs, one at a time, then 200 g (7 oz, 1¾ cups) plain (all-purpose) flour sifted with 1 teaspoon baking powder, and finally stir in 1 tablespoon orange-flower water. Butter and lightly flour some madeleine moulds and spoon in the mixture. Bake in a preheated oven at 220°C (425°F, gas 7) for about 10 minutes. Turn out the madeleines on to a wire rack to cool.

Conversations

Conversations are small pastries with an almond filling, a coating of icing (frosting) and a topping of pastry lattice.

Separate 3 eggs. Work 150 g (5 oz, ⅔ cup) butter into a paste with a wooden spatula, adding 150 g (5 oz, ⅔ cup) caster (superfine) sugar, then the 3 yolks one by one. Mix well, then add 175 g (6 oz, 1½ cups) ground almonds, 50 g (2 oz, ½ cup) cornflour (cornstarch) and 1 teaspoon vanilla-flavoured sugar. Beat thoroughly to obtain a well blended mixture. Cut 400 g (14 oz) puff pastry into three portions, two of them equal, the third smaller. Roll out the equal portions into sheets and use one of them to line 8 greased tartlet moulds. Fill each tartlet with the almond cream and moisten the edges of the pastry with water. Then place the moulds close together and cover them with the second sheet of pastry. Pass the rolling pin over this, cutting the pastry off on the rims of the moulds.

Whisk 2 of the egg whites until stiff, adding 200 g (7 oz, 1¼ cups) icing (confectioner's) sugar. Spread this icing (frosting) over the tartlets. Roll out the remaining pastry, cut it into thin strips and intertwine these in diamond shapes on the icing. Leave for 15 minutes before cooking in a preheated oven at 190°C (375°F, gas 5) for 30 minutes. Allow the tarts to cool before serving.

Damier

A gâteau made of rum-flavoured Genoese sponge filled with butter cream and covered with praline. The sides are coated with flaked almonds and the top is decorated in a chequerboard pattern. Make a Genoese cake using 40 g (1½ oz, 3 tablespoons) butter, 3 egg yolks, 90 g (3½ oz, 7 tablespoons) caster (superfine) sugar, 90 g (3½ oz, 1 cup) plain (all-purpose) flour and a pinch of salt. Allow the cake to rest in the tin (pan) for 24 hours. Prepare a syrup by boiling 300 g (11 oz, 1⅓ cups) caster sugar in 300 ml (½ pint, 1¼ cups) water, allow to cool and then add 3 tablespoons rum.

Prepare a *crème au beurre* using 3 egg yolks, 150 g (5 oz, ⅔ cup) butter, 125 g (4½ oz, ½ cup) caster (superfine) sugar, 2 tablespoons water and 50 g (2 oz, ¼ cup) ground praline. Gently melt 250 g (9 oz, 9 squares) dark chocolate in a bowl over hot water. Prepare some royal icing (frosting) using 1 egg white and 75 g (3 oz, ½ cup) icing (confectioner's) sugar. Toast some flaked almonds and coarsely chop them.

Cut the sponge into two equal rounds and sprinkle the rum syrup over them. Spread half the *crème au beurre* over one of the rounds with a palette knife (spatula). Cover with the second round and decorate this with the remaining *crème au beurre*. Sprinkle the sides of the gâteau with flaked almonds. Using a piping (pastry) bag, pipe the royal icing over the butter cream to form a chequerboard pattern of 3 cm (1¼ in) squares. Fill alternate squares with royal icing and the rest with the melted chocolate.

Danicheff gâteau

Prepare a Genoese sponge using 4 egg yolks, 50 g (2 oz, ¼ cup) butter, 125 g (4½ oz, ½ cup) caster (superfine) sugar and 125 g (4½ oz, 1 cup) plain (all-purpose) flour; leave the cake to rest for 24 hours.

Boil 300 g (11 oz, 1¼ cups) caster sugar with 300 ml (½ pint, 1¼ cups) water in a saucepan, then allow to cool and add 2½ tablespoons kirsch. Prepare some confectioner's custard (pastry cream) using 250 ml (8 fl oz, 1 cup) milk, 2 egg yolks, 50 g (2 oz, ¼ cup) caster sugar, and 1–1½ tablespoons cornflour (cornstarch). Also make an Italian meringue using 4 egg whites, 200 g (7 oz, 1 cup) caster sugar, and 3 tablespoons water.

Cut the sponge cake into two equal rounds and spoon the sugar syrup over them. Place one of the rounds on a baking sheet and thickly spread with the confectioner's custard. Dice a large can of pineapple rings, sprinkle with kirsch, place them on top of the confectioner's custard and cover with about 100 g (4 oz, ⅓ cup) apricot jam (preserve). Place the other round of sponge cake on top and completely coat the surface of the gâteau, including the sides, with the Italian meringue paste, spreading it with a palette knife (spatula). Sprinkle with about 200 g (7 oz, 2 cups) flaked almonds and dust with icing (confectioner's) sugar. Brown in a preheated oven at 200°C (400°F, gas 6) for about 5 minutes. Allow to cool before transferring to a serving dish.

Duchesse petits fours

Grease 3 baking sheets and dust with flour. Mix together 100 g (4 oz, 1 cup) ground almonds, 100 g (4 oz, ½ cup) caster (superfine) sugar, and 40 g (1½ oz, 6 tablespoons) plain (all-purpose) flour. Whisk 6 egg whites until very stiff and fold into the mixture with a metal spoon. Melt 40 g (1½ oz, 3 tablespoons) butter and add to the mixture. Put the mixture into a piping (pastry) bag and pipe small rounds on to the baking sheets. Cook in a preheated oven at 190°C (375°F, gas 5) for 7–8 minutes, remove from the oven and carefully lift off the rounds of meringue with a palette knife (spatula). Mix 200 g (7 oz, 1 cup) ground praline with 225 g (8 oz, 1 cup) French butter cream and use to sandwich the duchesses together. Store in a cool place.

Dundee cake

Cream 225 g (8 oz, 1 cup) butter with 225 g (8 oz, 1¼ cups) caster (superfine) sugar and the grated zest of 1 orange until pale and soft. Sift 225 g (8 oz, 2 cups) self-raising flour with 100 g (4 oz, 1 cup) plain (all-purpose) flour. Beat 4 eggs with 1–2 drops oil of bitter almonds. Stir the eggs into the butter mixture, adding the occasional spoonful of the sifted flours to prevent the mixture from curdling. Mix 225 g (8 oz, 1½ cups) each of raisins and sultanas (golden raisins) with 100 g (4 oz, ¾ cup) chopped mixed candied orange, lemon and citrus peel. Add 100 g (4 oz, 1 cup) chopped blanched almonds, 100 g (4 oz, 1 cup) ground almonds and a spoonful of the measured flours, then mix well. Fold the remaining flour into the cake mixture, then stir in the fruit and almond mixture.

Line and grease a 20 cm (8 in) round deep cake tin (pan) and turn the mixture into it. Spread the mixture out evenly. Cover the top with whole blanched almonds, starting with a circle around the edge and working in towards the middle. Press the nuts lightly into the mixture, placing them close together as they separate slightly when the cake rises during baking. Bake in a preheated oven at 160°C (325°F, gas 3) for about 4 hours. Cover the top of the cake loosely with foil, if necessary, to prevent the nuts from becoming too dark. Insert a clean metal skewer into the middle of the cake to check if it is cooked: if the skewer is clean the cake is cooked; if it has sticky mixture on it, the cake is not ready, continue baking for 15 minutes before testing again.

Leave the cake to cool in the tin (pan) for 30 minutes, then turn it out on to a wire rack and leave to cool completely. Wrap the cake in greaseproof (wax) paper and place in an airtight container, then leave to mature for 2–4 weeks before serving.

English madeleines

Cream 100 g (4 oz, ½ cup) butter with 100 g (4 oz, ½ cup) caster (superfine) sugar until pale and creamy. Stir in 2 eggs and a little self-raising flour taken from 100 g (4 oz, 1 cup). Then fold in the remaining flour. Divide the mixture between 10 well-greased dariole moulds and bake in a preheated oven at 180°C (350°F, gas 4) for about 20 minutes, until risen, golden and springy to the touch. Cool on a wire rack. When cold, coat each cake with a thin layer of warmed and sieved raspberry jam (preserve), then roll in desiccated (shredded) coconut. Top each cake with ½ glacé (candied) cherry.

Filled Genoese sponge à la normande

Bake a Genoese sponge, allow to cool completely, then slice it into 2 rounds and sprinkle each half with a little Calvados-flavoured sugar syrup. Prepare a very dry apple compote, press it through a sieve, then add half its weight of warm confectioner's custard (pastry cream) flavoured with Calvados. Allow this to cool, then spread a thick layer over the bottom half of the cake. Replace the top half. Spread the surface with sieved apricot jam (preserve), then ice (frost) with fondant and leave to cool completely. Decorate with thin slices of apple cooked in very concentrated syrup, flaked (slivered) almonds and diamond-shaped pieces of candied angelica.

French cassonade tart

Mix together 125 g (4½ oz, ½ cup) melted butter, 2 egg yolks and a pinch of salt. Sprinkle in 250 g (9 oz, 2¼ cups) sifted self-raising flour and add sufficient water to give a smooth firm dough – about 3½ tablespoons. Roll the dough into a ball, wrap it in a cloth and leave to rest for 1 hour. Butter a baking sheet and roll out the pastry into a circle. Pinch around the rim and, with the tip of a knife, lightly trace diamond shapes on the top. Sprinkle evenly with 150 g (5 oz, ¾ cup) cassonade (raw brown sugar) and divide 50 g (2 oz, 4 tablespoons) butter into small balls and place these on top of the sugar. Place in a preheated oven at 200°C (400°F, gas 6) and bake for about 35–40 minutes.

Fruit cake

Soften 125 g (4½ oz, ½ cup) butter at room temperature. Cream it with 125 g (4½ oz, ½ cup) caster (superfine) sugar and a pinch of salt until pale and soft. Add 3 eggs, one at a time. Mix 175 g (6 oz, 1½ cups) plain (all-purpose) flour with 1 teaspoon baking powder. Wash and dry 250 g (9 oz, 1½ cups) currants or mixed dried fruit and add them to the flour. Mix well and stir into the mixture of butter, sugar and eggs. Refrigerate the mixture for 30 minutes.

Butter a loaf tin (pan) about 23 cm (9 in) long, line it with buttered greaseproof (wax) paper and fill with the mixture. Bake in a preheated oven at 240°C (475°F, gas 9) for about 12 minutes, then reduce the temperature to 180°C (350°F, gas 4) and bake for 45 minutes. Check that the cake is sufficiently cooked with the point of a knife, which should come out clean. Allow the cake to become lukewarm before removing from the tin. Cool on a rack.

Galette de plomb

Galette is a term used for biscuits (cookies) made with butte (a great Breton speciality); for tradional buckwheat crêpes from Brittany; and, most commonly, for a flat, round cake of variable size. As a type of cake, the galette probably dates from the Neolithic era, when thick cereal pastes were cooked by spreading them out on hot stones.

Make a well in 300 g (11 oz, 2¾ cups) sifted plain (all-purpose) flour and add 1 teaspoon caster (superfine) sugar, 2 teaspoons salt dissolved in 1 tablespoon single (light) cream, and 200 g (7 oz, ¾ cup) softened butter cut into small pieces (dot these pieces all over the flour). Mix all the ingredients together with the tips of the fingers. Beat together 1 egg and 1 yolk. Add them to the dough and knead towards the centre. If necessary, add another tablespoon of cream. Work the dough into a ball, cover with a cloth and leave to stand for 30 minutes.

Flour the work surface, spread out the dough with the flat of the hand into a rectangle, fold it 3 times upon itself, roll it into a ball again and flatten it into a round shape, 2–3 cm (¾–1¼ in) thick. Place it on a buttered tart dish, trace rosettes on the top with the point of a knife, brush it with beaten egg and bake in a preheated oven at 220°C (425°F, gas 7) for about 30 minutes. Serve lukewarm or cold.

Galette fondante

Mix 300 g (11 oz, 2¾ cups) sifted plain (all-purpose) flour with 50 g (2 oz, ¼ cup) softened butter. Add 1 beaten egg and 1 yolk, 6 tablespoons single (light) cream, 20 g (¾ oz, 1½ tablespoons) sugar and a generous pinch of salt. Roll the dough into a ball and leave to stand for 30 minutes. Roll it out and incorporate 200 g (7 oz, ¾ cup) butter, as for puff pastry. Fold and roll the dough a further 4 times, as for puff pastry, allowing it to rest for 10 minutes between the first 2 turns but rolling the final 2 turns without resting. Roll the dough out into a circle and score a lattice pattern on the top with the point of a knife. Brush with beaten egg and bake in a preheated oven at 240°C (475°F, gas 9) until golden brown. Sprinkle the galette with icing (confectioner's) sugar and put it back in the oven for a moment to glaze it.

Galettes bretonnes

In a bowl, mix 1 egg yolk and 3 eggs with 600 g (1 lb 5 oz, 2⅔ cups) sugar and 1 teaspoon ground cinnamon. Mix in 750 g (1 lb 10 oz, 3¼ cups) softened slightly salted Breton butter until the mixture is smooth. Add a little brown rum, vanilla essence (extract) and essential oil of bergamot. Sift 1 kg (2¼ lb, 9 cups) plain (all-purpose) flour, add a generous pinch of baking powder and work into the butter mixture. Turn out the resulting dough on to a cloth dusted with flour. Fold the cloth over and knead the dough inside the cloth for 3 minutes, adding flour to the cloth occasionally to prevent the dough from sticking. Leave the dough wrapped in the cloth overnight in a cool place but not in the refrigerator. (Too cold an environment hardens the butter.)

The following day, divide the dough into 5 lumps, each about 500 g (18 oz), flatten them into shallow pie dishes, glaze with beaten egg and a little milk and decorate by scoring with a fork. Bake in a preheated oven at 220°C (425°F, gas 7) for about 20 minutes, until deep golden brown. Take care not to allow the galettes to burn.

Galicien

Prepare a round Genoese sponge cake using 40 g (1½ oz, 3 tablespoons) butter, 3 eggs, 90 g (3½ oz, ½ cup) caster (superfine) sugar, 90 g (3½ oz, scant 1 cup) plain (all-purpose) flour, and a pinch of salt. Slice the cake in half horizontally, then sandwich it back together with a layer of confectioner's custard (pastry cream) flavoured with finely chopped pistachio nuts. Spread the cake with apricot jam (preserve). Make an icing (frosting) with 3 egg whites, the juice of 1 lemon, 300 g (11 oz, 2¾ cups) icing (confectioner's) sugar, and 3 drops of green colouring. Cover the cake with the icing, decorate with chopped pistachios and keep cool until ready to serve.

Gâteau Alexandra

Gently melt 100 g (4 oz, 4 squares) sweetened chocolate in a bowl over hot water. Whisk 3 egg yolks, 1 egg and 125 g (4½ oz, ⅔ cup) caster (superfine) sugar in a basin until the mixture is almost white and very thick. Blend in 75 g (3 oz, ¾ cup) ground almonds, then the chocolate, 3 tablespoons plain (all-purpose) flour, and 75 g (3 oz, ⅔ cup) cornflour (cornstarch). Whisk 3 egg whites with a pinch of salt until stiff, then gently blend them into the chocolate mixture together with 75 g (3 oz, ⅓ cup) melted butter.

Grease and flour an 18 cm (7 in) square cake tin (pan) and pour in the mixture. Bake in a preheated oven at 180°C (350°F, gas 4) for 50 minutes. When cool, cover the cake with 200 g (7 oz, ⅔ cup) apricot jam (preserve), then refrigerate for about 10 minutes.

Meanwhile, melt 75 g (3 oz, 3 squares) chocolate with 2 tablespoons water and, in another saucepan, very gently warm through 200 g (7 oz, 1 cup) fondant. Add the melted chocolate to the fondant: the mixture must be liquid enough to be spread easily. Cover the cake with this chocolate fondant, then store in a cool place until ready to serve.

Gâteau le parisien

Pare the zest from a lemon, blanch it for 1 minute, cool, dry and cut into short very fine julienne strips. Whisk 3 egg yolks with 100 g (4 oz, ½ cup) caster (superfine) sugar until the mixture is almost white. Pour in 25 g (1 oz, ¼ cup) plain (all-purpose) flour, 40 g (1½ oz, ⅓ cup) cornflour (cornstarch), 1 teaspoon vanilla sugar and the zest, then carefully fold in the 3 egg whites, whisked with a pinch of salt until very stiff. Pour this mixture into a buttered fairly deep 23 cm (9 in) sandwich tin (layer cake pan) or manqué mould and bake in a preheated oven at 200°C (400°F, gas 6) for 40 minutes.

Make a frangipane cream with 3 egg yolks, 75 g (3 oz, 6 tablespoons) caster sugar, 25 g (1 oz, ¼ cup) cornflour, 400 ml (14 fl oz, 1¾ cups) milk, 1 teaspoon vanilla sugar and 125 g (4½ oz, 1 cup) ground almonds. Blend in 125 g (4½ oz, ½ cup) chopped crystallized (candied) fruits.

When the cake is cooked, leave it to cool. Make some Italian meringue with 3 egg whites, 2 tablespoons icing (confectioner's) sugar, and 175 g (6 oz, ¾ cup) caster sugar. Cut the cooled cake into 3 equal rounds. Cover each layer with the frangipane cream and crystallized fruit mixture and re-form the cake. Spread some meringue on the top, then fill a fluted piping (pastry) bag with the rest of the meringue and decorate all round the cake with regular motifs. Sprinkle the meringue with icing sugar and put in a preheated oven at 180°C (350°F, gas 4). Take out the cake as soon as the meringue turns brown. Leave to cool completely.

Gâteau 'le prélat'

Prepare 1 litre (1¾ pints, 4⅓ cups) strong, lightly sweetened coffee, flavoured with white rum. Allow to cool. Beat together 2 eggs and 6 egg yolks, add 300 g (11 oz, 1½ cups) sugar boiled to the thread stage and whisk until cold. Blend in 300 g (11 oz, 2 cups) melted bitter (semisweet) chocolate pieces, some grated orange zest and 750 ml (1¼ pints, 3¼ cups) lightly whipped double (heavy) cream. Mix well.

Cover the bottom of a buttered rectangular mould with sponge fingers (ladyfingers) soaked in a little of the cold coffee. Cover with some of the chocolate mixture. Top with another layer of soaked sponge fingers and continue layering until the mould is full, finishing with a layer of sponge fingers. Place in the refrigerator for 24 hours before turning out of the mould. Melt 450 g (1 lb) dark chocolate and mix with 150 g (5 oz, ⅔ cup) butter and 2 tablespoons light oil. Coat the gâteau with this mixture.

Gâteau manqué

Manqués are sponge cakes that are a speciality of Paris.

Melt 100 g (4 oz, ½ cup) butter without browning. Separate 6 eggs. Put the yolks into a bowl with 200 g (7 oz, scant 1 cup) caster (superfine) sugar and 1 teaspoon vanilla sugar. Whisk until the mixture becomes light and frothy. Then fold in 150 g (5 oz, 1¼ cups) plain (all-purpose) flour, the melted butter and half a liqueur glass of rum, mixing until evenly blended. Whisk the egg whites together with a pinch of salt into firm peaks and gently fold them into the manqué mixture.

Grease a deep sandwich tin (layer cake pan) or a manqué mould with butter, pour in the mixture, and bake in a preheated oven at 200°C (400°F, gas 6) for 40–45 minutes. Leave for a few minutes in the tin, then turn out on to a wire rack to cool completely.

Gâteau Montmorency

Montmorency is the name given to various savoury or sweet dishes that include the sour Montmorency cherries

Separate the yolks from the whites of 3 eggs. Whisk the 3 yolks with 50 g (2 oz, ½ cup) ground almonds and 125 g (4½ oz, scant ⅔ cup) caster (superfine) sugar. Drain 400 g (14 oz) cherries in syrup, halve, stone (pit) and roll them in flour. Incorporate 50 g (2 oz, ½ cup) plain (all-purpose) flour and the cherries into the almond mixture, then carefully fold in the 3 egg whites stiffly whisked with a pinch of salt. Pour the mixture into a buttered cake tin (pan) and bake in a preheated oven at 200°C (400°F, gas 6) for about 30 minutes. Turn the cake out on to a wire rack and allow to cool.

Melt 200 g (7 oz) fondant over a low heat, stirring all the time. Add a liqueur glass of kirsch and 2–3 drops of cochineal (red food colouring). Spread the fondant over the cake with a spatula and decorate with 12 glacé (candied) cherries and a few pieces of angelica.

Alternatively, the cake may be cut into 2 layers, steeped in kirsch, and sandwiched together with butter cream mixed with cherries in brandy.

Gâteau Montpensier

Gâteau Montpensier is a Genoese sponge enriched with ground almonds, raisins and crystallized (candied) fruits.

Steep 50 g (2 oz, ⅓ cup) crystallized (candied) fruits and 50 g (2 oz, ⅓ cup) sultanas (golden raisins) in 6 tablespoons rum. With the fingertips, work 125 g (4½ oz, generous 1 cup) plain (all-purpose) flour with 75 g (3 oz, 6 tablespoons) butter cut into small pieces. Beat 7 egg yolks with 125 g (4½ oz, scant ⅔ cup) caster (superfine) sugar until the mixture is white, then mix in 100 g (4 oz, 1 cup) ground almonds and finally 3 stiffly whisked egg whites. Drain the fruit and sultanas, then add them to the mixture, together with the flour-and-butter mixture. Work together briskly with a wooden spoon for a short time.

Butter a 22 cm (8½ in) cake tin (pan) and sprinkle it with 50 g (2 oz, ½ cup) flaked (slivered) almonds. Pour the mixture into the tin and bake in a preheated oven at 200°C (400°F, gas 6) for 30 minutes. Turn out the cake on to a wire rack and allow to cool. Melt 150 g (5 oz, ½ cup) apricot jam (preserve) over a low heat, strain and spread over the surface of the cake. Keep cold until ready to serve.

Geneva sponge fingers

Beat 125 g (4½ oz, ½ cup) caster (superfine) sugar with a little grated lemon zest, a pinch of salt, 1 whole egg and 3 egg yolks until the mixture is thick enough to form a ribbon trail. Add 50 g (2 oz, ¼ cup) clarified butter, 40 g (1½ oz, ⅓ cup) ground almonds, 125 g (4½ oz, 1 cup) plain (all-purpose) flour and 3 stiffly whisked egg whites. Pour into finger-shaped moulds that have been buttered and dusted with caster sugar and cornflour (cornstarch) and bake in a preheated oven at 180°C (350°F, gas 4) for about 10 minutes. Turn the sponge fingers out of the moulds and leave to dry at the front of the oven with the oven door open. Leave them to cool completely and store in an airtight container until needed.

Genoa cake

A type of rich sponge cake made with ground almonds, not to be confused with Genoese sponge cake. Of varying degrees of lightness, depending on whether or not the beaten egg whites are incorporated separately, Genoa cake is traditionally cooked in a round mould with a fluted edge. It is served plain or with various decorations and fillings.

Work 125 g (4½ oz, ½ cup) butter into a soft paste with 150 g (5 oz, ⅔ cup) caster (superfine) sugar, then whisk until the mixture becomes white. Blend in 100 g (4 oz, 1 cup) ground almonds, then add 3 eggs, one by one, 40 g (1½ oz, ⅓ cup) cornflour (cornstarch) and a pinch of salt. Work everything well together. Flavour the mixture with 1 tablespoon liqueur (such as Curaçao).

Butter a round cake tin (pan), line the bottom with a circle of buttered greaseproof (wax) paper, and pour in the mixture. Bake in a preheated oven at 180°C (350°F, gas 4) for 40 minutes. Turn out immediately on to a wire rack and remove the paper.

Genoese sponge

A light sponge cake that takes its name from the city of Genoa. Genoese sponge is made of eggs and sugar whisked over heat until thick, then cooled and combined with flour and melted butter. It can be enriched with ground almonds or crystallized (candied) fruits and flavoured with liqueur, the rind (zest) of citrus fruits or vanilla.

Genoese sponge differs from ordinary sponge cake in that the eggs are beaten whole, whereas in the latter the yolks and whites are usually beaten separately. Genoese sponge is the basis of many filled cakes. Cut into two or more layers, which may be covered with jam (preserve), cream or fruit purée, it is coated, iced (frosted) and decorated as required.

Melt 125 g (4½ oz, ½ cup) butter gently without allowing it to become hot. Put 275 g (10 oz, 1⅓ cups) caster (superfine) sugar, 8 beaten eggs, 2 large pinches of salt and 1 teaspoon vanilla sugar into a basin and place it in a tepid bain marie; whisk the mixture until it becomes thick, pale and foamy. Remove from the heat and continue to whisk until it cools down completely. Carefully fold in 250 g (9 oz, 2¼ cups) sifted flour and then trickle in the tepid melted butter at the side of the bowl. Mix in gently until it is evenly blended. Pour this mixture into a large buttered sandwich tin (layer cake pan) and bake in a preheated oven at 200°C (400°F, gas 6) for 10–15 minutes.

Genoese sponge with coffee filling

Prepare a Genoese sponge cake using half the given quantity in the recipe and bake it in a large sandwich tin (layer cake pan). Allow it to cool completely. Slice it into 2 layers of equal thickness and cover each layer with coffee butter cream. Reassemble the cake and cover the sides with *crème au beurre*. Decorate the top and sides with chopped toasted almonds and pipe a rosette of butter cream on the top.

Genoese sponge with crystallized fruits

Make a Genoese sponge mixture with 125 g (4½ oz, ½ cup) sugar, 4 eggs, a pinch of salt, ½ teaspoon vanilla sugar, 125 g (4½ oz, 1 cup) sifted plain (all-purpose) flour and 100 g (4 oz, ½ cup) butter. Chop 150 g (5 oz, 1 cup) crystallized (candied) fruits into very small pieces. Roll them in flour, shake in a sieve to remove the excess flour and add to the sponge mix. Pour the mixture into a buttered deep sandwich tin (layer cake pan) or manqué mould and bake in a preheated oven at 200°C (400°F, gas 6) for 25–30 minutes. Make a syrup with 150 g (5 oz, ⅔ cup) sugar and 150 ml (¼ pint, ⅔ cup) water and boil for 4–5 minutes. When cool, add 2½ tablespoons white rum and pour this syrup over the cake while it is still warm.

Ginger cake

Cut 100 g (4 oz, ½ cup) preserved ginger into fine dice. Soften 100 g (4 oz, ½ cup) butter with a wooden spatula. Vigorously whisk together 3 large eggs, 1 tablespoon rum and 2 tablespoons hot water. When the mixture is thick and foamy, gradually add 175 g (6 oz, ¾ cup) caster (superfine) sugar, continuing to whisk. Sift together 250 g (9 oz, 2 cups) plain (all-purpose) flour and 2 teaspoons baking powder, make a well in the middle and mix in the beaten eggs, softened butter and ginger. Pour into a buttered manqué mould or deep sandwich tin (layer cake pan) 22 cm (8¾ in) in diameter. Bake in a preheated oven at 220°C (425°F, gas 7) for about 40 minutes.

Gingerbread

Warm together 100 g (4 oz, ½ cup) margarine or lard (shortening) and 200 g (7 oz, ¾ cup) black treacle or molasses. Add 150 ml (¼ pint, ⅔ cup) milk and allow to cool. Sift 200 g (7 oz, 2 cups) plain (all-purpose) flour, 1 teaspoon mixed spice, 2 teaspoons ground ginger and 1 teaspoon bicarbonate of soda (baking soda) into a bowl. Add the treacle mixture, 50 g (2 oz, ¼ cup) brown sugar and 2 eggs. Beat well. Pour into a 18 cm (7 in) square tin (pan) lined with greaseproof (wax) paper. Bake in a preheated oven at 150°C (300°F, gas 2) for 1¼–1½ hours, until firm to the touch.

Hazelnut cake

Spread 50 g (2 oz, ½ cup) ground hazelnuts on a baking sheet and brown them lightly in a preheated oven at 140°C (275°F, gas 1). Whisk 5 egg yolks with 150 g (5 oz, ⅔ cup) caster (superfine) sugar for 5 minutes, then beat in 150 g (5 oz, 1¼ cups) sifted plain (all-purpose) flour and the ground hazelnuts. Melt 90 g (3½ oz, 7 tablespoons) butter over a very low heat, blend in the nut mixture, then carefully fold in 5 egg whites whisked to stiff peaks. Pour this mixture into a 20 cm (8 in) buttered, deep, round sandwich tin (layer cake pan) and bake in a preheated oven at 180°C (350°F, gas 4) for 30–35 minutes. Turn the cake out on to a wire rack and leave to cool.

Meanwhile, make *crème au beurre* using 4 egg yolks, 150 g (5 oz, ⅔ cup) caster sugar, 175 g (6 oz, ¾ cup) butter and 50 g (2 oz, ½ cup) ground hazelnuts. Then prepare the dough for the decoration: soften 50 g (2 oz, 4 tablespoons) butter and blend in 50 g (2 oz, 4 tablespoons) caster sugar, 1 teaspoon vanilla sugar and 1 egg; using a whisk, beat in 50 g (2 oz, ½ cup) plain flour. Roll this dough out, cut it into small rounds with a biscuit (cookie) cutter, and place the rounds well apart on a lightly buttered baking sheet. Bake in a preheated oven at 240°C (475°F, gas 9). Remove the rounds when cooked and leave to cool.

Cut the cake into 3 equal layers, spread *crème au beurre* over each layer, then reassemble the cake. Coat the sides with the remaining cream and decorate with the baked rounds. The spaces between the rounds can be filled with toasted hazelnuts. Store in a cool place.

Honey and cherry cake

Soften 100 g (4 oz, ½ cup) butter at room temperature, divide into small pieces, and then cream with 100 g (4 oz, ½ cup) caster (superfine) sugar, a large pinch of salt and 2 tablespoons liquid honey. Mix in 1 teaspoon baking powder, 200 g (7 oz, 1¾ cups) plain (all-purpose) flour and 3 eggs, added one at a time. Flavour with 2 tablespoons rum. Halve 125 g (4½ oz, ½ cup) glacé (candied) cherries and add them to the cake mixture. Pour immediately into a buttered loaf tin (pan) and bake in a preheated oven at 190°C (375°F, gas 5) for about 45 minutes. If the cake is browning too quickly, cover it with a piece of foil. Turn the cooked cake out of the tin when lukewarm and leave to cool on a rack. Decorate with glacé cherries and pieces of angelica.

Italian sponge cake

In a large bowl, use a spatula to beat 500 g (18 oz, 2¼ cups) caster (superfine) sugar with 1½ teaspoons vanilla sugar and 10 egg yolks. Whisk 10 egg whites with a pinch of salt until stiff and fold into the mixture. Quickly fold in 125 g (4½ oz, 1 cup) plain (all-purpose) flour and 125 g (4½ oz, 1 cup) cornflour (cornstarch) sifted together. Butter a charlotte mould and dust the inside with caster sugar and cornflour. Pour the mixture into the mould, no more than two-thirds full. Bake in a preheated oven at 160°C (325°F, gas 3) until risen, golden and firm – about 1¼ hours depending on the size of the mould.

Italian sponge drops

Put 250 g (9 oz, 1 cup) granulated sugar into a small saucepan with 500 ml (17 fl oz, 2 cups) water and boil until the syrup reaches the 'hard ball' stage. Partially cool, then add 4 egg yolks and 125 g (4½ oz, 1 cup) plain (all-purpose) flour. Whisk 4 egg whites stiffly with a pinch of salt and add to the mixture. Pipe into small flat rounds and finish as for lemon sponge drops.

Crème caramel
Recipe on page 47

Diplomat pudding (baked)
Recipe on page 55

Floating islands
Recipe on page 61

Peaches à la bordelaise
Recipe on page 82

Pineapple surprise
Recipe on page 89

Rice with almond milk and citrus fruit jelly
Recipe on page 100

Vanilla meringues with exotic fruit
Recipe on page 114

Passion fruit sorbet
Recipe on page 137

Redcurrants in a tulip
Recipe on page 161

Black Forest gâteau
Recipe on page 169

Orange sandwich cake
Recipe on page 201

Linzertorte
Recipe on page 244

Strawberry délices
Recipe on page 261

Individual tangerine barquettes
Recipe on page 262

Kugelhopf
Recipe on page 279

Rum babas
Recipe on page 284

Lemon délice

Melt 100 g (4 oz, ½ cup) butter. Measure 250 g (9 oz, 2¼ cups) self-raising flour into a mixing bowl, then add the melted butter, 4 eggs, 200 g (7 oz, 1 cup) caster (superfine) sugar, the grated zest and juice of 1 lemon, and 100 g (4 oz, ¾ cup) crystallized (candied) fruits cut into very small dice. Mix until evenly blended, then turn the mixture into a 25 cm (10 in) round loose-bottomed cake tin (pan) and cook for 40 minutes in a preheated oven at 190°C (375°F, gas 5).

Meanwhile, prepare a *crème au beurre* using 125 g (4½ oz, ½ cup) caster sugar cooked to the thread stage in 3 tablespoons water, 4 egg yolks, 125 g (4½ oz, ½ cup) butter and the grated zest and juice of 1 lemon.

When the cake is cooked, turn out on to a wire rack, allow to cool and cut into three rounds. Cover two of the rounds with a thick layer of the lemon butter cream and sandwich together. Dust generously with icing (confectioner's) sugar and keep in a cool place (not the refrigerator) until ready to serve. (The layers may be sprinkled with lemon sugar syrup if liked.)

Lemon manqué

Remove the peel (zest) from a lemon and blanch for 2 minutes in boiling water. Refresh in cold water, dry and shred very finely. Finely dice 100 g (4 oz, ½ cup) candied citron peel. Melt 100 g (4 oz, ½ cup) butter without allowing it to brown. Separate 6 eggs. Put the yolks into a bowl with 200 g (7 oz, scant 1 cup) caster (superfine) sugar and 1 teaspoon vanilla sugar. Whisk until the mixture becomes light and frothy. Then fold in 150 g (5 oz, 1¼ cups) plain (all-purpose) flour, the lemon and diced citron, the melted butter and half a liqueur glass of rum, mixing until evenly blended. Whisk the egg whites together with a pinch of salt into firm peaks and gently fold them into the manqué mixture.

Bake the cake, remove from the tin (pan) while still warm, and cool completely. Lightly whisk 2 egg whites and mix in 1 tablespoon lemon juice, then some icing (confectioner's) sugar, until the mixture has a spreading consistency. Coat the cake with the icing (frosting) and decorate with small pieces of candied citron peel.

Lemon sponge drops

Using a large bowl and a spatula, beat 250 g (9 oz, 1 cup) caster (superfine) sugar with 8 egg yolks until the mixture is thick enough to form a ribbon trail. Add the grated zest of 1 lemon, 125 g (4½ oz, 1 cup) sifted plain (all-purpose) flour, 75 g (3 oz, ¾ cup) cornflour (cornstarch), 1½ tablespoons ground almonds and 8 egg whites stiffly whisked with a pinch of salt.

Using a piping (pastry) bag with a smooth nozzle, pipe small flat rounds, 2.5 cm (1 in) in diameter, on to a baking sheet and dust with caster sugar. Bake in a preheated oven at 180°C (350°F, gas 4) for about 10 minutes, or until lightly browned and set. Cool completely and store in an airtight container.

Macaroons (1)

This is the classic macaroon recipe.

Line a baking sheet with rice paper or buttered greaseproof (wax) paper. Mix 350 g (12 oz, 1½ cups) caster (superfine) sugar with 250 g (9 oz, 2½ cups) ground almonds. Lightly whisk 4 egg whites with a pinch of salt and mix thoroughly with the sugar and almond mixture. If liked, a little finely chopped candied orange peel or cocoa powder can be added to the mixture before cooking. Pipe or spoon small heaps of this mixture on to the baking sheet, spacing them so that they do not run into one another during cooking.

Cook in a preheated oven at 200°C (400°F, gas 6) for about 12 minutes. Lift the macaroons off the baking sheet with a spatula, transfer to a wire rack and leave to cool. Macaroons can be stored in an airtight container for several days in the refrigerator, or for several months in the freezer.

Macaroons (2)

This recipe gives softer macaroons.

Mix together 250 g (9 oz, 2½ cups) ground almonds, 450–500 g (16–18 oz, 3⅓–3⅔ cups) icing (confectioner's) sugar, and 1 teaspoon vanilla sugar or a few drops of vanilla essence (extract) in a bowl with 4 lightly whisked egg whites. Whisk 4 additional egg whites into stiff peaks with a pinch of salt and fold very gently into the mixture. Place the mixture in a piping (pastry) bag with a smooth nozzle 5 mm (¼ in) in diameter. Pipe small amounts of the mixture on to a baking sheet lined with rice paper or greaseproof (wax) paper, spacing them so that they do not stick together during cooking. Cook in a preheated oven at 180°C (350°F, gas 4) for about 12 minutes. Finish as for classic macaroons. A little finely chopped angelica can be added to the almond mixture.

Madeleines

This is the classic French recipe for these small sponge cakes.

Melt 100 g (4 oz, ½ cup) butter without allowing it to become hot. Butter a tray of madeleine moulds with 20 g (¾ oz, 1½ tablespoons) butter. Put the juice of ½ a lemon in a bowl with a pinch of salt, 125 g (4½ oz, scant ⅔ cup) caster (superfine) sugar, 3 eggs and an extra egg yolk. Mix well together with a wooden spatula and then sprinkle in 125 g (4½ oz, scant 1¼ cups) sifted self-raising flour and mix until smooth; finally add the melted butter. Spoon the mixture into the moulds but do not fill more than two-thirds full. Bake in a preheated oven at 180°C (350°F, gas 4) for about 25 minutes. Turn out the madeleines and cool on a wire rack.

Marble cake

Melt 175 g (6 oz, ¾ cup) butter very slowly, without letting it become hot. Whisk in 200 g (7 oz, ¾ cup) caster (superfine) sugar and then 3 egg yolks. Sift 175 g (6 oz, 1½ cups) plain (all-purpose) flour and 1 teaspoon baking powder and stir into the egg mixture. Whisk 3 egg whites with a pinch of salt until stiff and fold them into the mixture. Divide the mixture in half. Fold 25 g (1 oz, ¼ cup) cocoa into one portion. Pour the two mixtures into a greased 20 cm (8 in) cake tin (pan) in alternate thin layers. Bake in a preheated oven at 180°C (350°F, gas 4) for 1–1¼ hours.

Marignan

This is a savarin cake spread with sieved apricot jam (preserve) and covered with Italian meringue; it is traditionally decorated with a ribbon of angelica fashioned like the handle of a basket.

Soak 75 g (3 oz, ½ cup) raisins in warm water until plump. Weigh out 250 g (9 oz, 2¼ cups) strong plain (bread) flour. Dissolve 15 g (½ oz) fresh yeast (1 cake compressed yeast) in a very small amount of water, stir in a little of the flour, then cover the mixture with the rest of the flour and leave to rise. When cracks appear in the flour (after about 15 minutes), transfer the yeast and flour to a mixing bowl and add 25 g (1 oz, 2 tablespoons) caster (superfine) sugar, a pinch of salt and 3 very lightly whisked eggs. Knead the dough well until it becomes elastic, then gradually incorporate about 4½ tablespoons water to make a very soft smooth dough. Stand for 30 minutes.

Melt 75 g (3 oz, 6 tablespoons) butter and add this to the dough, together with the drained and dried raisins. Turn the dough into a buttered and floured manqué mould or deep-sided cake tin (pan), 19 cm (7½ in) in diameter, and leave it to rise. When the dough has doubled in volume, bake in a preheated oven at 190°C (375°F, gas 5) for about 40 minutes.

Prepare a syrup with 100 g (4 oz, ½ cup) sugar, 250 ml (8 fl oz, 1 cup) water, and 6 tablespoons rum. Pour this over the warm cake. Spread the cake with warmed and sieved apricot jam (about half a jar is required). Prepare an Italian meringue mixture with 400 g (14 oz, 1¾ cups) caster sugar, 4 egg whites and 1 liqueur glass of rum. Completely cover the sides and top of the cake with this mixture. Bend a long strip of angelica over the cake to resemble the handle of a basket, and fix it to the cake at each end.

Mascotte

Make a Genoese mixture with 4 eggs, 125 g (4½ oz, scant ⅔ cup) granulated sugar, a pinch of salt and 125 g (4½ oz, generous 1 cup) plain (all-purpose) flour. Bake in a buttered round cake tin (pan) 23 cm (9 in) in diameter.

Prepare a syrup with 100 g (4 oz, ½ cup) granulated sugar and 6 tablespoons water. When it has cooled, blend in 6 tablespoons rum. Make a coffee *crème au beurre* with 4 tablespoons instant coffee powder, 250 g (9 oz, generous 1 cup) sugar, 6 egg yolks, 300 g (11 oz, scant 1½ cups) softened butter and 3 tablespoons rum. Divide into half and add 2 tablespoons toasted crushed almonds to one half.

Cut the cake horizontally into 2 halves and soak them in the rum-flavoured syrup. Sandwich together with the *crème au beurre* without almonds and coat the top and sides of the cake with the remaining cream.

Mocha cake

Melt 90 g (3½ oz, 7 tablespoons) butter, taking care not to let it get too hot. Whisk 5 egg yolks with 150 g (5 oz, ⅔ cup) caster (superfine) sugar until the mixture has turned white and thick. Mix in 150 g (5 oz, 1¼ cups) plain (all-purpose) flour and 50 g (2 oz, ½ cup) ground hazelnuts, then incorporate the melted butter and fold in 5 stiffly whisked egg whites. Pour this mixture into a deep 22 cm (8½ in) buttered cake tin (pan) and bake in a preheated oven at 180°C (350°F, gas 4) for about 35 minutes. As soon as the cake is cooked, turn it out on to a wire rack and leave to cool completely. Then cover and refrigerate for at least 1 hour.

Dissolve 150 g (5 oz, ⅔ cup) sugar with 2 tablespoons water and very slowly bring it to the boil. Gently mix the boiling syrup with 4 egg yolks and beat briskly until it has cooled and is thick and mousse-like. Now whisk in 175 g (6 oz, ¾ cup) soft butter, cut into small pieces, and 1 teaspoon coffee essence (extract). Finely grind 150 g (5 oz, 1¼ cups) toasted hazelnuts. Cut the cake into 3 layers. Mix two-thirds of the ground nuts into half the cream and spread on 2 of these layers. Sandwich the cake together and cover it completely with half the remaining cream. Sprinkle the surface of the cake with the remaining ground hazelnuts, put the rest of the cream into a piping (pastry) bag with a fluted nozzle and pipe a regular design of rosettes on the cake. Place a coffee bean covered in bitter chocolate at the centre of every rosette. Refrigerate the cake in a sealed container for at least 2 hours and then serve it very cold.

Mocha cake can also be filled and coated with coffee cream, then decorated with toasted flaked (slivered) almonds and crystallized (candied) violets and mimosa. Mocha cake is best eaten the day after its preparation.

Nantes cakes

Cream 100 g (4 oz, ½ cup) butter, 100 g (4 oz, ½ cup) caster (superfine) sugar, a pinch of salt, ½ teaspoon bicarbonate of soda (baking soda) and the zest of 1 lemon or 1 orange until pale and soft. Beat in 2 eggs and 125 g (4½ oz, 1 cup) sifted plain (all-purpose) flour, beating the mixture well. Butter some tartlet moulds and sprinkle with slivered almonds. Pour in the mixture and cook in a preheated oven at 190°C (375°F, gas 5) for about

20 minutes. Turn the cakes out on to a wire rack. Coat them with warmed apricot jam (preserve), then ice (frost) them with fondant flavoured with maraschino and dust with coloured sugar grains.

Napolitain cake

A large cylindrical or hexagonal French cake with a hollow centre. It is made of layers of almond pastry sandwiched together with apricot jam (preserve), redcurrant jelly or other preserve, and usually lavishly decorated with marzipan (almond paste) and crystallized (candied) fruits.

Pound 375 g (13 oz, 2½ cups) sweet almonds in a mortar, together with 5 g (¼ oz, 1 teaspoon) bitter almonds, if desired. Gradually incorporate 1 egg white to prevent the almonds from becoming oily. Then add 200 g (7 oz, 1 cup) caster (superfine) sugar, the very finely grated zest of 1 lemon, 250 g (9 oz, generous 1 cup) softened butter and 500 g (18 oz, 4½ cups) sifted plain (all-purpose) flour. Work all the ingredients together in the mortar. Add 4 whole eggs, one by one, until the dough is very smooth but still firm.

Leave the dough in a cool place for 2 hours. Then roll it out to a thickness of 1 cm (½ in) on a lightly oiled surface and cut out circles 20–25 cm (8–10 in) in diameter. Leaving 2 rounds whole, cut out the centres of the remaining rounds with a pastry (cookie) cutter 6 cm (2½ in) in diameter. Place all the rounds on a baking sheet, in batches if necessary, and bake in a preheated oven at 200°C (400°F, gas 6) for 20–25 minutes.

When cold, cover one of the whole rounds with very reduced sieved apricot jam, then build up the cake by placing the rounds with the centres cut out one on top of the other, covering each of them with apricot jam. Place the remaining whole round on the top and cover it with apricot jam. Put the cake in a cool place. Finish by covering the cake with marzipan or royal icing (frosting) and decorate the top with crystallized (candied) apricot halves.

Orange galettes

Make a well in 250 g (9 oz, 2¼ cups) sifted plain (all-purpose) flour. In the centre place 125 g (4½ oz, ½ cup) sugar, 150 g (5 oz, ⅔ cup) butter, a pinch of salt, the rind (zest) of 2 oranges rubbed on lumps of sugar and 6 egg yolks. Mix these ingredients together and gradually blend the flour into the mixture. Knead the dough into a ball and allow it to stand for a few hours in a cool place. Roll out the dough to a thickness of about 5 mm (¼ in). Cut it into rounds with a fluted cutter 5–6 cm (2–2½ in) in diameter. Place the galettes on a buttered baking sheet, brush with egg beaten with a pinch of sugar and bake in a preheated oven at 240°C (475°F, gas 9) for about 6 minutes until lightly golden.

Orangine

Make a Genoese sponge with 150 g (5 oz, ⅔ cup) caster (superfine) sugar, 6 eggs, 150 g (5 oz, 1¼ cups) plain (all-purpose) flour, 50 g (2 oz, ¼ cup) butter and a pinch of salt. Leave it to cool completely. Make 250 ml (8 fl oz, 1 cup) Curaçao-flavoured confectioner's custard (pastry cream) and mix in 250 ml (8 fl oz, 1 cup) double (heavy) cream, whisked with 1 teaspoon vanilla sugar and 25 g (1 oz, 2 tablespoons) caster sugar. Put this cream into the refrigerator. Slice the sponge into 3 equal layers. Soak each layer with 2 tablespoons Curaçao-flavoured syrup. Spread the cream over 2 of the layers and build up the cake again. Ice (frost) the top and sides with Curaçao-flavoured fondant. Decorate the cake with candied orange peel and angelica.

Orange pound cake

Butter and flour a cake tin (pan). Weigh 3 eggs, then weigh out the same amount of caster (superfine) sugar, butter and sifted plain (all-purpose) flour. Break the eggs, keeping whites and yolks separate. Beat the yolks with the sugar and a pinch of salt until the mixture becomes white and creamy. Beat in the butter, which should be melted but not hot, then the flour and the blanched, finely grated rind (zest) from 2 oranges or 75 g (3 oz, ½ cup) chopped candied orange peel. Finally add 3 tablespoons Cointreau, Grand Marnier or Curaçao. Whisk the egg whites to stiff peaks and fold them in carefully. Pour the mixture into the cake tin and bake for about 45 minutes in a preheated oven at 200°C (400°F, gas 6); the temperature can be increased to 220°C (425°F, gas 7) when the cake has risen. Turn the cake out of the tin as soon as it is removed from the oven and leave it to cool on a wire rack.

Heat 400 g (14 oz, 1¼ cups) orange marmalade, boil until it is reduced to three-quarters of its volume, then pour it over the cake. Leave until cold, then refrigerate for 1 hour before serving.

Orange sandwich cake

In a large bowl use a spatula to beat 500 g (18 oz, 2¼ cups) caster (superfine) sugar with 1½ teaspoons vanilla sugar and 10 egg yolks. Whisk 10 egg whites with a pinch of salt until stiff and fold into the mixture. Quickly fold in 125 g (4½ oz, 1 cup) plain (all-purpose) flour and 125 g (4½ oz, 1 cup) cornflour (cornstarch) sifted together. Butter a charlotte mould and dust generously with icing (confectioner's) sugar. Pour the mixture into the mould, no more than two-thirds full. Bake in a preheated oven at 160°C (325°F, gas 3) until risen, golden, and firm – about 1¼ hours depending on the size of the mould. Turn the cake out on to a wire rack and leave until just warm.

Cut the cake horizontally into 2 rounds of equal thickness. Pour a little Curaçao on to the bottom half and spread with a thick layer of orange jam (preserve) or marmalade. Place the other half on top. Coat the top and sides with orange jam or warmed sieved marmalade. Coat with fondant icing (frosting) flavoured with Curaçao. Decorate with candied orange and mint sprigs, and serve with a blackcurrant and raspberry coulis. Instead of making a large cake, the mixture can be baked in individual moulds or soufflé dishes.

Pain d'épice

Heat 500 g (18 oz, 1½ cups) honey to boiling point, then skim it. Place in an earthenware bowl 500 g (18 oz, 4½ cups) sifted plain (all-purpose) flour, make a well in the centre, pour the honey into it and mix with a wooden spoon. (Some flours absorb more liquid than others; it may be necessary to add more liquid in order to obtain a firm paste.) Gather the paste into a ball, wrap it in a cloth and let it stand for 1 hour. Then add 2½ teaspoons baking powder and knead the paste thoroughly. Mix in 2 teaspoons aniseed, a generous pinch of cinnamon, the same amount of powdered cloves and ½ teaspoon grated lemon or orange zest.

Alternatively, mix the sifted flour directly with the same weight of liquid honey. Let the paste stand, then knead it hard with 100 g (4 oz, ½ cup) caster (superfine) sugar, 2 teaspoons cream of tartar, 1 teaspoon bicarbonate of soda (baking soda), 50 g (2 oz, ½ cup) skinned and chopped almonds and 65 g (2½ oz, ½ cup) mixed and chopped candied orange and lemon peel.

Pour the mixture into a 23 cm (9 in) square cake tin (pan) or a buttered manqué mould. Bake in a preheated oven at 190°C (375°F, gas 5) for about 30 minutes. As soon as the cake is cooked, quickly brush the top with some milk sweetened to a thick syrup or with sugar cooked to the fine thread stage and glaze for a few seconds in a cool oven.

Palets de dames

Palets are small, crisp petit fours flavoured with rum, aniseed, vanilla or brown sugar; ground almonds, candied peel or other ingredients may be added. *Palets de dames* are traditionally made with currants.

Wash 75 g (3 oz, ½ cup) currants and macerate them in a little rum. Mix 125 g (4½ oz, ½ cup) softened butter and 125 g (4½ oz, ½ cup) caster (superfine) sugar. Work with a whisk, then blend in 2 eggs, one after the other, and mix well. Next add 150 g (5 oz, 1¼ cups) plain (all-purpose) flour, the currants with their rum and a pinch of salt. Mix thoroughly. Butter a baking sheet, dust it lightly with flour and arrange the mixture on it in small balls, well separated from each other. Cook in a preheated oven at 220°C (425°F, gas 7) for 25 minutes or until the edges of the palets are golden.

Pineapple manqué

Melt 100 g (4 oz, ½ cup) butter without allowing it to brown. Separate 6 eggs. Put the yolks into a bowl with 200 g (7 oz, scant 1 cup) caster (superfine) sugar and 1 teaspoon vanilla sugar. Whisk until the mixture becomes light and frothy. Then fold in 150 g (5 oz, 1¼ cups) plain (all-purpose) flour, 100 g (4 oz, ½ cup) finely chopped, crystallized (candied) pineapple, the melted butter and half a liqueur glass of rum, mixing until evenly blended. Whisk the egg whites together with a pinch of salt into firm peaks and gently fold them into the manqué mixture.

Bake the cake. When it is cold, ice (frost) with 100 g (4 oz) fondant mixed with half a liqueur glass of rum heated to 35°C (95°F). Decorate the top with pieces of crystallized pineapple and glacé (candied) cherries.

Plum cake

Soften 500 g (18 oz, 2¼ cups) butter until creamy and beat until it turns very pale. Add 500 g (18 oz, 2¼ cups) caster (superfine) sugar and beat again for a few minutes. Then incorporate 8 eggs, one at a time, beating well after each addition. Add 250 g (9 oz, 1½ cups) chopped candied peel (orange, citron or lemon), 200 g (7 oz, 1¼ cups) seedless raisins, 150 g (5 oz, 1 cup) sultanas (golden raisins) and 150 g (5 oz, 1 cup) currants. Mix in 500 g (18 oz, 4½ cups) plain (all-purpose) flour sifted with 1½ teaspoons baking powder, the grated zest of 2 lemons and 3 tablespoons rum.

Line a 25 cm (10 in) round cake tin (pan) with greaseproof (wax) paper so that the paper extends 4 cm (1½ in) above the rim. Pour the mixture into the tin, taking care not to fill it above two-thirds. Bake in a preheated oven at 180°C (350°F, gas 4) for about 2 hours or until a skewer inserted in the centre of the cake comes out clean. Cover with a piece of foil if the cake is browning too much during cooking. Leave to cool in the tin for 10 minutes, then turn out on to a wire rack to cool completely.

Pogne de romans

Also known as *pognon* or *pougnon*, this is a type of brioche that is sometimes filled with crystallized (candied) fruit and served either hot or cold, often with redcurrant jelly.

Arrange 500 g (18 oz, 4½ cups) plain (all-purpose) flour in a circle on the worktop. In the middle of this circle put 1½ teaspoons salt, 1 tablespoon orange-flower water, 25 g (1 oz) fresh yeast (2 cakes compressed yeast), 250 g (9 oz, 1 cup) softened butter and 4 whole eggs. Mix together thoroughly, working the dough vigorously to give it body. Add 2 more eggs, one after the other, and finally incorporate 200 g (7 oz, ¾ cup) caster (superfine) sugar, little by little, kneading the dough all the while. Place this dough in a bowl sprinkled with flour, cover with a cloth and leave it to rise for 10–12 hours at room temperature away from draughts.

Turn the dough out on to the table and knock it back (punch down) with the flat of the hand. Make into 'crowns': shape two-thirds of the dough into balls, then use the remainder to shape smaller balls to place on top, like brioches. Place these crowns in buttered baking tins (pans). Leave the dough to rise for a further 30 minutes in a warm place. Brush with beaten egg and bake in a preheated oven at 190°C (375°F, gas 5) for about 40 minutes. Serve with redcurrant jelly.

Pound cake

Butter and flour a cake tin (pan). Weigh 3 eggs, then weigh out the same amount of caster (superfine) sugar, butter and sifted plain (all-purpose) flour. Break the eggs, keeping whites and yolks separate. Beat the yolks with the sugar and a pinch of salt until the mixture becomes white and creamy. Beat in the butter, which should be melted but not hot, then the flour and finally 3 tablespoons rum or brandy. Whisk the egg whites to stiff peaks and fold them in carefully. Pour the mixture into the cake tin and bake for about 45 minutes in a preheated oven at 200°C (400°F, gas 6); the temperature can be increased to 220°C (425°F, gas 7) when the cake has risen. Turn the cake out of the tin as soon as it is removed from the oven and leave it to cool completely on a wire rack.

Instead of mixing in the yolks and whites separately, the whole eggs can be lightly beaten and mixed with the sugar: the result is not quite so light.

Punch cakes

Using a large bowl and a spatula, beat together 375 g (13 oz, 1⅔ cups) caster (superfine) sugar, 1½ teaspoons orange-flavoured sugar, 1½ teaspoons lemon-flavoured sugar, 3 eggs and 12 egg yolks until light and fluffy. Continue beating and add 3 tablespoons rum and 375 g (13 oz, 3¼ cups) sifted plain (all-purpose) flour, then 8 stiffly whisked egg whites and 300 g (11 oz, 1⅓ cups) clarified butter. Butter some small paper cases and fill them with the mixture. Bake in a preheated oven at 180°C (350°F, gas 4) for about 15 minutes, until risen and golden.

Sachertorte

A famous Viennese gâteau, created at the Congress of Vienna (1814–15) by Franz Sacher, Metternich's chief pastrycook. Sachertorte (literally, 'Sacher's cake') is a sort of chocolate Savoy sponge cake, filled or spread with apricot jam (preserve), then covered with chocolate icing (frosting); it is traditionally served with whipped cream and a cup of coffee.

(From Joseph Wechsberg's recipe in *Viennese Cookery*, Time-Life) Line two 20 cm (8 in) round sandwich tins (layer cake pans) with buttered greaseproof (wax) paper. Melt 200 g (7 oz, 7 squares) plain cooking (semisweet) chocolate, broken into small pieces, in a bain marie. Lightly beat 8 egg yolks and mix in 125 g (4½ oz, ½ cup) butter, melted, and the melted chocolate. Whisk 10 egg whites until stiff with a pinch of salt and add 150 g (5 oz, ⅔ cup) caster (superfine) sugar, slightly vanilla-flavoured, beating all the time until the mixture stands up in stiff peaks. Fold one-third of the egg whites into the chocolate mixture, then gradually fold in the remaining whites. Add 125 g (4½ oz, 1 cup) sifted plain (all-purpose) flour, sprinkling it on gradually and lightly mixing and folding together all the ingredients until all traces of white disappear. Pour equal quantities of the mixture into the 2 tins and bake in a preheated oven at 180°C (350°F, gas 4) for about 45 minutes, until the cakes are well risen and a skewer inserted in the centres comes out clean. Turn out the cakes on to a wire rack and allow to cool.

To make the icing (frosting), put 150 g (5 oz, 5 squares) plain cooking chocolate, broken into pieces, in a saucepan together with 250 ml (8 fl oz, 1 cup) double (heavy) cream and 200 g (7 oz, ¾ cup) vanilla sugar. Stir over a moderate heat until the chocolate has melted, then cook for 5 minutes without stirring. Beat 1 egg, mix in 3 tablespoons of the chocolate mixture, and pour this back into the saucepan. Cook for 1 minute, stirring, then leave to cool at room temperature.

Spread 175 g (6 oz, ½ cup) sieved apricot jam over one of the halves of the chocolate cake, then put the other half on top. Cover the whole cake with the chocolate icing, smoothing it out with a metal spatula. Slide the cake on to a plate and chill in the refrigerator for 3 hours, until the icing hardens. Remove 30 minutes before serving.

Savoy sponge cake

Savoy sponge cake is extremely light due to the large proportion of stiffly whisked egg whites in the recipe.

Beat 500 g (18 oz, 2¼ cups) caster (superfine) sugar, 1 tablespoon vanilla-flavoured sugar and 14 egg yolks until the mixture is pale and thick. Add 175 g (6 oz, 1½ cups) potato flour or cornflour (cornstarch). Finally, fold in 14 egg whites stiffly whisked with a pinch of salt until they stand in peaks. Pour the mixture into Savoy cake tins (pans), which have been buttered and dusted with potato flour, filling them only two-thirds full. Bake in a preheated oven at 180°C (350°F, gas 4) for about 40 minutes.

Singapour

This is a large Genoese sponge filled with jam (preserve) and fruit in syrup, coated with warmed apricot jam and generously decorated with crystallized (candied) fruits.

Bring 750 ml (1¼ pints, 3¼ cups) water to the boil with 575 g (1¼ lb, 2½ cups) granulated sugar. Drain a large can of pineapple slices, add the slices and simmer for 1½ hours. Leave the slices to cool, then drain them.

Whisk 4 eggs with 125 g (4½ oz, ½ cup) granulated sugar in a bain marie until the mixture reaches 40°C (104°F), then remove from the heat and cool completely. Mix in 125 g (4½ oz, 1 cup) plain (all-purpose) flour, stirring with a wooden spoon, then add 50 g (2 oz, ¼ cup) melted butter. Pour the batter into a buttered and floured 23 cm (9 in) cake tin (pan). Bake in a preheated oven at 200°C (400°F, gas 6) for about 20 minutes, or until the cake is well risen and golden and the centre springs back when lightly pressed.

Meanwhile, melt 250 g (9 oz, 2¼ cups) apricot jam (preserve) over a gentle heat and grill (broil) 150 g (5 oz, 1¼ cups) chopped almonds. Prepare a syrup with 300 ml (½ pint, 1¼ cups) water and 300 g (11 oz, 1⅓ cups) granulated sugar and allow to cool, then add 3 tablespoons kirsch.

Cut the sponge in half horizontally and let it soak up the kirsch syrup. Spread the lower half with some of the apricot jam; cut the slices of pineapple into small dice, set a few aside and sprinkle the rest over the jam. Place the upper half of the sponge in position and coat the whole cake with more of the jam. Sprinkle with chopped almonds and decorate the top with the remaining diced pineapple, together with glacé (candied) cherries and candied angelica. Serve on the day it is made.

Sponge cake mixture

Using a large bowl and a spatula, beat 500 g (18 oz, 2¼ cups) caster (superfine) sugar with 2 tablespoons vanilla sugar and 10 egg yolks until the mixture is very pale and thick enough to form a ribbon trail. Then carefully fold in 125 g (4½ oz, 1 cup) plain (all-purpose) flour and an equal quantity of cornflour (cornstarch), 10 stiffly whisked egg whites and a pinch of salt.

Alternatively, a slightly heavier mixture can be made using 250 g (9 oz, 1 cup) granulated sugar, 8 eggs (separated), 125 g (4½ oz, 1 cup) plain flour and a pinch of salt.

Sponge fingers (ladyfingers)

Beat 250 g (9 oz, 1 cup) caster (superfine) sugar with 8 egg yolks until the mixture is thick enough to form a ribbon trail. Flavour with 1 tablespoon orange-flower water. Add 200 g (7 oz, 1¾ cups) plain (all-purpose) flour and fold in 8 egg whites stiffly whisked with a pinch of salt. Using a piping (pastry) bag with a smooth nozzle, pipe short lengths of the mixture on to baking sheets lined with greaseproof (wax) paper. Dust with icing (confectioner's) sugar and gently lift and tap the sheets of paper to remove any excess sugar. Bake in a preheated oven at 160°C (325°F, gas 3) for about 10 minutes, or until pale golden. The mixture can be flavoured with orange or lemon zest, if liked.

Strawberry gâteau

Wash, hull and dry 1 kg (2¼ lb) large strawberries. Bring 150 g (5 oz, ⅔ cup) granulated sugar and 5½ tablespoons water to the boil, add 2 tablespoons of kirsch and 2 tablespoons wild strawberry liqueur. Place an 18 × 23 cm (7 × 9 in) rectangle of sponge cake on a baking sheet lined with greaseproof (wax) paper. Soak it with one-third of the syrup. Whip 500 g (18 oz, 2¼ cups) butter cream to make it lighter and, using a wooden spatula, incorporate 100 g (4 oz, ½ cup) of confectioner's custard (pastry cream). Spread one-third of this mixture on the sponge cake. Arrange the strawberries on top, very close together and pointing upwards, pressing them well into the cream. Pour 2 tablespoons kirsch on top and sprinkle on 25 g (1 oz, 2 tablespoons) caster (superfine) sugar. Level the top of the strawberries using a serrated knife and cover with the remaining butter cream mixture, smoothing the top and sides with the spatula. Cover with another rectangle of sponge cake the same size and pour the remaining syrup over it. Coat the gâteau with a thin layer of pistachio-flavoured almond paste (75 g, 3 oz, ⅓ cup). Leave the strawberry gâteau for at least 8 hours in the refrigerator. Before serving, tidy the edges with a knife dipped in hot water. Decorate with strawberries sliced into a fan shape and coated with 100 g (4 oz, ⅓ cup) of apricot glaze, applied with a pastry brush.

Succès

A French round cake made from two layers of meringue mixture containing almonds, separated by a layer of praline-flavoured butter cream and topped with a smooth layer of the butter cream. It is decorated with flaked (slivered) almonds, sugar, hazelnuts, marzipan leaves and, traditionally, by a rectangle of almond paste with the word *succès* piped in royal icing (frosting).

The succès mixture is also used for making petits fours, usually filled with butter cream, as well as for various pastries.

To make the base, crush 250 g (9 oz, 2 cups) blanched almonds with 250 g (9 oz, 1 cup) sugar until reduced to a powder. Fold in 350 g (12 oz) egg whites (about 8) whisked into very stiff peaks with a pinch of salt. Pour this mixture into two 18–20 cm (7–8 in) flan (pie) rings set on buttered and floured baking sheets; it should form a layer about 5 mm (¼ in) thick. Cook in a preheated oven at 180°C (350°F, gas 4) for 12–15 minutes. Cool on a wire rack after removing the rings.

Swiss roll

Beat 250 g (9 oz, 1 cup) caster (superfine) sugar with ½ tablespoon vanilla sugar and 5 egg yolks until very pale and thick enough to form a ribbon trail. Fold in 50 g (2 oz, ½ cup) each of flour and cornflour (cornstarch), then 5 egg whites stiffly whisked with a pinch of salt. Line a rectangular baking sheet with greaseproof (wax) paper and brush with clarified butter. Spread the mixture evenly using a metal spatula until it covers the whole buttered area to a thickness of about 1 cm (½ in). Cook in a preheated oven at 180°C (350°F, gas 4) for 10 minutes. The top of the cake should be just golden.

Meanwhile, prepare a syrup using 75 g (3 oz, ⅓ cup) granulated sugar, 60 ml (2 fl oz, ¼ cup) water and 3 tablespoons rum. Lightly toast 125 g (4½ oz, 1½ cups) flaked (slivered) almonds. When the cake is cooked, turn it out on to a cloth and sprinkle with the syrup. Spread it with apricot jam (preserve) or raspberry jelly. Using the cloth, roll up the cake and trim the ends. Cover all the Swiss (jelly) roll with apricot glaze and decorate with the toasted almonds.

Tourons

Pound 250 g (9 oz, 2 cups) blanched almonds with 2 egg whites; add 200 g (7 oz, 1 cup) caster (superfine) sugar and knead the mixture on a marble worktop. Sprinkle with 2 tablespoons icing (confectioner's) sugar and roll out to a thickness of 5 mm (¼ in). Mix 100 g (4 oz, 1 cup) chopped pistachios with 200 g (7 oz, 1 cup) caster sugar and the zest of ½ an orange, very finely chopped. Add 100 g (4 oz) royal icing (frosting) and 2 whole eggs. Mix with a spatula and spread evenly over the almond paste. Cut into circles or rings and arrange on a buttered and floured baking sheet. Dry in a very cool oven.

Truffles in paprika

Melt 150 g (5 oz, 5 squares) bitter (bittersweet) chocolate. Add 175 ml (6 fl oz, ¾ cups) boiling whipping cream and mix well. Leave to cool. Finely chop 40 g (1½ oz, 3 tablespoons) prunes in Armagnac and incorporate into the paste. Shape into small balls and roll in a mixture of half unsweetened cocoa, half mild paprika. Store in a cold place.

Visitandines

A small round or boat-shaped cake, made of a rich mixture of egg whites, ground almonds, butter and sugar. After cooking, it is sometimes glazed with apricot jam (preserve) and iced (frosted) with fondant flavoured with kirsch. Visitandines, which were first made in monasteries, were invented as a means of using up surplus egg whites. Mix 500 g (18 oz, 2¼ cups) caster (superfine) sugar and 500 g (18 oz, 4½ cups) sifted plain (all-purpose) flour, then mix in

12 very lightly beaten egg whites little by little, stirring in well, and finally 800 g (1¾ lb, 3½ cups) melted butter (barely tepid). To finish, add 4 stiffly whisked egg whites. Fill buttered barquette moulds with small quantities of the mixture, using a piping (pastry) bag with a large smooth nozzle. Cook in a preheated oven at 220°C (425°F, gas 7) for about 10 minutes or just long enough for the cakes to be browned with the insides remaining soft.

Walnut cake

Cream 125 g (4½ oz, generous ½ cup) butter, then beat in 300 g (11 oz, 1½ cups) caster (superfine) sugar, 5 eggs (one by one), 125 g (4½ oz, generous 1 cup) ground almonds and 125 g (4½ oz, generous 1 cup) ground green walnut kernels. Then fold in 2 tablespoons rum and 75 g (3 oz, ¾ cup) sifted self-raising flour and mix well until smooth.

Butter a 20 cm (8 in) sandwich tin (layer cake pan), line the base with a circle of buttered greaseproof (wax) paper and transfer the mixture to the tin. Bake in a preheated oven at 200°C (400°F, gas 6) for 35–40 minutes. Allow the cake to cool in the tin before turning it out. Decorate with walnut halves.

Walnut surprises

In a heavy-based saucepan heat 250 g (9 oz, 1 cup) granulated sugar, 750 ml (1¼ pints, 3¼ cups) water and 25 g (1 oz) glucose. When the temperature reaches 115°C (240°F), take the pan off the heat and add, all at once, 125 g (4½ oz, 1 cup) ground almonds. Stir until the mixture acquires a sandy texture, then knead it by hand, blending in 5 drops of coffee essence (strong black coffee). Roll the paste out into a long thin sausage and cut it into 50 equal slices; roll each slice into a ball and flatten it slightly; moisten each side and press in a walnut half. Store in a cool place. To serve, put each petit four into a pleated paper case.

Pastries

Alcazar gâteau

This is a French gâteau made with a base of enriched shortcrust pastry (basic pie dough) covered with a layer of apricot marmalade and topped with a kirsch-flavoured almond meringue mixture. The gâteau is decorated with apricot marmalade and a lattice of almond paste. It keeps for two or three days.

Line a flan tin (pie pan) with 250 g (9 oz) *pâte sucrée*. Prick the base and spread with 2 tablespoons apricot marmalade or jam (preserve). Whisk 4 egg whites and 125 g (4½ oz, ½ cup) caster (superfine) sugar over heat to a stiff meringue, then fold in 50 g (2 oz, ½ cup) ground almonds, 50 g (2 oz, ½ cup) plain (all-purpose) flour and 2 tablespoons melted butter mixed with 1 tablespoon kirsch. Pour this mixture into the prepared flan (pie) case and cook in a preheated oven at 200°C (400°F, gas 6) until the top has browned. Turn the gâteau out of the tin and cool it on a wire tray.

Using a piping (pastry) bag with a fluted nozzle, pipe softened almond paste into a diamond-shaped lattice over the top of the gâteau and then as a border around the edge. Replace it in the oven to brown the almond paste. Over a low heat reduce 200 g (7 oz, ¾ cup) apricot marmalade or jam and fill each of the diamond shapes, then place half a pistachio nut in the centre of each one. If desired, the border may also be glazed with apricot jam and coated with chopped roasted pistachio nuts.

Almond choux fritters

To make about 20 fritters, use 500 g (18 oz) choux paste and 100 g (4 oz, 1 cup) shredded almonds. Scatter the almonds over a baking sheet and bake in a preheated oven at 220°C (425°F, gas 7) until golden. Mix these almonds with the choux paste. In a deep pan, heat some oil to 175°C (345°F). Drop teaspoonfuls of paste into the oil to make the fritters, which turn over by themselves in the oil when they are cooked (about 6 minutes). Cook them in batches of 10. Drain the fritters on paper towels and serve them hot, sprinkled with plenty of icing (confectioner's) sugar. They may be accompanied with a fruit sauce, such as apricot, cherry or raspberry.

Almond darioles

Lightly butter 6 dariole moulds and line them with puff pastry. Prepare some frangipane cream using 75 g (3 oz, 6 tablespoons) caster (superfine) sugar, 75 g (3 oz, ¾ cup) plain (all-purpose) flour, 1 whole egg, 3 egg yolks, 500 ml (17 fl oz, 2 cups) milk, 6 crushed macaroons, 1 tablespoon ground almonds and 25 g (1 oz, 2 tablespoons) butter. Allow to cool completely, then fill the pastry-lined moulds with this mixture. Bake in a preheated oven at 220°C (425°F, gas 7) for about 30 minutes. Remove the pastries from the moulds and dust with icing (confectioner's) sugar. Alternatively, the moulds may be filled simply with frangipane cream, without the puff pastry.

Alsace tart

Beat 1 egg with 250 g (9 oz, 1 cup) caster (superfine) sugar, then add 125 g (4½ oz, ½ cup) melted butter. Work the mixture together. Gradually blend in 250 g (9 oz, 2¼ cups) sifted plain (all-purpose) flour, then 250 g (9 oz, generous 2¼ cups) ground almonds. Knead thoroughly, adding 1–2 tablespoons water if the dough is difficult to work. Roll out three-quarters of the dough to form a circle 1 cm (½ in) thick; place this on a buttered baking sheet. Roll out the remaining dough very thinly and cut it into narrow strips. Surround the pastry circle with one of the strips and arrange the others crisscross fashion on the disc. Fill each section with a different jam (preserve) (such as strawberry or plum) and bake in a preheated oven at 200°C (400°F, gas 6) for 20 minutes. Serve lukewarm or cold.

Amandines à la duchesse

Make a dough with 150 g (5 oz, 1¼ cups) plain (all-purpose) flour, 75 g (3 oz, 6 tablespoons) softened butter, 3 tablespoons caster (superfine) sugar, a pinch of salt, 1 egg yolk and 4 teaspoons water. Roll it into a ball and place in the refrigerator. Beat 100 g (4 oz, ½ cup) butter until soft and mix into it 100 g (4 oz, ½ cup) caster sugar. Add 2 eggs, one at a time, and beat the mixture. Stir in 100 g (4 oz, 1 cup) ground almonds, then 50 g (2 oz, ½ cup) cornflour (cornstarch), and mix well. Add 100 ml (4 fl oz, 7 tablespoons) kirsch and mix until combined.

Roll out the chilled dough to a thickness of about 3 mm (⅛ in) and cut out 8 rounds with a pastry (cookie) cutter. Use these to line 8 buttered tartlet moulds and prick the bottom of each one with a fork. Put a few cooked redcurrants into each of the tartlets and cover with the almond mixture. Bake in a preheated oven at 200°C (400°F, gas 6) for 20 minutes. Allow the amandines to cool completely before turning them out of the moulds. Warm 100 g (4 oz, ⅓ cup) redcurrant jelly and use to glaze the amandines. Decorate the tops with redcurrants and keep in a cool place.

Apple and prune turnovers

Soak 250 g (9 oz, 1¾ cups) stoned (pitted) prunes in tepid water and 50 g (2 oz, ⅓ cup) washed currants in 4 tablespoons rum. Peel and thinly slice 4 good apples, then place in a stewpan with 5 tablespoons water and 50 g (2 oz, ¼ cup) caster (superfine) sugar. Leave to cook for 20 minutes, then blend and return to the pan with the drained currants and 25 g (1 oz,

2 tablespoons) butter; stir over a gentle heat to dry out. Put the drained prunes in another pan with 100 ml (4 fl oz, 7 tablespoons) weak tea, 50 g (2 oz, ¼ cup) sugar and the grated zest of 1 lemon; boil gently for 10 minutes, then blend and return to the pan to dry uncovered over a gentle heat.

Roll out 500 g (18 oz) puff pastry thinly on a floured board. Cut out 8 rounds, using a cutter 15 cm (6 in) in diameter, and elongate them slightly. Brush over the edges of the rolled-out pastry with beaten egg and fill half of each round with stewed apples and stewed prunes, without mixing them. Fold over the pastry and join the edges together, tucking them over each other and pressing down well. Arrange the turnovers on a moistened baking sheet and brush with beaten egg. Trace light diamond-shaped cuts in the pastry. Bake in a preheated oven at 220°C (425°F, gas 7) for about 25 minutes and serve them either warm or cold and dusted with icing (confectioner's) sugar.

Apple cream puffs

Fill some choux with a well-blended mixture of thick apple purée and a third of its weight of confectioner's custard (pastry cream) flavoured with Calvados. Dust the choux generously with icing (confectioner's) sugar.

Apple flan grimaldi

Peel and core 4 dessert (eating) apples and cut into quarters. Cook in a vanilla-flavoured syrup. Make a pastry dough with 250 g (9 oz, 2¼ cups) plain (all-purpose) flour, 125 g (4½ oz, ½ cup) butter, 1 egg yolk, a pinch of salt and 2 tablespoons water. Roll into a ball and leave in a cool place for 1 hour. Roll it out, line a 22 cm (9 in) flan ring (pie pan), and bake blind.

Prepare some rice in milk using 150 g (5 oz, ¾ cup) round-grain rice. When it is cold, mix in 100 g (4 oz, ½ cup) chopped crystallized (candied) fruit, 100 g (4 oz, ½ cup) chopped candied orange peel, a small liqueur glass of Curaçao and 50 g (2 oz, ¼ cup) butter. Fill the flan (pie) case with this mixture, level it off, then arrange the drained apple quarters on top. Sprinkle with crushed macaroons and caster (superfine) sugar and glaze in a preheated oven at 240°C (475°F, gas 9).

Apple puffs à la normande

Roll out 575 g (1¼ lb) puff pastry to a thickness of 2 cm (¾ in), cut it into two 20 cm (8 in) squares, prick them with a fork and place them side by side on a baking sheet. Blend 1 egg white with 75 g (3 oz, ¾ cup) icing (confectioner's) sugar for 2 minutes using a wooden spoon. Spread this icing (frosting) over one of the squares, then bake both squares for 12–15 minutes in a preheated oven at 200°C (400°F, gas 6).

Peel and slice 675 g (1½ lb) apples and cook them in 50 g (2 oz, ¼ cup) melted butter with 150 g (5 oz, ⅔ cup) caster (superfine) sugar for 15 minutes. Brown 25 g (1 oz, ¼ cup) flaked (slivered) almonds in a frying pan over a low heat, stirring them with a wooden spoon. Spread the cooked apples over the plain square, cover with the iced square and sprinkle with the toasted almonds. Serve warm.

Apple strudel

Mix 150 ml (¼ pint, ⅔ cup) tepid water in a bowl with a pinch of salt, 1 teaspoon vinegar and 1 egg yolk; add 1 tablespoon oil. Make a well in 250 g (9 oz, 2¼ cups) strong plain (bread) flour in a mixing bowl; pour the egg mixture into the centre, mix with the blade of a knife, then knead until the dough is elastic. Gather it into a ball and place it on a floured board; cover it with a scalded basin and leave it to stand for 1 hour.

Peel and dice 1 kg (2¼ lb) cooking apples; sprinkle with 3 tablespoons caster (superfine) sugar. Wash and wipe 200 g (7 oz, 1⅓ cups) raisins.

Spread a large floured tea towel (dish cloth) over the worktop and place the dough on it. Stretch the dough carefully using your knuckles; working from underneath it, brush with melted butter, then keep on stretching it until it is very thin, taking care not to tear it. Trim the edges to the shape of a large even rectangle.

Lightly brown a handful of breadcrumbs and 100 g (4 oz, 1 cup) chopped walnuts in 75 g (3 oz, 6 tablespoons) melted butter; spread this mixture evenly over the dough. Sprinkle with the prepared apples and raisins, then dust with 1 teaspoon cinnamon and 8 tablespoons caster sugar. Roll up the dough carefully to enclose all the ingredients, then slide the strudel on to a buttered baking sheet. Brush with 2 tablespoons milk. Cook in a preheated oven at 200°C (400°F, gas 6) for 40–45 minutes. When golden, take it out of the oven, dust with icing (confectioner's) sugar and serve lukewarm.

Apple tart

In a food processor blend 250 g (9 oz, 2¼ cups) plain (all-purpose) flour, 125 g (4½ oz, ½ cup) butter cut into pieces, and a large pinch of salt until the dough sticks to the sides of the bowl. Add 3 tablespoons water (or a little more) and operate the food processor again until the dough begins to bind together. Quickly shape the dough into a ball, wrap it in foil and chill for at least 2 hours.

Peel and finely slice 800 g (1¾ lb) apples and sprinkle with lemon juice. Roll out the dough to a thickness of 5 mm (¼ in) and use it to line a buttered and floured 25 cm (10 in) tart tin (pie pan). Arrange the slices of apple over the pastry base in concentric circles; sprinkle generously with granulated sugar and 50 g (2 oz, ¼ cup) melted butter. Bake in a preheated oven at 220°C (425°F, gas 7) for about 30 minutes, until the apples caramelize slightly. Serve lukewarm, accompanied by crème fraîche.

Apricot barquettes

Barquettes are small boat-shaped tarts made of shortcrust pastry (basic pie dough) or puff pastry, baked and filled with sweet or savoury ingredients.

For 15 barquettes, prepare pastry using 225 g (8 oz, 2 cups) sifted flour, 1 teaspoon salt, 1 tablespoon sugar, 1 egg yolk, 100 g (4 oz, ½ cup) butter, and about 7 tablespoons water. Roll out the pastry to a thickness of 3 mm (⅛ in). Cut with a fluted oval pastry (cookie) cutter. Line the moulds with the pastry, prick the bottom of each one, and sprinkle with a little icing (confectioner's) sugar. Remove the stones (pits) from the apricots and cut each one into four. Lay the apricot quarters lengthways in the pastry boats, skin-side down. Bake in a preheated oven at 200°C (400°F, gas 6) for about 20 minutes. Turn out and allow to cool on a wire rack. Coat each barquette with sieved apricot jam (preserve) and decorate with 2 blanched almonds. Puff pastry can also be used. Alternatively, the pastry boats may be baked blind, filled with French butter cream and topped with apricots cooked in syrup.

Apricot jam Dartois

Prepare 500 g (1 lb 2 oz) puff pastry and chill for 1 hour. Then divide the pastry in half and roll each half into a rectangle 15 cm (6 in) wide, 25 cm (10 in) long and 3 mm (⅛ in) thick. Place one of the rectangles on a baking sheet and cover with about 400 g (14 oz, 1¼ cups) apricot jam (preserve). Cover with the second rectangle of pastry and bake in a preheated oven at 220°C (425°F, gas 7) for about 15 minutes. Dust with icing (confectioner's) sugar and return to the oven to caramelize for 5 minutes. Serve warm.

Apricot tart

Make 350 g (12 oz) shortcrust pastry (basic pie dough) Roll it out to a thickness of 5 mm (¼ in) and use it to line a 24 cm (9½ in) buttered and floured flan tin (pie pan). Chill for 30 minutes. Prick the bottom with a fork. Stone (pit) 800 g (1¾ lb) very ripe apricots and arrange the halves on the bottom of the tart case, with the cut sides against the pastry. Sprinkle with 5 tablespoons caster (superfine) sugar. Bake in a preheated oven at 200°C (400°F, gas 6) for about 40 minutes. Turn out on to a wire rack. Spread the top with 3 tablespoons apricot compote, sieved and boiled down. Serve cold.

Apricot tourte

Place some thinly rolled-out shortcrust pastry (basic pie dough) in a *tourtière* or deep flan dish (pie pan) lightly moistened in the middle. Trim it to size, prick the base and moisten the edge, fixing around it a band of puff pastry 3 cm (1¼ in) wide and 1 cm (½ in) thick to form the rim. Fill the tourte with stoned (pitted) fresh apricots, without letting the fruit touch the pastry rim (which would prevent it from rising evenly during cooking). Brush the upper surface of the rim with egg and score it lightly with the point of a knife. Bake in a preheated oven at 190°C (375°F, gas 5) for about 45 minutes. About 5 minutes before it is cooked, sprinkle lightly with icing (confectioner's) sugar to provide a glaze.

Many other fruits can be used, cooked or uncooked, whole or cut up: pineapple, cherries, nectarines, pears, apples or plums.

Baklavas with pistachio nuts

In a food processor mix 575 g (1¼ lb, 5 cups) plain (all-purpose) flour, 25 g (1 oz) salt and enough water to obtain a firm, elastic dough. Make 12 balls of equal size. Flatten the first ball with the hand. Sprinkle a pinch of cornflour (cornstarch) over it to prevent it from sticking. Place a second ball on top. Flatten this with the hand and sprinkle a pinch of cornflour over it. Repeat with the other 10 balls. This results in a pastry consisting of 12 layers.

Gradually flatten this pastry with a rolling pin, taking care not to crush or tear it, stretching it gently along the edges in order to obtain a circle of about 30 cm (12 in) in diameter. Cover the pastry with a cloth and allow to rest for about 1 hour.

Then remove the first layer of the pastry, turn it over and sprinkle it with a pinch of cornflour. Repeat with the other layers, so that both sides of each layer are coated with cornflour, and pile them on top of each other again. Sprinkle cornflour on a marble surface and place the stack of pastry on top, then stretch it out gently with the hands into a circle 50 cm (20 in) in diameter and 3–4 cm (1¼–1½ in) thick. Because the top stretches more than the bottom, turn the stack of pastry over and repeat the stretching operation. Roll out carefully with a very long rolling pin into a circle about 80 cm (32 in) in diameter. Place the rolling pin in the middle of the pastry and roll 6 layers around it, one by one, sprinkling each with cornflour, then roll them on the table. Repeat the operation with a second rolling pin and the 6 remaining layers. Finally, bring the 12 layers together; by now they will have become extremely thin.

Chop shelled pistachio nuts. Place the pastry over an ovenproof dish 70 cm (28 in) in diameter. The edges will overhang by about 20 cm (8 in); cut out the circle of pastry and set aside. Cut the rest into 4–6 diamond shapes. Divide these shapes in two (6 layers) and place half in the dish. Decorate with the chopped pistachio nuts and cover with the other half (6 layers). Cover the diamonds with the circle of pastry. Melt 1.5 kg (3¼ lb, 6½ cups) butter and pour slowly on to the pastry. Allow to rest for 30 minutes.

Bake in a preheated oven at 180°C (350°F, gas 4) for 20–30 minutes. Take the baklavas out of the oven and allow to cool. Mix 7 parts of sugar, 2 parts of water and 2 tablespoons orange flower water and cook gently for 5 minutes. Pour the hot syrup over the baklavas and leave them to cool.

Basque tart

In a mixing bowl blend 300 g (11 oz, 2¾ cups) sifted plain (all-purpose) flour, 4 egg yolks, a pinch of salt, 2 teaspoons baking powder, 100 g (4 oz, ½ cup) caster (superfine) sugar and 50 g (2 oz, ¼ cup) softened butter; gradually add sufficient milk to obtain a pliable yet firm dough. Put aside for 1 hour. Roll out the dough and line a buttered 25 cm (10 in) flan tin (pie pan). Prick the base with a fork and bake blind in a preheated oven at 200°C (400°F, gas 6) for 20 minutes.

Meanwhile, peel and quarter 12 apples. Remove the cores and sprinkle with the quarters with lemon juice. Melt 100 g (4 oz, ½ cup) butter in a saucepan, cook the apples to a pale golden colour, sprinkle with 100 g (4 oz, ½ cup) caster sugar and gently stir. Arrange the apples on the tart base in a rosette and sprinkle with the butter they were cooked in. Sprinkle with 2 tablespoons granulated sugar and glaze for 5 minutes, in a very hot oven or under the grill (broiler).

Beauharnais barquettes

Bake some pastry barquette cases blind. Peel some bananas, mash the flesh and add lemon juice and a little white rum. Fill the barquettes with the mixture and bake in a preheated oven at 240°C (475°F, gas 9) for 7–8 minutes, then sprinkle with a little stale, finely crumbled brioche and melted butter. Bake for a further 5 minutes in a very hot oven.

Belgian cassonade tart

Make some pastry using 250 g (9 oz, 2¼ cups) plain (all-purpose) flour, 125 g (4½ oz, ½ cup) butter, a pinch of salt, and 4 tablespoons cold water. Roll into a ball and leave to rest for 3–4 hours. Then use it to line a tart tin (pan) and bake blind in a preheated oven at 200°C (400°F, gas 6). Grind 150–200 g

(5–7 oz, 1¼–1¾ cups) almonds in a blender and mix with 3 egg yolks, 200 ml (7 fl oz, ¾ cup) double (heavy) cream, and 300 g (11 oz, 1⅔ cups) cassonade (raw brown sugar). Beat 3 egg whites until they form stiff peaks and add to the mixture. Pour into the tart case and bake for about 40 minutes.

Bilberry flan

Make some shortcrust pastry (basic pie dough) with 200 g (7 oz, 1¾ cups) plain (all-purpose) flour, 100 g (4 oz, ½ cup) butter cut into pieces, a pinch of salt, 1 tablespoon caster (superfine) sugar and 3 tablespoons cold water. Form into a ball and leave it to stand for 2 hours.

Wash and dry 300 g (11 oz, 2¾ cups) fresh bilberries (or use frozen fruit). Prepare a syrup with 100 g (4 oz, ½ cup) sugar and 250 ml (8 fl oz, 1 cup) water. Simmer for 5 minutes, then add the bilberries and leave to soak for 5 minutes. Return to a gentle heat and cook for 8 minutes, until all the syrup has been absorbed.

Roll out the pastry and line a buttered 23 cm (9 in) flan tin (pie pan). Line with greaseproof (wax) paper, sprinkle with baking beans and bake blind in a preheated oven at 200°C (400°F, gas 6) for 12 minutes. Remove the paper and beans, and continue cooking for a further 6–7 minutes until the flan base is golden. Leave until lukewarm before unmoulding.

Fill the cold pastry case with the bilberries, smoothing the top. Warm together 2 tablespoons apricot purée and 1 teaspoon water, sieve and coat the bilberries with the glaze. Leave until cold.

Prepare a Chantilly cream by whipping 7 tablespoons double (heavy) cream with 1 tablespoon chilled milk, 1 teaspoon vanilla sugar and 1 tablespoon icing (confectioner's) sugar. Using a piping (pastry) bag fitted with a fluted nozzle, pipe the cream on top of the tart and decorate with a few sugared violets, if wished.

Blackberry tartlets

Put into a food processor 200 g (7 oz, 1¾ cups) plain (all-purpose) flour, 5 tablespoons sugar and 1 egg, and work to a coarse dough. Add 100 g (4 oz, ½ cup) softened butter cut into small pieces and work quickly until smooth. Form into a ball and leave it to stand for 2 hours.

Roll out the dough and use to line 6 buttered tartlet tins (moulds). Prick the bottom with a fork, sprinkle with caster (superfine) sugar and fill with 800 g (1¾ lb) washed blackberries, packing them closely together. Sprinkle with sugar again. Bake the tartlets in a preheated oven at 200°C (400°F, gas 6) for about 30 minutes. Remove from the oven, leave until lukewarm, then unmould them on to a wire rack. Serve warm or cold accompanied by crème fraîche, or with piped Chantilly cream. A tart is prepared in the same manner.

Bourdaloue pear tart

Roll out some shortcrust pastry (basic pie dough) thinly. Use to line a buttered pie dish, making a little crest along the edge. Cover the pastry with a layer of frangipane cream and arrange thinly sliced pears in syrup on top. Cook in a preheated oven at 190°C (375°F, gas 5) for 30 minutes. Leave to cool, then coat with apricot glaze.

British-style apple pie

Make shortcrust pastry (basic pie dough) using 225 g (8 oz, 2 cups) plain (all-purpose) flour and 100 g (4 oz, ½ cup) butter. Instead of all butter, half white vegetable fat (shortening) and half butter can be used. Roll out a small portion of pastry into a strip and press this on to the dampened rim of a deep pie dish. Peel, core and slice 900 g (2 lb) cooking apples, such as Bramleys, and place them in the dish, adding 100 g (4 oz, ½ cup) sugar between the layers. Distribute 6 cloves among the layers of apple.

Roll out the remaining pastry and use to cover the top of the pie, dampening the pastry rim with water and pressing the edge firmly to seal in the fruit. Make several slits or a hole in the middle of the pie and decorate the top with pastry trimmings. Brush with milk and bake in a preheated oven at 200°C (400°F, gas 6) for 15 minutes. Reduce the oven temperature to 180°C (350°F, gas 4) and cook for a further 30 minutes, until browned. Sprinkle with caster (superfine) sugar and cool slightly before serving.

Chantilly cream puffs

These pastries are made to resemble swans. Prepare some choux paste, using the quantities in the basic recipe, and place it in a piping (pastry) bag fitted with a plain 1.5 cm (⅝ in) diameter nozzle. On to a lightly oiled baking sheet, pipe 10 oval-shaped buns, each about the size of a soup spoon. Now replace the nozzle with one 4–5 mm (about ¼ in) in diameter and pipe 10 'S' shapes, 5–6 cm (2–2½ in) long on to another oiled baking sheet. Cook the 'S' shapes, which will form the swans' necks, following the basic recipe, allowing about 15 minutes for the 'S' shapes once the temperature has been reduced and 20–25 minutes for the buns.

During this time, prepare the Chantilly cream, using 400 ml (14 fl oz, 1¾ cups) very cold double (heavy) cream, 100 ml (4 fl oz, 7 tablespoons) extremely cold milk, 40 g (1½ oz, 3 tablespoons) caster (superfine) sugar and 1 tablespoon vanilla-flavoured sugar. Place the cream, milk and vanilla sugar into a chilled bowl and begin to whip. When the cream starts to thicken, add the caster sugar while continuing to whip. Place the cream in cool place until it is needed.

Split and cool the buns. Cut the top off each bun and cut the tops in half lengthways to form the swans' wings. Fit the piping bag with a large-diameter fluted nozzle, fill the bag with the Chantilly cream and fill the buns with it, forming a dome on each. Place a 'neck' at one end of each bun and stick the 'wings' into the cream on either side. Dust with icing (confectioner's) sugar.

Cherry cream puffs

Prepare some confectioner's custard (pastry cream), flavour it with kirsch and add some stoned (pitted) well-drained cherries in syrup. Separately prepare some white fondant icing (frosting) flavoured with kirsch. Fill some cooked choux buns with the cherry cream. Heat the fondant icing until it is runny, ice the tops of the puffs and leave to cool completely.

Cherry flan

Line a flan ring (pie pan) with sweetened pastry (*pâte sucrée*) and bake blind. Remove the stalks and stones (stems and pits) from 400 g (14 oz, 2 cups) black cherries (Bing cherries). Boil 300 ml (½ pint, 1¼ cups) milk with a vanilla pod (bean) split in two and then stir in 3 tablespoons double (heavy) cream. Beat 3 eggs with 100 g (4 oz, ½ cup) caster (superfine) sugar in a bowl, add the vanilla-flavoured milk and whisk until the mixture has cooled completely. Place the cherries in the flan case (pie shell) and carefully pour the mixture over. Cook in a preheated oven at 190°C (375°F, gas 5) for 35–40 minutes. Serve either lukewarm or cold, sprinkled with sugar if wished.

Cherry tart

Line a flan tin (pie pan) with shortcrust pastry (basic pie dough) and fill with ripe stoned (pitted) cherries. Whisk together 100 g (4 oz, ½ cup) caster (superfine) sugar and 2 whole eggs, then blend in 200 ml (7 fl oz, ¾ cup) milk and 50 g (2 oz, ½ cup) plain (all-purpose) flour. Pour this cream over the cherries and bake the tart in a preheated oven at 200°C (400°F, gas 6) for about 30 minutes.

Chestnut barquettes

Barquettes are small boat-shaped tarts made of shortcrust pastry (basic pie dough) or puff pastry, baked and filled with sweet or savoury ingredients.

Bake some pastry barquette cases blind and then fill them with chestnut cream. They can be decorated with piped whipped cream and a sugar violet. Alternatively, shape the cream into a dome with two sides and ice (frost) one side with coffee icing (frosting) and the other with chocolate icing and top with piped *crème au beurre*.

Chiboust coffee cream puffs

Prepare enough choux paste for 12 puffs. Using a piping (pastry) bag, pipe the paste into balls on a buttered baking sheet and sprinkle with shredded almonds. Cook them, leave to cool, then fill with Chiboust cream flavoured with coffee. Cool before serving so that the cream becomes firm.

Chocolate cream puffs

Prepare some confectioner's custard (pastry cream) and flavour it with melted chocolate. Separately prepare some chocolate fondant icing (frosting) using 200 g (7 oz, ¾ cup) fondant icing and 50 g (2 oz, ½ cup) cocoa blended with 2 tablespoons water. Fill some choux buns with the chocolate custard and coat with the fondant icing. Leave to set.

Chocolate éclairs

Prepare some choux paste with 125 g (4½ oz, 1 cup) plain (all-purpose) flour, 65 g (2½ oz, 5 tablespoons) butter, a large pinch of salt, 250 ml (8 fl oz, 1 cup) water and 4 eggs. Using a piping (pastry) bag with a smooth nozzle, 2 cm (¾ in) in diameter, pipe thick fingers of dough, 6–7.5 cm (2½–3 in) long, on to a baking sheet, well spaced apart so that they will be able to rise without sticking together. Beat an egg yolk with a little milk and use to glaze the éclairs. Bake the éclairs in a preheated oven at 190°C (375°F, gas 5) until pale golden in colour. This will take 20 minutes at the most. The inside must still be soft. Leave the éclairs to cool, then split them down one side.

Make a confectioner's custard (pastry cream) with 50 g (2 oz, ½ cup) plain flour, 1 egg, 2 egg yolks and 50 g (2 oz, ¼ cup) caster (superfine) sugar. Add 1 tablespoon cocoa (unsweetened cocoa) to the mixture. Leave to cool, then put into a piping bag and use to fill the éclairs. Heat 200 g (7 oz, 1 cup) fondant icing (frosting) over a low heat, add 50 g (2 oz, 2 squares) melted dark chocolate, and mix well. Coat the top of the éclairs and leave to cool.

Chocolate mille-feuille

Mix 1.5 kg (3¼ lb, 13 cups) plain (all-purpose) flour, 2 tablespoons fine salt and 575 g (1¼ lb, 2½ cups) butter. Add 3 tablespoons milk and 400 ml (14 fl oz, 1¾ cup) double (heavy) cream. Stir without giving too much shape to the dough. Rest for 4 hours.

Work 300 g (11 oz, 3½ cups) cocoa powder into 1.25 kg (2¾ lb, 5½ cups) butter. Roll out the dough into a square and put in a cool place. Now place the marbled butter in the middle of the square and fold the ends of the dough over the butter to enclose it. Roll out again, fold into three again, then allow to rest for 30 minutes. Repeat this operation 5 times, allowing the pastry to rest each time for 30 minutes between operations. Finally roll out the pastry to a thickness of 3 mm (⅛ in). Cut into 3 strips and allow to rest for 30 minutes. Trim the ends of the strips and place on a baking sheet. Bake in a preheated oven at 200°C (400°F, gas 6) for 5 minutes, then at 150°C (300°F, gas 2) for 1 hour 10 minutes. Cool on a wire rack.

Bring 750 ml (1¼ pints, 3¼ cups) milk to the boil. In a mixing bowl, beat 8 egg yolks with 100 g (4 oz, ½ cup) caster (superfine) sugar until the mixture turns a pale yellow. Add 50 g (2 oz, ½ cup) plain flour, then 150 g (5 oz, 1¾ cups) cocoa powder but without stirring. Pour the boiling milk into the egg mixture, stir, bring to the boil and cook for 3 minutes. Pour into a bowl and cover with cling film (plastic wrap). Allow to cool.

Sandwich the chocolate pastry together with the chocolate confectioner's custard (pastry cream), spreading it thickly. Decorate with mint leaves and cocktail cherries, and serve with a chocolate sauce.

Chocolate profiteroles

Prepare some choux paste with 250 ml (8 fl oz, 1 cup) water, a pinch of salt, 2 tablespoons sugar, 125 g (4½ oz, 1 cup) plain (all-purpose) flour and 4 eggs. Using a piping (pastry) bag with a plain nozzle, pipe out balls of dough the size of walnuts on to a greased baking sheet and brush them with beaten egg. Cook in a preheated oven at 200°C (400°F, gas 6) for about 20 minutes until crisp and golden; allow to cool in the oven.

Meanwhile melt 200 g (7 oz, 7 squares) plain (semisweet) chocolate with 100 ml (4 fl oz, 7 tablespoons) water in a bain marie; add 100 ml (4 fl oz, 7 tablespoons) double (heavy) cream and stir well. Prepare some Chantilly cream by whipping 300 ml (½ pint, 1¼ cups) double cream with 100 ml (4 fl oz, 7 tablespoons) very cold milk, then 75 g (3 oz, 6 tablespoons) caster (superfine) sugar and 1 teaspoon vanilla sugar. Split the profiteroles on one side and fill them with the Chantilly cream, using a piping bag. Arrange in a bowl and serve with the hot chocolate sauce.

Chocolate tart

Prepare a chocolate pâte sablée with 125 g (4½ oz, ½ cup) butter, 50 g (2 oz, ⅓ cup) icing (confectioner's) sugar, 50 g (2 oz, ½ cup) ground almonds, 1 egg, 175 g (6 oz, 1½ cups) plain (all-purpose) flour and 3 tablespoons sifted cocoa powder. Allow to rest for 2 hours in a cool place. Roll out the pastry and line a flan tin (pie pan). Bake blind in a preheated oven at 180°C (350°F, gas 4) for about 40 minutes and leave to cool.

Bring 250 ml (8 fl oz, 1 cup) single (light) cream to the boil with 100 g (4 oz, ⅔ cup) glucose. Pour on to 200 g (7 oz, 7 squares) cooking chocolate with 80% cocoa content, broken up into small pieces, and 50 g (2 oz, ¼ cup) pure cocoa paste. Add 50 g (2 oz, ¼ cup) butter. Allow to cool but not thicken. Sprinkle 25 g (1 oz, ¼ cup) toasted chopped almonds in the bottom of the pastry case and pour the chocolate ganache on top. Allow to set.

Choux à la cévenole

Prepare some sweet choux buns. Mix together equal volumes of chestnut cream and whipped cream sweetened with vanilla-flavoured sugar and fill the choux with it.

Coffee cream puffs

Fill some cooked choux buns with confectioner's custard (pastry cream) flavoured with coffee essence (strong black coffee). Prepare 200 g (7 oz, ¾ cup) fondant icing (frosting), flavour it with coffee essence (or instant coffee made up with 2 tablespoons of water) and heat until it is runny. Ice the tops of the puffs with the fondant and leave to cool completely.

Coffee éclairs

Prepare some choux paste with 125 g (4½ oz, 1 cup) plain (all-purpose) flour, 65 g (2½ oz, 5 tablespoons) butter, a large pinch of salt, 250 ml (8 fl oz, 1 cup) water and 4 eggs. Using a piping (pastry) bag with a smooth nozzle, 2 cm (¾ in) in diameter, pipe thick fingers of dough, 6–7.5 cm (2½–3 in) long, on to a baking sheet, spaced well apart so that they will be able to rise without sticking together. Beat an egg yolk with a little milk and use to glaze the éclairs. Bake the éclairs in a preheated oven at 190°C (375°F, gas 5) until pale golden in colour. This will take 20 minutes at the most. The inside must still be soft. Leave the éclairs to cool, then split them down one side.

Make a confectioner's custard (pastry cream) with 50 g (2 oz, ½ cup) plain flour, 1 egg, 2 egg yolks and 50 g (2 oz, ¼ cup) caster (superfine) sugar. Flavour the cream filling with 2 teaspoons instant coffee dissolved in 250 ml (8 fl oz, 1 cup) milk brought to the boil with 40 g (1½ oz, 3 tablespoons) unsalted butter. Leave to cool completely, then put into a piping bag and use to fill the eclairs. Heat 200 g (7 oz, 1 cup) fondant icing (frosting) over a low heat and add coffee essence (extract), drop by drop to taste, mixing well. Coat the top of the éclairs and leave to cool.

Coffee or chocolate tartlets

Line some greased tartlet tins (pans) with pâte sablée. Prick the bottom with a fork and bake blind for about 10 minutes. Allow to cool. Then, using a piping (pastry) bag, fill some of the cases with coffee *crème au beurre* and the remainder with Chantilly cream flavoured with chocolate and rum.

Coffee religieuses

Make some choux paste with 250 ml (8 fl oz, 1 cup) water, a pinch of salt, 65 g (2½ oz, 5 tablespoons) butter, 1 teaspoon sugar, 125 g (4½ oz, 1 cup) plain (all-purpose) flour and 3–4 eggs. Pipe bun shapes on to a baking sheet so that half of them are twice the size of the others. Bake in a preheated oven at 200°C (400°F, gas 6) for 30 minutes, then leave to cool in the oven with the door ajar.

Make some *crème au beurre* with 4 egg yolks, 125 g (4½ oz, ½ cup) caster (superfine) sugar, 60 ml (2 fl oz, ¼ cup) water, 125 g (4½ oz, ½ cup) creamed butter and 1 teaspoon vanilla sugar.

Prepare some Chiboust cream with 6 egg yolks, 200 g (7 oz, 1 cup) caster sugar, 75 g (3 oz, ¾ cup) flour or 50 g (2 oz, ½ cup) cornflour (cornstarch), 1 litre (1¾ pints, 4⅓ cups) milk, 4 leaves of gelatine and 4 egg whites. Flavour it with ½ teaspoon coffee essence (strong black coffee) and allow to cool completely. Fill all the choux pastries with the Chiboust cream.

Melt 400 g (14 oz) fondant icing (frosting), flavour it with ½ teaspoon coffee essence and use it to ice all the choux pastries. Before the icing sets, stick the small buns on to the larger ones. Using a piping (pastry) bag with a fluted nozzle, decorate the top of each cake with a rosette of *crème au beurre*, then run a ribbon of butter cream around the joint of the 2 buns. Keep in a cool place until ready to serve.

Condé cakes

Roll out some puff pastry to a thickness of about 5 mm (¼ in). Cut out strips 7.5–10 cm (3–4 in) wide and cut these into rectangles 4 cm (1½ in) wide. Coat the top of the rectangles with Condé icing (frosting) (royal icing with almonds) and then sprinkle with icing (confectioner's) sugar. Place the cakes on a baking sheet and cook in a preheated oven at 200°C (400°F, gas 6) until they are just golden. They may be split while still warm and filled with a little sieved strawberry jam (preserve).

Curd cheese (me'gin) tart à la mode de Metz

Prepare a shortcrust pastry (basic pie dough) tart base (shell). Mix 200 g (7 oz, 1 cup) well-drained curd cheese (called *fremgin* or *me'gin*), 100–200 ml (4–7 fl oz, ½–¾ cup) crème fraîche, 3 beaten eggs, 2–3 tablespoons caster (superfine) sugar and a pinch of salt; flavour, if desired, with 1 teaspoon vanilla sugar or some vanilla essence (extract). Fill the base with this mixture and bake in a preheated oven at 200°C (400°F, gas 6) for about 35 minutes.

Danish cherry flan

Remove the stones (pits) from some bigarreau cherries and macerate the fruit with sugar and a pinch of cinnamon. Line a flan dish (pie pan) with shortcrust pastry (basic pie dough) and fill with the stoned cherries. Mix 125 g (4½ oz, ½ cup) butter, 125 g (4½ oz, ½ cup) caster (superfine) sugar, 125 g (4½ oz, 1 cup) ground almonds, 2 beaten eggs and the juice from the cherries. Cover the cherries with this mixture and bake in a preheated oven at 220°C (425°F, gas 7) for 35–40 minutes. Leave to cool, then cover with redcurrant jelly and a white rum-flavoured icing (frosting).

Doullins

Mix 500 g (18 oz, 4½ cups) plain (all-purpose) flour, 350 g (12 oz, 1½ cups) softened butter, 2 eggs, 3 tablespoons milk, 1½ tablespoons caster (superfine) sugar and 1 teaspoon salt to make a smooth dough. Roll it into a ball and place in the refrigerator while cooking the pears.

Peel and core 8 small pears and place a knob of butter in the centre of each. Cook in a preheated oven at 190°C (375°F, gas 5) for 10 minutes. Remove and allow them to get completely cold. (Do not turn the oven off.)

Roll out the pastry to a thickness of about 3 mm (⅛ in) and cut it into 8 squares of equal size. Place a well-drained pear in the centre of each square and fold the corners upwards, stretching the pastry a little. Pinch the sides and the top with damp fingers to seal. Draw lines on the pastry with the point of a knife. Glaze with an egg yolk beaten in 2 tablespoons milk and bake in the oven for 25–30 minutes. Serve hot, warm, or cold, with crème fraîche.

Fig tart

Prepare 350 g (12 oz) shortcrust pastry (basic pie dough) and use it to line a 23 cm (9 in) flan ring (pie pan). Prick and bake blind. Allow it to cool. Peel and halve some fresh figs and leave for 30 minutes. Mix a little rum with some apricot jam (preserve), sieve the mixture and spread it over the base of the flan. Arrange the drained fig halves on top, coat them with apricot jam and decorate with Chantilly cream.

Frangipane Dartois

Prepare 500 g (1 lb 2 oz) puff pastry and chill for 1 hour. To make the frangipane, soften 100 g (4 oz, ½ cup) butter with a wooden spatula. Blend 2 egg yolks in a mixing bowl with 125 g (4½ oz, 1 cup) ground almonds, 125 g (4½ oz, ½ cup) caster (superfine) sugar, a little vanilla essence (extract) and the softened butter. Cut the pastry into two rectangles 25 cm (10 in) long and 15 cm (6 in) wide. Place one of the rectangles on a baking sheet and cover with about 400 g (14 oz, 1¼ cups) frangipane. Cover with the second rectangle of pastry and bake in a preheated oven at 220°C (425°F, gas 7) for about 15 minutes. Dust with icing (confectioner's) sugar and return to the oven to caramelize for 5 minutes. Serve warm.

French-style double-crust apple pie

Rub 100 g (4 oz, ½ cup) butter into 200 g (7 oz, 1¾ cups) plain (all-purpose) flour. Add ½ teaspoon salt and gradually add about 4 tablespoons water. Knead to form a soft ball of dough that does not stick to the bowl. Allow the pastry to rest in a cool place for at least 20 minutes, then divide it into two pieces, one larger than the other.

Butter a china manqué mould or deep ovenproof dish. Roll out the larger piece of dough and line the bottom and the sides of the mould. Mix 2 heaped tablespoons plain flour, 2 heaped tablespoons soft brown sugar, a pinch of vanilla powder, ½ teaspoon ground cinnamon and a pinch of grated nutmeg. Sprinkle half of this mixture over the pastry. Peel 800 g (1¾ lb) pippin (eating) apples, cut into quarters, then into slices. Arrange these on the pastry, forming a dome in the centre. Add a dash of lemon juice and sprinkle with the remaining spice mixture. Roll out the second piece of pastry and cover the pie, sealing the edges with beaten egg. Make an opening in the centre. Glaze the top with the beaten egg. Put in a preheated oven at 230°C (450°F, gas 8). After 10 minutes, reduce the oven temperature to 180°C (350°F, gas 4), glaze again with the egg and return to the oven. It may be glazed again a third time if desired. Cook for a total of 50 minutes. Serve on its own, with crème fraîche, blackberry coulis or some ice cream.

Galette des rois

Galette des rois or *gâteau des rois* is the traditional French Twelfth-Night cake, with the bean to be found in one lucky portion. The person finding the bean is appointed king or queen for the occasion.

Roll out 500 g (18 oz) puff pastry and cut out 2 circles. Place one on a baking sheet and brush the edge with beaten egg. Mix 100 g (4 oz, ½ cup) softened butter with 100 g (4 oz, ½ cup) sugar, 100 g (4 oz, 1 cup) ground almonds, a few drops of vanilla essence (extract) and 1 tablespoon rum. Mix in 200 g (7 oz) confectioner's custard (pastry cream). Spread the almond mixture on the pastry on the baking sheet, leaving the glazed edge uncovered, and put in a dried bean. Cover with the other circle of pastry and press the edges together, then trim them with a pastry cutter. Brush with beaten egg. Allow to rest for 1 hour in the refrigerator and bake in a preheated oven at 190°C (375°F, gas 5) for 25 minutes.

Gâteau flamand

Make a smooth pastry dough by mixing 175 g (6 oz, 1½ cups) sifted plain (all-purpose) flour, 65 g (2½ oz, 5 tablespoons) butter, 50 g (2 oz, ¼ cup) sugar, 1 egg and a pinch of salt. Roll it out to a thickness of 3 mm (⅛ in) and use to line a buttered manqué mould or sandwich tin (layer cake pan) 20 cm (8 in) in diameter. Place it in the refrigerator.

For the filling, mix together 125 g (4½ oz, ⅔ cup) caster (superfine) sugar, 1 teaspoon vanilla sugar and 100 g (4 oz, 1 cup) ground almonds. Whisk in 3 egg yolks, one by one, then add 3 tablespoons kirsch and continue to whisk the mixture until it turns white. Then add 25 g (1 oz, ¼ cup) cornflour (cornstarch). Whisk 3 egg whites until very stiff and blend them into the mixture together with 40 g (1½ oz, 3 tablespoons) melted butter.

Pour the filling into the lined mould and bake in a preheated oven at 200°C (400°F, gas 6) for about 45 minutes. Then remove from the oven and allow to cool for at least 15 minutes before taking out of the mould. Melt 200 g (7 oz, 1 cup) fondant very slowly in a saucepan. Blend in 3 tablespoons kirsch and spread the fondant over the cake. Decorate with glacé (candied) cherries and sticks of angelica.

Gâteau nantais

A cake made of *pâte sablée* mixed with ground almonds or chopped crystallized (candied) fruit and flavoured with kirsch or rum. It may be baked as a large flat cake or as small biscuits (cookies) cut out with a round fluted pastry (cookie) cutter and decorated with chopped almonds, chopped crystallized fruit or raisins.

Cream 150 g (5 oz, ⅔ cup) butter with a spatula. Mix 250 g (9 oz, 2¼ cups) plain (all-purpose) flour, 150 g (5 oz, ⅔ cup) sugar and a pinch of salt in a bowl. Add the butter, 3 egg yolks, 1 tablespoon rum and 125 g (4½ oz, 1 cup) diced candied angelica. Work these ingredients together to make a smooth paste, roll it into a ball, flatten it out with the palms of the hands, again roll into a ball, and leave in a cool place for 2 hours. Roll the paste out into a circle 2 cm (¾ in) thick and place it on an oiled baking sheet. Mix 1 egg yolk with 1 tablespoon water and brush it over the surface of the gâteau. Sprinkle with chopped almonds. Cook in a preheated oven at 200°C (400°F, gas 6) for 35 minutes. Serve when cold.

Gâteau polka

A gâteau consisting of a ring of choux pastry on a base of shortcrust pastry (basic pie dough), filled with confectioner's custard (pastry cream) or frangipane cream, then dusted with sugar and caramelized with a red-hot skewer forming a crisscross pattern. Small polkas can also be made.

Make a short pastry with 50 g (2 oz, ¼ cup) softened butter, 125 g (4½ oz, 1 cup) plain (all-purpose) flour, 1 tablespoon caster (superfine) sugar and 1 egg yolk. When smooth, roll it into a ball and chill in the refrigerator. Make a confectioner's custard (pastry cream) with 1 litre (1¾ pints, 4⅓ cups) milk, 6 eggs, 200 g (7 oz, ¾ cup) caster sugar, 175 g (6 oz, 1½ cups) plain flour and 100 ml (4 fl oz, 7 tablespoons) rum. Leave to cool.

Roll the dough thinly into a circle 20 cm (8 in) in diameter. Place on a buttered baking sheet and prick. Make some choux pastry with 120 ml (4½ fl oz, ½ cup) water, 25 g (1 oz, 2 tablespoons) butter, 1 tablespoon caster sugar, a pinch of salt, 65 g (2½ oz, ⅔ cup) plain flour and 2 beaten eggs. Place in a piping (pastry) bag with a plain nozzle 1.5 cm (⅝ in) in diameter. Brush the rim of the pastry circle with beaten egg and pipe the choux pastry in a border 5 mm (¼ in) from the edge. Brush this border with beaten egg.

Bake in a preheated oven at 200°C (400°F, gas 6) for 20 minutes, covering the centre of the circle with foil if the pastry browns too quickly. Leave to cool completely, then pour the confectioner's custard into the centre. Sprinkle with granulated sugar. Carefully heat a metal skewer in a flame until it is red hot and then mark a criss-cross pattern on the top of the custard.

German cherry tart

Prepare some puff pastry and roll it out to a thickness of 5 mm (¼ in). Use it to line a flan tin (pie pan), moistening the edges of the pastry and pinching them to make a border. Prick the base with a fork. Sprinkle with a little caster (superfine) sugar and a pinch of powdered cinnamon. Over the base arrange some stoned (pitted) cherries (fresh or canned, well-drained) and bake in a preheated oven at 200°C (400°F, gas 6) for about 30 minutes. Allow to cool, then coat the top with a generous layer of sweetened cherry purée, prepared by cooking some cherries in sugar. To finish, bake some fine breadcrumbs to a pale golden colour in the oven and sprinkle them over the tart.

The cherries may be replaced by apricot halves if desired.

German gooseberry tart

Clean some large ripe gooseberries. Prepare a puff-pastry tart base and bake blind. Mix the gooseberries in a saucepan with an equal weight of sugar cooked to the crack stage: when the sugar has melted, drain the fruit and boil down the juice until it sets into a jelly. Put the gooseberries back into the syrup, boil together for a moment, then pour into a basin. When cool, use it to fill the tart; mask with whipped cream.

Grande religieuse à l'ancienne

Religieuse is a cake classically consisting of a large choux pastry filled with coffee- or chocolate-flavoured confectioner's custard (pastry cream) or Chiboust cream surmounted by a smaller choux pastry, similarly filled; the whole is iced (frosted) with fondant (the same flavour as the filling) and decorated with piped butter cream. The *religieuse* can be made either as a large cake or as small individual cakes. In one old version, the choux pastry was cooked in the form of éclairs, rings or buns, filled with coffee or chocolate cream, and stacked on top of each other or arranged in a pyramid on a base of sweet pastry; the whole was then decorated with piped butter cream.

Make some sweet pastry with 125 g (4½ oz, 1 cup) plain (all-purpose) flour, 1 egg yolk, a pinch of salt, 40 g (1½ oz, 3 tablespoons) caster (superfine) sugar and 50 g (2 oz, ¼ cup) butter cut into small pieces. Roll the pastry into a ball and leave it in a cool place.

Make some choux paste with 250 ml (8 fl oz, 1 cup) water, 65 g (2½ oz, 5 tablespoons) butter, a pinch of salt, 1 teaspoon sugar, 125 g (4½ oz, 1 cup) plain flour and 3–4 eggs. Using a piping (pastry) bag with a smooth nozzle, 1 cm (½ in) in diameter, pipe on to a baking sheet 12 strips 10 cm (4 in) long, 1 small round bun, and 4 rings decreasing in size from a diameter of 15 cm (6 in). Bake in a preheated oven at 200°C (400°F, gas 6) for 30 minutes, then leave to cool in the oven with the door ajar.

Meanwhile, butter a deep 19-cm (7½-in) sandwich tin (layer cake pan), using 25 g (1 oz, 2 tablespoons) butter. Roll out the sweet pastry to a thickness of 3 mm (⅛ in) and use it to line the sandwich tin; prick the bottom, cover with dried haricot (navy) beans and bake blind for 10 minutes. Remove the beans, leave to cool, then turn it out of the tin.

Prepare some *crème au beurre* by boiling 60 ml (2 fl oz, ¼ cup) water with 125 g (4½ oz, generous ½ cup) caster sugar; when the temperature reaches 110°C (225°F), pour slowly on to 4 egg yolks and whisk briskly until the mixture is cold; then whisk in 150 g (5 oz, ⅔ cup) softened butter.

Prepare some Chiboust cream with 6 egg yolks, 200 g (7 oz, 1 cup) caster sugar, 75 g (3 oz, ¾ cup) cornflour (cornstarch), 1 litre (1¾ pints, 4⅓ cups) milk, 4 leaves of gelatine and 4 egg whites. Mix half of this cream with 50 g (2 oz, 2 squares) melted chocolate and the other half with ½ teaspoon coffee essence (strong black coffee). Slit the cooked choux pastries: into half of them pipe the chocolate cream and into the other half pipe the coffee cream.

Put 200 g (7 oz) fondant icing (frosting) in a saucepan with 1 tablespoon water and heat to 40°C (104°F), stirring constantly; add 50 g (2 oz, 2 squares) melted chocolate. Prepare the same quantity of fondant flavoured with ½ teaspoon coffee essence. Ice the éclairs, rings and bun with the fondant to match to their filling. Boil 150 g (5 oz, ⅔ cup) caster sugar in 60 ml (2 fl oz, ¼ cup) water; when the temperature reaches 145°C (293°F), brush the syrup over the bottom of the éclairs. Stick these together side by side vertically inside the pastry base, alternating the flavours, then put the 4 rings on top, beginning with the largest; place the bun at the very top. Using a fluted nozzle, pipe the butter cream along the joints of the éclairs, the rings and the bun.

Grape tart

Make a tart pastry with 250 g (9 oz, 2¼ cups) plain (all-purpose) flour, a generous pinch of salt, 100 g (4 oz, ½ cup) caster (superfine) sugar, 1 egg yolk, ½ glass water and 125 g (4½ oz, ½ cup) softened butter. Roll the dough into a ball and chill it for 1 hour. Wash and seed 500 g (18 oz) white grapes.

In a bowl mix 3 eggs with 100 g (4 oz, ½ cup) caster (superfine) sugar and 250 ml (8 fl oz, 1 cup) single (light) cream. Whisk and gradually add 250 ml (8 fl oz, 1 cup) milk, then 6 tablespoons kirsch. Roll out the dough and use it to line a 24 cm (9½ in) tart tin (pan). Prick the bottom with a fork, spread the grapes over the tin and bake in a preheated oven at 200°C (400°F, gas 6) for 10 minutes. Pour the cream into the tart and continue to cook for 25–30 minutes (cover with foil if the cream browns too fast). Leave to get cold, then unmould it on to a serving dish and sprinkle with icing (confectioner's) sugar.

Iced bâtons

Roll puff pastry out to a thickness of about 3 mm (⅛ in). Cut into strips 8 cm (3 in) wide and coat with royal icing (frosting). Cut across these strips to make sticks 4 cm (1¾ in) wide. Place on a buttered baking sheet and bake in a preheated oven at about 200°C (400°F, gas 6) for about 5 minutes until the pastry puffs up and the icing turns white.

Iced sweet allumettes

Roll out some puff pastry to a thickness of 3 mm (⅛ in), and cut it into strips 8 cm (⅛ in) wide. Spread with a thin layer of royal icing (frosting). Cut the strips into 2.5–3 cm (1–1¼ in) lengths and place them on a baking sheet. Bake in a preheated oven at 180°C (350 F, gas 4) until the icing turns cream-coloured (about 10 minutes).

Individual diplomats with crystallized fruit

Individual diplomats are barquettes filled with a cream containing crystallized fruit, glazed with apricot jam (preserve), covered with fondant icing (frosting) and decorated with a crystallized cherry.

Make a short pastry with 125 g (4½ oz, 1 cup) plain (all-purpose) flour, a pinch of salt, 3 tablespoons caster (superfine) sugar, 1 egg yolk and 75 g (3 oz, 6 tablespoons) softened butter. Roll the dough into a ball; wrap and chill.

Mix 75 g (3 oz, 6 tablespoons) softened butter with 75 g (3 oz, 6 table-spoons) caster sugar, 1 egg and 75 g (3 oz, ¾ cup) ground almonds. Roll 50 g (2 oz, ⅓ cup) sultanas (golden raisins) and 50 g (2 oz, ¼ cup) diced crystal-lized (candied) fruit in 3 tablespoons plain flour. Stir the fruit into the almond mixture, then add 3 tablespoons light rum and mix well.

Roll out the pastry until it is about 3 mm (⅛ in) thick, then cut out about 10 oval shapes with a pastry (cookie) cutter. Butter some barquette moulds and line them with the pastry shapes, leaving an excess of about 3 mm (⅛ in) around the edges. Fill with the fruit-almond mixture and bake in a preheated oven at 200°C (400°F, gas 6) for 30 minutes. Remove the moulds from the oven and cool. Turn the barquettes out of the moulds and glaze with apricot jam that has been melted over a low heat.

Heat 100 g (4 oz) fondant icing (frosting) very gently so that it melts, and use to coat the diplomats. Decorate each diplomat with a glacé (candied) cherry and keep in a cool place.

Jalousies with apricot jam

Roll out 500 g (18 oz) puff pastry into a rectangle about 3 mm (⅛ in) thick and cut it into 2 equal strips about 10 cm (4 in) wide. Brush all round the edges of one of the strips with beaten egg and spread 500 g (18 oz, 1½ cups) apricot jam (preserve) in the centre. Fold the second piece of pastry in half lengthways, and with a knife make slanting cuts from the folded side to within 1 cm (½ in) of the other edge. Unfold the strip and place it over the first one. Press the edges firmly together to seal them, trimming if necessary to a neat rectangle, then make decorative indentations with the point of a knife. Brush the top with beaten egg, put in a preheated oven at 200°C (400°F, gas 6), and bake for 25–30 minutes. When it is done, brush the top lightly with apricot jam that has been mixed with double its volume of water and boiled to reduce it slightly; finally, sprinkle the top with caster (superfine) sugar.

Cut the strip into 4 cm (1¾ in) slices and serve warm or cold.

Le jeu de pommes

Make a fine pastry by combining in a processor 200 g (7 oz, 1¾ cups) plain (all-purpose) flour, 150 g (5 oz, ⅔ cup) rather firm butter, a pinch of salt, 1 teaspoon sugar and a little olive oil. Incorporate 100 ml (4 fl oz, ½ cup) water and work together briefly (the particles of butter should still be visible). Remove the dough and roll it out finely; cut out 16 circles about 12 cm (5 in) in diameter using a pastry (cookie) cutter. Place them on nonstick baking sheets, cover them with very thin slices of apple, brush with 50 g (2 oz, ¼ cup) melted butter and sprinkle lightly with caster (superfine) sugar. Bake in a preheated oven at 220°C (425°F, gas 7) for 15 minutes.

Turn each tartlet over on the baking sheet using a spatula and dust the reverse side with icing (confectioner's) sugar. Put under the grill (broiler): as it caramelizes, the sugar forms a glossy crackly film. Leave to cool for 15 minutes. Take 4 dessert plates and place 4 tartlets on top of each other on each plate (apples upwards). Just before serving, cover each *jeu de pommes* with 1 tablespoon warmed acacia honey and sprinkle with a little Calvados and a few drops of lemon juice. This dessert may be accompanied by a lemon sorbet.

Lemon meringue pie

Butter a baking tin (cake pan) 23–25 cm (9–10 in) in diameter and line it with 350 g (12 oz) shortcrust pastry (basic pie dough). Cook the pastry case (pie shell) blind in a preheated oven at 200°C (400°F, gas 6) for 10 minutes.

Boil 350 ml (12 fl oz, 1½ cups) water in a saucepan. In another saucepan, mix 65 g (2½ oz, ½ cup plus 2 tablespoons) plain (all-purpose) flour, 65 g (2½ oz, ½ cup plus 2 tablespoons) cornflour (cornstarch) and 250 g (9 oz, 1 cup) caster (superfine) sugar and gradually add the boiling water, stirring all the time. Bring to the boil, still stirring, then remove from the heat and leave to cool slightly.

Wash and wipe 2–3 lemons, grate the zest and squeeze the juice. Add the grated zest, the juice, 4 egg yolks and 25 g (1 oz, 2 tablespoons) butter to the cooled mixture and cook in a bain marie for 15 minutes, whisking from time to time. Pour the mixture into the pastry case, bake in a preheated oven at 200°C (400°F, gas 6) for 10 minutes, then leave to cool.

Add a pinch of salt to 4 egg whites, whisk into stiff peaks, then gradually fold in 125 g (4½ oz, ½ cup) caster (superfine) sugar and 20 g (¾ oz, 2 tablespoons) icing (confectioner's) sugar. Spread this meringue over the pie using a metal spatula, then return to the oven for 10 minutes, to brown lightly. Serve lukewarm or cold.

Lemon tart

Make a tart case (shell) of shortcrust pastry (basic pie dough) and bake blind until the pastry is crisp but not completely cooked. Mix together 3 eggs, 100 g (4 oz, ½ cup) sugar, 75 g (3 oz, 6 tablespoons) melted butter, the juice of 5 lemons and their grated zest. Whisk and pour into the tart case. Bake in a preheated oven at 240°C (475°F, gas 9) for 10–15 minutes. This recipe can be made using 3 oranges or 7 tangerines instead of the lemons.

Linzertorte

Leave 75 g (3 oz, 6 tablespoons) butter to reach room temperature. Remove the rind (zest) from a lemon and shred two-thirds of it into fine julienne strips. Blanch, drain and chop these strips. Sift 175 g (6 oz, 1½ cups) plain (all-purpose) flour on to the work surface and add 75 g (3 oz, ¾ cup) ground almonds, 75 g (3 oz, 6 tablespoons) caster (superfine) sugar, 1 egg, 2 teaspoons powdered cinnamon, the softened butter, the lemon rind, and a pinch of salt. Knead the ingredients thoroughly, cover and refrigerate for 2 hours.

Butter a 23 cm (9 in) round flan tin (pie pan). Roll the dough out to a thickness of 3–4 mm (⅛–¼ in) and line the flan tin carefully, trimming off the excess around the top. Prick with a fork and fill with 125 g (4½ oz, ⅓ cup) raspberry jam (preserve). Gather the pastry trimmings together and roll them out into a rectangle about 3 mm (⅛ in) thick. Cut it into strips a little under 1 cm (½ in) wide and make a lattice pattern on top of the flan, pressing the ends into the top of the pastry case. Bake in a preheated oven at 200°C (400°F, gas 6) for about 30 minutes.

Remove the flan from the tin, place on a serving dish and allow to cool completely. The tart may be lightly brushed with an apricot glaze.

• *variation:* instead of strips of pastry, a piped dough can be applied over the jam filling. Make a half quantity of the dough with an additional 50 g (2 oz, ¼ cup) butter and 1 egg yolk, creaming the ingredients in a bowl to a stiff piping consistency. Fit a piping (pastry) bag with a star tube and pipe the mixture on the tart.

Maple syrup tart

Boil 7 tablespoons maple syrup with a little water for 5 minutes. Blend in 3 tablespoons cornflour (cornstarch) mixed with cold water, then 50 g (2 oz, ¼ cup) butter. Line a tart plate (pie pan) with shortcrust pastry (basic pie dough) and spread the lukewarm syrup mixture over it. Decorate with chopped almonds. Cover with a fairly thin pastry lid, pinch round the edge, prick with a fork, and bake in a preheated oven at 220°C (425°F, gas 7) for about 20 minutes.

Mille-feuille gâteau

Prepare some puff pastry with 300 g (11 oz, 2¾ cups) plain (all-purpose) flour, a generous pinch of salt, 6 tablespoons water and 225 g (8 oz, 1 cup) softened butter. Divide the dough into 3 equal portions and roll them out to a thickness of 2 cm (¾ in). Cut out 3 circles 20 cm (8 in) in diameter, place them on a baking sheet and prick them with a fork. Sprinkle with 50 g (2 oz, ½ cup) icing (confectioner's) sugar and bake in a preheated oven at 220°C (425°F, gas 7) for 15 minutes.

Meanwhile, prepare 750 ml (1¼ pints, 3¼ cups) rum-flavoured confectioner's custard (pastry cream) and allow it to cool. Roughly chop 100 g (4 oz, 1 cup) blanched almonds and brown them gently in a frying pan. Leave the circles of pastry to cool completely. Use two-thirds of the custard to cover two circles of pastry, arrange them one on top of the other and cover with the third circle. Cover the entire gâteau with the remaining custard, sprinkle with the browned almonds and some icing sugar, and store in a cool place.

Mince pies

Line some tartlet tins (moulds) with shortcrust pastry (basic pie dough) and fill with mincemeat. Cover with a thin layer of puff pastry and seal the edges. Make a small hole in the centre of each pie to allow the steam to escape. Brush with egg and bake in a preheated oven at 220°C (425°F, gas 7) for 15–20 minutes. Serve hot.

Muscat grape tartlets

Make a *pâte sablée*, roll it out very thinly, cut out 4 circles 18 cm (7 in) in diameter and use them to line 4 tartlet tins (pans). Prick the bottom of each lined tin, leave to rest, then bake blind for 15 minutes.

Mix together 250 ml (8 fl oz, 1 cup) black Muscat grape juice, 150 ml (¼ pint, ⅔ cup) single (light) cream, 100 g (4 oz, ½ cup) melted butter, 2 egg yolks, 2 eggs and 2 tablespoons sugar. Fill the tarts with this mixture and bake in a preheated oven at 180°C (350°F, gas 4) for 20 minutes.

Nut délices

Combine 125 g (4½ oz, 1 cup) plain (all-purpose) flour with 50 g (2 oz, ¼ cup) softened butter, 1 egg yolk, 1 tablespoon water, 3 tablespoons caster (superfine) sugar and a pinch of salt. When the dough is smooth, roll it into a ball and chill.

Cream 65 g (2½ oz, 5 tablespoons) butter; add 65 g (2½ oz, ⅓ cup) caster sugar and 1 egg, then 65 g (2½ oz, ½ cup) ground almonds, and finally 25 g

(1 oz, ¼ cup) potato flour; mix well. Roll out the chilled dough to a thickness of 3 mm (⅛ in). Cut out 8 discs and line tartlet moulds with them. Prick the bottoms and cover with the almond cream. Cook in a preheated oven at 190°C (375°F, gas 5) for 15 minutes.

Meanwhile, prepare a French butter cream using 125 g (4½ oz, ½ cup) sugar cooked to the thread stage in 3 tablespoons water, 4 egg yolks, 125 g (4½ oz, ½ cup) butter and 1 teaspoon coffee essence. Chop 100 g (4 oz, 1 cup) fresh walnuts and mix with the cream. Allow the tartlets to cool, then turn out and top each with a dome of the walnut cream. Put in a cold place for 30 minutes.

Warm 250 g (9 oz) fondant icing (frosting) to about 32°C (90°F), flavour it with a few drops of coffee essence and add just enough water to make it spread easily. Dip the top of each tartlet into the fondant, smoothing it evenly over the cream with a palette knife (spatula). Place a fresh walnut on each *délice* and store in a cool place.

Oreillettes de Montpellier

Oreillettes are pastry fritters traditionally made in the Languedoc region of France at carnival time. They are made from sweetened dough cut into long rectangles with a slit in the centre (sometimes one end is passed through this hole to form a sort of knot) and fried in oil. The oreillettes of Montpellier, flavoured with rum and orange or lemon zest, are famous.

Pour 1 kg (2¼ lb, 9 cups) plain (all-purpose) flour into a heap and make a well in the centre. Pour 300 g (11 oz, 1⅓ cups) melted butter into the well and work it in, gradually drawing the flour to the centre; continue to work in 5 eggs, 2 tablespoons caster (superfine) sugar, a few tablespoons of rum, a small glass of milk and the finely grated zest of 2 oranges. Knead well to obtain a smooth dough. Continue to work the dough until it becomes elastic, then form it into a ball and leave it to rest for 2 hours. Roll out the dough very thinly and cut it into rectangles 5 × 8 cm (2 × 3¼ in). Make 2 incisions in the centre of each rectangle. Fry the oreillettes in very hot oil at 175°C (345°F): they will puff up immediately and rapidly become golden. Drain them on paper towels, sprinkle with icing (confectioner's) sugar and arrange them in a basket lined with a napkin.

Palmiers

Palmiers are small pastries made of a sugared and double-rolled sheet of puff pastry cut into slices, the distinctive shape of which resembles the foliage of a palm tree. First made at the beginning of the 20th century, palmiers are served with tea or as an accompaniment to ices and desserts.

Prepare some puff pastry and give it 4 extra turns, dusting it generously with icing (confectioner's) sugar between each rolling. Roll it out to a thickness of 5 mm (¼ in), into a rectangle 20 cm (8 in) wide (the length will depend on the quantity used). Dust again with icing sugar. Roll each of the long sides to the centre and flatten slightly, then fold the strip in half. Cut this into sections 1 cm (½ in) thick and place on a baking sheet, leaving enough space between them so that they do not stick to each other during cooking. Cook the palmiers in a preheated oven at 220°C (425°F, gas 7) for about 10 minutes, turning them over halfway through cooking to colour both sides.

Paris-Brest

Sprinkle 100 g (4 oz, 1 cup) flaked (slivered) almonds over a baking sheet and cook them in a preheated oven at 200°C (400°F, gas 6) until golden. Prepare a choux paste with 100 g (4 oz, ½ cup) butter, 2 tablespoons caster (superfine) sugar, a generous pinch of salt, 200 g (7 oz, 1¾ cups) plain (all-purpose) flour, 350 ml (12 fl oz, 1½ cups) water and 5 or 6 eggs, according to their size.

Fill a piping (pastry) bag, fitted with a nozzle 1.5 cm (¾ in) in diameter, with this mixture and pipe 2 rings, 18 cm (7 in) in diameter. Glaze them with beaten egg, sprinkle them with the flaked almonds and cook in a preheated oven at 180°C (350°F, gas 4) for 35–40 minutes. Turn off the oven and leave the rings to cool with the door ajar, then remove from the oven and leave them to get completely cold.

Prepare a confectioner's custard (pastry cream) with 65 g (2½ oz, ½ cup) plain flour, 175 g (6 oz, ¾ cup) caster sugar, 15 g (½ oz, 1 tablespoon) butter, 4 whole eggs, a generous pinch of salt and 500 ml (17 fl oz, 2 cups) boiling milk. In another bowl make a praline-flavoured *crème au beurre* with 200 ml (7 fl oz, ¾ cup) milk, 6 eggs, 200 g (7 oz, 1 cup) caster sugar, 400 g (14 oz, ¾ cup) butter and 75 g (3 oz, ⅓ cup) praline. Finally, prepare 150 g (5 oz) Italian meringue.

Leave the three preparations to cool thoroughly, then mix them together. Cut the choux rings in half horizontally and fill the lower halves with the meringue mixture using a piping bag with a large fluted nozzle.

Replace the top halves of the rings, dust with icing (confectioner's) sugar and put in a cool place until time to serve.

• *individual Paris-Brest:* instead of making large pastries, pipe rings measuring 7.5 cm (3 in) in diameter. Bake as above, allowing about 30 minutes. Fill and serve with a custard sauce. Hazelnuts can be used instead of almonds in the praline (with chopped hazelnuts on top of the choux rings) and the dessert can be decorated with a few whole caramelized nuts.

Pastry cream puffs

Prepare 12 choux buns and fill them with confectioner's custard (pastry cream) made using 250 ml (8 fl oz, 1 cup) milk, 3 egg yolks, 50 g (2 oz, ¼ cup) caster (superfine) sugar, 100 g (4 oz, 1 cup) plain (all-purpose) flour.

Flavour the custard to taste. The filled puffs may be dusted with icing (confectioner's) sugar or iced with fondant and, if desired, decorated with crystallized (candied) fruits.

Pastry cream puffs with grapes

Prepare some confectioner's custard (pastry cream), flavour it slightly with marc brandy and add some fresh grapes with the skins and seeds removed. Fill some choux buns with the custard and then sprinkle them generously with icing (confectioner's) sugar.

Peaches à la duchesse

Make a dough with 150 g (5 oz, 1¼ cups) plain (all-purpose) flour, a pinch of salt, 3 tablespoons caster (superfine) sugar, 75 g (3 oz, 6 tablespoons) softened butter, 1 tablespoon water and 1 egg yolk. Roll into a ball and place in the refrigerator. Dice 8 slices canned pineapple and macerate them in kirsch. Put 50 g (2 oz, ½ cup) flaked (slivered) almonds on to a baking sheet, moisten with water, dust with sugar and bake in a preheated oven at 200°C (400°F, gas 6) until golden brown, turning often.

Roll out the chilled dough to a thickness of about 3 mm (⅛ in) and cut out 8 circles with a pastry (cookie) cutter. Use to line 8 tartlet moulds, prick the bottom of each one with a fork, place a piece of greaseproof (wax) paper in each and fill with baking beans. Cook for 5 minutes in the oven, remove the paper and baking beans, and cook for a further 7 minutes. Cool and then turn out of the moulds.

Prepare a zabaglione by whisking 100 g (4 oz, ½ cup) caster sugar and 3 egg yolks in a bain marie until the mixture is warm and frothy. Add 3 table-spoons of both kirsch and Maraschino, whisking until the mixture has thickened. Soften 500 ml (17 fl oz, 2 cups) vanilla ice cream by crushing it with a wooden spatula. Add the diced pineapple. Place some of the ice cream mixture in the bottom of each tartlet, put a canned peach half on each, and coat with the zabaglione. Sprinkle with flaked almonds and chill briefly.

The peaches may be replaced by pears.

Pear pie

Peel and core 4 pears, cut into slices and sprinkle with lemon juice. Arrange the pear slices in a buttered pie dish and sprinkle with 2 tablespoons caster (superfine) sugar; a little ground cinnamon may also be added. Dot with 25 g (1 oz, 2 tablespoons) butter.

Prepare some shortcrust pastry (basic pie dough) and put a border around the rim of the dish, brush it with beaten egg and cover the dish with a lid of pastry. Press down to seal the edges, then crimp between finger and thumb, brush with beaten egg and bake in a preheated oven at 180°C (350°F, gas 4) for 1 hour. When cooked, dust with sugar and serve very hot.

Pets-de-nonne

Make some choux paste with 250 ml (8 fl oz, 1 cup) water, a pinch of salt, 2 tablespoons caster (superfine) sugar, 65 g (2½ oz, 5 tablespoons) butter, 125 g (4½ oz, 1 cup) plain (all-purpose) flour and 3 or 4 eggs. Heat up some oil in a deep-fat fryer to 180°C (356°F). Drop teaspoonfuls of the paste into the hot oil; when golden brown on one side (after about 2½ minutes), turn them over, if necessary, to cook the other side (another 2 minutes). Drain the fritters on paper towels and sprinkle with icing (confectioner's) sugar.

Pineapple tart

Prepare some shortcrust pastry (basic pie dough) with 150 g (5 oz, 1¼ cups) plain (all-purpose) flour, 75 g (3 oz, 6 tablespoons) softened butter, a pinch of salt and a little cold water. When it is pliable and well-mixed, roll it and use it to line a 22 cm (8½ in) buttered flan tin (pie pan); prick the base. Leave in a cool place for 2 hours, then bake blind in a preheated oven at 200°C (400°F, gas 6) for 20 minutes.

Meanwhile, mix together 2 egg yolks, 75 g (3 oz, 6 tablespoons) caster (superfine) sugar, 1 teaspoon flour and 175 ml (6 fl oz, ¾ cup) milk. Stir over a low heat until it thickens, then add the juice of ½ a lemon and 60 ml (2 fl oz, ¼ cup) reduced pineapple syrup. Take the tart case (shell) out of the oven, allow to cool, then pour in the pineapple cream and arrange on top 6 slices of canned pineapple, well-drained. Whisk 2 egg whites to stiff peaks, pour over the fruit and sprinkle with 25 g (1 oz, 2 tablespoons) caster (superfine) sugar. Return to the oven at the same temperature and cook for 10 minutes to brown the meringue mixture. Leave in a cool place until just before serving.

Pine-nut flan

Spread 2 tablespoons blackcurrant jelly over a base of sweetened rich shortcrust pastry (basic pie dough). Cover with equal quantities of confectioner's custard (pastry cream) and ground almonds. Scatter 100 g (4 oz, 1 cup) pine nuts over the top. Cook in a preheated oven at 200°C (400°F, gas 6) for about 20 minutes.

Pithiviers

A large, round, puff-pastry tart with scalloped edges, filled with an almond cream. A speciality of Pithiviers, in the Orléans region, it traditionally serves as a Twelfth-Night cake, when it contains a broad (fava) bean.

Cream 100 g (4 oz, ½ cup) butter with a spatula and mix with 100 g (4 oz, ½ cup) caster (superfine) sugar. Then beat in 6 egg yolks, one at a time, 40 g (1½ oz, ¼ cup) potato flour, 100 g (4 oz, 1 cup) ground almonds and

2 tablespoons rum. Mix this cream thoroughly. Roll out 200 g (7 oz) puff pastry and cut out a circle 20 cm (8 in) in diameter. Spread this with the almond paste, leaving a 1 cm (½ in) border all round. Beat 1 egg yolk and brush it around the rim of the circle. Roll out a further 300 g (11 oz) pastry and cut another circle the same size as the first but thicker. Place it on the first circle and seal the rim. Decorate the edge with the traditional scalloped pattern and brush with beaten egg. Score diamond or rosette patterns on the top with the point of a knife. Cook in a preheated oven at 220°C (425°F, gas 7) for 30 minutes. Dust with icing (confectioner's) sugar and return it to the oven for a few minutes to glaze. Serve warm or cold.

Plum tart

Prepare a lining pastry with 200 g (7 oz, 1¾ cups) plain (all-purpose) flour, 90 g (3½ oz, 6½ tablespoons) softened butter, a pinch of salt, 1 egg and 1 tablespoon water. Roll the dough into a ball and refrigerate for 2 hours. Wash 500 g (18 oz) ripe plums and stone (pit) them without separating the halves completely. Roll out the dough to a thickness of 5 mm (¼ in) and use it to line a buttered tart tin (pan). Trim off the excess pastry and mark the edge with a criss-cross pattern. Prick the bottom with a fork, sprinkle with 40 g (1½ oz, 3 tablespoons) caster (superfine) sugar, and arrange the plums in the tart, opened out with curved sides downwards. Sprinkle the fruit with 40 g (1½ oz, 3 tablespoons) caster sugar. Cook in a preheated oven at 200°C (400°F, gas 6) for 30 minutes. Remove from the oven, leave until lukewarm, then coat the top with apricot jam (preserve).

Plum tart à l'alsacienne

Prepare a sweet pastry with 125 g (4½ oz, ½ cup) softened butter, 250 g (9 oz, 1 cup) caster (superfine) sugar, 1 whole egg, 250 g (9 oz, 2¼ cups) plain (all-purpose) flour and 250 g (9 oz, 2 cups) ground almonds. Add just enough very cold water to bind the dough, roll it into a ball and place in the refrigerator for 2 hours.

Set aside a quarter of the dough and roll out the rest to a thickness of 5 mm (¼ in). Use it to line a tart tin (pie pan) 23 cm (9 in) in diameter. Roll out the remaining dough very thinly and cut it into long narrow strips. Spread a thick layer of quetsch or mirabelle plum jam (preserve) over the tart and arrange the strips of pastry in a criss-cross pattern over the top. Cook in a preheated oven at 220°C (425°F, gas 7) for 30 minutes. Dust with icing (confectioner's) sugar and serve hot, with whipped cream.

Ponts-neufs

Prepare a lining pastry with 200 g (7 oz, 1¾ cups) plain (all-purpose) flour, a pinch of salt, 25 g (1 oz, 2 tablespoons) caster (superfine) sugar, 100 g (4 oz, ½ cup) melted butter and 1 egg. Roll the dough into a ball and put it in the refrigerator. Prepare a confectioner's custard (pastry cream) with 400 ml (14 fl oz, 1¾ cups) milk, 4 eggs, 50 g (2 oz, ¼ cup) caster sugar, ½ a vanilla pod (bean) and 25 g (1 oz, ¼ cup) plain flour. Add 25 g (1 oz, ¼ cup) crushed macaroons and leave to cool. Prepare a choux paste with 100 ml (4 fl oz, 7 tablespoons) water, 25 g (1 oz, 2 tablespoons) butter, a pinch of salt, 65 g (2½ oz, ⅔ cup) plain flour, 3 eggs and ½ teaspoon caster sugar. Leave to cool.

Roll out the lining pastry very thinly, cut into 10 circles and line sections of patty tins (muffin pans) of a slightly smaller diameter. Roll the remaining pastry into a ball. Mix the choux pastry with the confectioner's custard and fill the tartlets. Glaze the tops with egg yolk. Roll out the remaining pastry very thinly and cut into 20 thin strips; use to make a pastry cross on each tartlet. Cook in a preheated oven at 190°C (375°F, gas 5) for 15–20 minutes and cool on a wire rack.

Melt 100 g (4 oz, ⅓ cup) redcurrant jelly over a gentle heat; coat the opposite quarters of each tartlet with the jelly and dust the remaining quarters with icing (confectioner's) sugar. Keep cool until ready to serve.

Puff-pastry apple tart

Prepare an apple compote with 800 g (1¾ lb) apples, the juice of ½ a lemon, 150 g (5 oz, ⅔ cup) caster (superfine) sugar and 1 teaspoon vanilla sugar. Sieve, heat gently to dry off the excess liquid. Prepare 400 g (14 oz) puff pastry. Roll it out to form a rectangle 30 × 13 cm (12 × 5 in). Make a border with a small strip of pastry about 1 cm (½ in) wide. Bake blind. Thinly slice 500 g (18 oz) crisp apples and sauté them in 50 g (2 oz, ¼ cup) butter until they are brown but still intact. Spread the apple compote over the cooked base, decorate with the slices of apple and sprinkle with 2 tablespoons icing (confectioner's) sugar, then glaze in the oven or under the grill (broiler).

Puff pastry croustades

Sprinkle the worktop with flour and roll out puff pastry to a thickness of about 1–2 cm (½–¾ in). Using a pastry (cookie) cutter, cut rounds 7.5–10 cm (3–4 in) in diameter. With a smaller cutter, on each round make a circle centred on the first, with a diameter 2 cm (¾ in) smaller, taking care not to cut right through the pastry: this smaller circle will form the lid of the croustades. Glaze with egg yolk and place in a preheated oven at 230°C, (450°F, gas 8). As soon as the crust has risen well and turned golden, take the croustades out of the oven. Leave until lukewarm, then take off the lid and, with a spoon, remove the soft white paste which is inside. Leave the croustades to cool completely.

Alternatively, roll the pastry to a thickness of only 5 mm (¼ in), then cut half of it into circles 7.5–10 cm (3–4 in) in diameter, and the rest into rings of the same external diameter and 1 cm (½ in) wide. Brush the base of the rings with beaten egg and place them exactly on the circles; glaze the whole with beaten egg and cook.

Puits d'amour

Roll out 500 g (18 oz) puff pastry into a 25 × 18 cm (10 × 7 in) rectangle. Cut out from it 12 circles, 6 cm (2½ in) in diameter. Place 6 of them on a buttered baking sheet and brush with beaten egg. Cut out the centres of the other 6 circles with a 3 cm (1¼ in) pastry (cookie) cutter; place these rings on the circles of pastry and brush with beaten egg. Cook in a preheated oven at 230°C (450°F, gas 8) for 15 minutes. Allow them to cool, then dust with icing (confectioner's) sugar and fill the centres with redcurrant jelly or vanilla-flavoured confectioner's custard (pastry cream).

Raisin tart

Soak 500 g (18 oz, 3 cups) raisins in brandy. Beat 8 whole eggs lightly, then whip them together with 1 litre (1¾ pints, 4⅓ cups) double (heavy) cream, 350 g (12 oz, 1½ cups) caster (superfine) sugar and 2 teaspoons vanilla sugar or a few drops of vanilla essence (extract). Line a flan tin (pie pan) at least 28 cm (11 in) in diameter with 450 g (1 lb) puff pastry. Pour the cream into the pastry case, add the raisins and bake in a preheated oven at 220°C (425°F, gas 7) for at least 30 minutes.

Raspberry and apple Dartois

Prepare 500 g (1 lb 2 oz) puff pastry and chill for 1 hour. Peel 575 g (1¼ lb) cooking apples, cut into quarters, core and slice finely, then toss in 2 tablespoons lemon juice. Put the apples into a saucepan with 125 g (4½ oz, ½ cup) caster (superfine) sugar, 40 g (1½ oz, 3 tablespoons) butter and ½ a vanilla pod (bean) cut in two. Add 1 tablespoon water and cook over a low heat, stirring from time to time. When the apples are reduced to a purée, remove the pieces of vanilla pod and allow to cool. Roll out the pastry to a rectangle, 3 mm (⅛ in) thick, and cut it into twelve 10 cm (4 in) squares. Mix the stewed apples with 2 tablespoons raspberry jam (preserve) and place a generous spoonful of the filling in the centre of six of the pastry squares. Moisten the edges of each square with water and cover with one of the remaining squares. Pinch the edges to seal the pastry. Cover with the second rectangle of pastry and bake in a preheated oven at 220°C (425°F, gas 7) for about 15 minutes. Dust with icing (confectioner's) sugar and return to the oven to caramelize for 5 minutes. Serve warm.

Raspberry barquettes

Barquettes are small, boat-shaped tarts made of shortcrust pastry (basic pie dough) or puff pastry, baked blind and then filled.

Prepare and cook some barquettes of shortcrust pastry and leave them to cool. Spread a little confectioner's custard (pastry cream) in each tartlet and top with fresh raspberries. Coat the fruit with some warmed redcurrant or raspberry jelly.

Raspberry tart

Prepare some short pastry (basic pie dough) using 300 g (11 oz, 2¾ cups) plain (all-purpose) flour, 1 egg, a pinch of salt, 125 g (4½ oz, ½ cup) butter and 5 tablespoons water. Roll it into a ball and leave it in a cool place for 1 hour. Then roll it out to a thickness of 3–4 mm (about ¼ in) and use to line a 24 cm (9½ in) tart tin (pie pan). Prick the base and bake blind. Prepare some confectioner's custard (pastry cream) using 50 g (2 oz, ½ cup) plain flour, 20 g (¾ oz, 1½ tablespoons) butter, 175 g (6 oz, ¾ cup) sugar, 4 eggs, 500 ml

(17 fl oz, 2 cups) milk and a vanilla pod (bean). Leave to cool. Pick over 500 g (18 oz, 3½ cups) raspberries, but do not wash. Cover the cooled tart with the confectioner's custard, put the raspberries on top and coat them with melted redcurrant and raspberry jelly. Serve chilled.

Rhubarb pie

Make 300 g (11 oz) shortcrust pastry (basic pie dough), shape it into a ball, and leave it to rest for at least 2 hours. Roll it out to a thickness of about 3 mm (⅛ in) and cut out a piece to cover a pie dish, and also a strip to go around the edge of the dish. Remove any stringy fibres from the rhubarb and cut it into pieces 4 cm (1½ in) long. Put the rhubarb in the buttered pie dish and sprinkle with caster (superfine) sugar or soft brown (coffee) sugar, using about 250 g (9 oz, 1 cup) sugar for 800 g (1¾ lb) rhubarb; moisten with 2–3 tablespoons water.

Cover the edge of the pie dish with the strip of pastry, brush it with beaten egg, then place the pastry lid over the dish, pressing down at the edges. Decorate the lid with a diamond-shaped design, brush with egg, then sprinkle lightly with caster sugar. Insert a small pie funnel in the lid for the steam to escape and bake the pie in a preheated oven at 200°C (400°F, gas 6) for 40–45 minutes.

Take the dish out of the oven, remove the funnel and pour in some double (heavy) cream. Alternatively, the cream can be served separately or crème anglaise can be served with the pie. Vanilla ice cream also goes well with rhubarb pie.

Rhubarb tartlets

Roll out 250 g (9 oz) puff pastry and cook between two baking sheets in a preheated oven at 200°C (400°F, gas 6). Cut into rectangles 12 × 7.5 cm

(4½ × 3 in). Sprinkle soft brown sugar on top and brown under the grill (broiler). Peel 500 g (18 oz) rhubarb and cut into pieces of the same length as the puff-pastry rectangles. Cook in the oven at 150°C (300°F, gas 2) until just tender, add a little water and 2 tablespoons caster (superfine) sugar, and continue cooking under a sheet of foil. Drain. Prepare a brown caramel sauce with 100 g (4 oz, ⅔ cup) icing (confectioner's) sugar and water. Add 50 g (2 oz, ¼ cup) butter: the caramel sauce must coat the spoon. Place the pieces of rhubarb on the puff pastry and put in a lukewarm oven for 1 minute. Using a pastry (piping) bag, pipe some very cold cream lengthways, then pour the lukewarm caramel in threads widthways.

Rice tart

Cut 200 g (7 oz, 1 cup) crystallized (candied) fruit into small dice and macerate in 2 tablespoons rum. Prepare some sweet pastry with 250 g (9 oz, 2¼ cups) sifted plain (all-purpose) flour, 125 g (4½ oz, ¾ cup) caster (superfine) sugar, 1 egg, a pinch of salt and 125 g (4½ oz, ½ cup) softened butter. Roll the pastry into a ball and chill.

Boil 400 ml (14 fl oz, 1¾ cups) milk with a vanilla pod (bean). Add 100 g (4 oz, ⅔ cup) washed round-grain rice to the boiling milk, together with a pinch of salt and 75 g (3 oz, 6 tablespoons) caster sugar, cover the pan and cook over a very low heat for 25 minutes. When the rice is completely cooked, allow it to cool slightly, then add a well-beaten egg, stirring it in thoroughly to mix. Then stir in 2 tablespoons crème fraîche and the crystallized fruit with the rum in which it was soaked.

Roll out the pastry and use to line a sponge tin (cake pan). Prick the pastry base and then put in the filling. Pour 50 g (2 oz, ¼ cup) melted butter over the top and sprinkle with 5 crushed sugar cubes. Cook in a preheated oven at 200°C (400°F, gas 6) for 30 minutes. Serve either warm or cold.

Rouen mirlitons

Roll out 250 g (9 oz) puff pastry to a thickness of about 3 mm (⅛ in). Line 10 tartlet tins (moulds). Mix 2 beaten eggs, 4 large crushed macaroons, 65 g (2½ oz, generous ¼ cup) caster (superfine) sugar, and 20 g (¾ oz, scant ¼ cup) ground almonds in a bowl. Three-quarters fill the tartlets with the almond mixture and leave to stand for 30 minutes in a cool place.

Halve 15 blanched almonds and arrange 3 halves on each tartlet. Sprinkle with icing (confectioner's) sugar and bake in a preheated oven at 200°C (400°F, gas 6) for 15–20 minutes. Serve warm or cold.

Saint-Honoré

A gâteau consisting of a layer of shortcrust pastry (basic pie dough) or puff pastry, on top of which is arranged a crown of choux paste garnished with small choux balls glazed with caramel. The inside of the crown is filled with Chiboust cream (also known as 'Saint-Honoré cream') or Chantilly cream.

Prepare the dough for the base with 125 g (4½ oz, 1 cup) plain (all-purpose) flour, 1 egg yolk, 50 g (2 oz, ¼ cup) softened butter, a pinch of salt, 15 g (½ oz, 1 tablespoon) granulated sugar and 2 tablespoons water. When the mixture is smooth, put it in the refrigerator.

Make some choux paste by heating 250 ml (8 fl oz, 1 cup) water, 50 g (2 oz, ¼ cup) butter, 15 g (½ oz, 1 tablespoon) caster (superfine) sugar and a pinch of salt until the butter has melted, then bring to the boil. Immediately add 125 g (4½ oz, 1 cup) plain flour, stirring, and remove from the heat. The paste should form a ball, leaving the sides of the pan clean. Cool slightly before beating in 4 beaten eggs, one by one.

Roll out the dough for the base into a circle 20 cm (8 in) in diameter and 3 mm (⅛ in) thick. Place on a buttered baking sheet, prick with a fork and brush the edge with beaten egg. Fit a piping (pastry) bag with a smooth nozzle the diameter of a finger and fill it with one-third of the choux paste. Pipe a border around the base 3 mm (⅛ in) from the edge. Brush this border with beaten egg. On a second buttered baking sheet, pipe 20 small choux balls, about the size of walnuts. Bake the base and choux balls in a preheated oven at 200°C (400°F, gas 6) for about 25 minutes, then leave to cool completely.

Prepare a light caramel sauce by cooking 250 g (9 oz, 1 cup) granulated sugar with 100 ml (4 fl oz, 7 tablespoons) water until it reaches 145°C (293°F). Dip the choux balls in the caramel and stick them on top of the choux border so that they touch each other.

To make the cream filling, soften 15 g (½ oz, 2 envelopes) gelatine in 5 tablespoons cold water. Boil 1 litre (1¾ pints, 4⅓ cups) milk with a vanilla pod (bean). Beat 6 egg yolks with 200 g (7 oz, 1 cup) caster (superfine) sugar until the mixture turns white and thick and then add 75 g (3 oz, ¾ cup) cornflour (cornstarch). Remove the vanilla pod from the milk and pour the milk over the mixture, beating hard. Return it to the saucepan and bring to the boil, whisking all the time. Stir in the softened gelatine until it has completely dissolved. Stiffly whisk 4 egg whites in a bowl. Bring the custard back to the boil and pour it over the egg whites, folding them in with a metal spoon. Leave until cold and on the point of setting, then fill the centre of the cake with this mixture, sprinkle with icing (confectioner's) sugar and grill (broil) rapidly until golden.

Put in a cool place until ready to serve, but do not keep for too long.

Strawberry délices

Work together in a mixing bowl 125 g (4½ oz, 1 cup) plain (all-purpose) flour with 1 egg, 50 g (2 oz, ¼ cup) caster (superfine) sugar, a pinch of salt, 1 tablespoon water and 50 g (2 oz, ¼ cup) butter cut into small pieces. When the mixture is a smooth dough, put it in the refrigerator to chill.

Meanwhile, wash and hull 175 g (6 oz, 1 cup) strawberries and macerate them in 50 g (2 oz, ⅓ cup) icing (confectioner's) sugar for about 1 hour.

Roll out the dough to a thickness of 3 mm (⅛ in), cut out 6 rounds and use them to line 6 buttered tartlet moulds; prick the bottom of each one with a fork and bake blind for about 10 minutes in a preheated oven at 190°C (375°F, gas 5). Remove the paper and baking beans and cook for a further 3–5 minutes. Cool on a wire rack. Sieve the macerated strawberries and gradually beat the purée into 125 g (4½ oz, ½ cup) unsalted butter. Fill the tartlet cases with this mixture and top with 175 g (6 oz, 1 cup) strawberries. Decorate with sprigs of mint and serve with a sweetened redcurrant coulis.

Strawberry tart

Sort, wash and hull 1 kg (2¼ lb, 7½ cups) strawberries. Put them in an earthenware bowl and sprinkle with the juice of 1 lemon and 50 g (2 oz, ¼ cup) caster (superfine) sugar. Prepare short pastry using 300 g (11 oz, 2¾ cups) plain (all-purpose) flour, 150 g (5 oz, ⅔ cup) softened butter, a pinch of salt and 2 tablespoons water. Roll it into a ball and leave it in a cool place for 2 hours. Then roll out the pastry and use it to line a buttered and floured 28 cm (11 in) tart tin (pie pan). Prick the base with a fork and bake blind. When the tart is cool, fill it with the strawberries. Mix 60 ml (2 fl oz, ¼ cup) redcurrant jelly with the juice drained from the strawberries and pour this syrup over the tart. The top can be decorated with whipped cream.

Tangerine gâteau

Grind 125 g (4½ oz, 1 cup) shelled almonds in a mortar and add 4 eggs, one by one. Add 4 pieces of candied tangerine peel, finely chopped, as well as 125 g (4½ oz, ⅔ cup) icing (confectioner's) sugar, 3 drops vanilla essence (extract), 2 drops bitter almond essence and 2 tablespoons apricot jam (preserve), strained through a fine sieve. Stir well. Roll some shortcrust pastry (basic pie dough) to line a flan ring (pie pan) mould. Spread a layer of tangerine compote on the bottom and cover with the almond mixture. Smooth the top. Bake in a preheated oven at 200°C (400°F, gas 6) for about 30 minutes. Take out of the oven and allow to cool. Press 3 tablespoons apricot compote through a sieve and spread over the top of the cake. Decorate with a few fresh mint leaves, quarters of tangerine cut in half horizontally, and flaked (slivered) almonds, briefly grilled (broiled) to colour them. Put in a cool place. Before serving, place the cake on a serving dish and cut a few slices so as to reveal the inside.

• *individual tangerine barquettes:* instead of making a large gâteau, line barquette or boat-shaped moulds with the pastry and fill as above. Reduce the cooking time to about 20 minutes. Decorate with flaked almonds. Serve with a scoop of tangerine sorbet or ice cream on a strawberry or raspberry coulis feathered with fine lines of single (light) cream.

Tarte au citron

Prepare a short pastry using 200 g (7 oz, 1¾ cups) plain (all-purpose) flour, 100 g (4 oz, ½ cup) butter, 4 tablespoons caster (superfine) sugar, 1 egg and a pinch of salt. Use it to line a well-buttered baking tin (pan).

Break 2 eggs into a mixing bowl containing 50 g (2 oz, ¼ cup) caster sugar and beat the mixture until it turns white. Remove the outer peel (zest) from a lemon and chop it finely; squeeze the juice from the pulp. To the eggs and sugar, add 100 g (4 oz, 1 cup) ground almonds, the lemon peel and the juice. Mix well. Fill the pastry case (shell) with this cream and bake in a preheated oven at 190°C (375°F, gas 5) for at least 30 minutes.

Meanwhile, wash 2 lemons and slice them very thinly. Place in a saucepan 200 g (7 oz, 1 cup) sugar, 250 ml (8 fl oz, 1 cup) water and 1 tablespoon vanilla-flavoured sugar. Cook for 10 minutes, then add the lemon slices and cook for a further 10 minutes. Leave to cool completely before using them and some glacé (candied) cherries to decorate the cooled tart.

Tarte Tatin

Mix 200 g (7 oz, scant 1 cup) sugar with 225 g (8 oz, 1 cup) butter. Smear this over the bottom and sides of a 23 cm (9 in) tarte Tatin tin (pan) or flameproof shallow baking tin or dish.

Peel and core 800 g (1¾ lb) apples and cut them into quarters or wedges, if large. Trim the pointed ends off the pieces of apple, then arrange them in concentric circles in the tin, adding the trimmed-off corners to fill in the gaps. When the apples are neatly packed in place, cook over a fairly high heat until the butter and sugar form a golden caramel. The mixture will rise as it boils and coat the apples: remove the tin from the heat to prevent it from boiling over. Leave until completely cold.

Make about 350 g (12 oz) shortcrust pastry (basic pie dough), roll it into a ball, and leave it in a cool place for 2 hours. (Alternatively, puff pastry can be used.) Roll out the pastry into a circle 3 mm (⅛ in) thick. Cover the apples with the pastry, tucking it inside the edge of the tin so the fruit is contained. Bake in a preheated oven at 200°C (400°F, gas 6) for 20–30 minutes.

Place a serving dish on top of the tin and turn the tart upside down. Remove the tin. Serve warm, with crème fraîche.

Three tatins with fresh pineapple and kiwi coulis

Cut 3 large fresh pineapples into quarters, then into slices 3 mm (⅛ in) thick. Make a brown caramel sauce with 125 g (4½ oz, ½ cup) caster (superfine) sugar and 60 ml (2 fl oz, ¼ cup) cold water. Pour the mixture into 18 tatin moulds or shallow individual tart tins (pans). Allow to cool, then fill with pieces of pineapple, gently pressing them down. Put a knob of butter and a pinch of sugar on top of each. Cook in a preheated oven at 200°C (400°F, gas 6) for 10 minutes. Remove from oven, and cool slightly, then cover with puff-pastry lids of the same size as the mould. Continue cooking at 220°C (425°F, gas 7) for about 15 minutes, or until the pastry is cooked.

Meanwhile, peel 6 kiwis and carefully crush the flesh. Press this purée through a sieve and add the juice of 1 lemon. Remove the small tatins from their moulds when cold. Pour kiwi coulis in the centre of each plate and arrange three tatins around it. Add a few pieces of fresh fruit and a spoonful of pineapple sorbet in the middle. Decorate with a sprig of fresh mint.

Timbales élysée

Prepare 8 pastry cups from a short biscuit-type (cookie-type) pastry made by thoroughly blending 100 g (4 oz, 1 cup) plain (all-purpose) flour, 100 g (4 oz, ½ cup) sugar, 1 egg and 50 g (2 oz, ¼ cup) rather soft butter. Flavour with vanilla. Divide the dough into 8, then roll into very thin rounds and arrange on a buttered and floured baking sheet. Bake in a preheated oven at 200°C (400°F, gas 6) for 6–8 minutes.

While the pastry rounds are still hot, mould each of them into a cup shape. Place a small slice of sponge cake soaked in a kirsch-flavoured syrup at the bottom of each pastry cup. Add a spoonful of vanilla ice cream and cover with fresh fruit, such as strawberries or raspberries. Coat this with a spoonful of kirsch-flavoured redcurrant jelly, then pipe rosettes of Chantilly cream round the inside edge of the cup.

Cover each of the filled cups with a cage of spun sugar: cook 200 g (7 oz, scant 1 cup) sugar and 40 g (1½ oz, ¼ cup) glucose to the 'hard crack' stage. Thread this sugar in a delicate lattice over the bowl of a ladle. Slide the sugar cage off the ladle when set.

Tourons

Pound 250 g (9 oz, 2 cups) blanched almonds with 2 egg whites; add 200 g (7 oz, 1 cup) caster (superfine) sugar and knead on a marble worktop. Sprinkle with 2 tablespoons icing (confectioner's) sugar and roll out to a thickness of 5 mm (¼ in). Mix 100 g (4 oz, 1 cup) chopped pistachios with 200 g (7 oz, 1 cup) caster sugar and the zest of ½ an orange, very finely chopped. Add 100 g (4 oz) royal icing (frosting) and 2 eggs. Mix with a spatula and spread evenly over the almond paste. Cut into circles or rings and arrange on a buttered and floured baking sheet. Dry in a very cool oven.

Trois-frères

Make 250 g (9 oz) *pâte sablée*. Put 7 whole eggs into a heatproof basin and whisk on the hob (stove top), over hot water, with 250 g (9 oz, 1 cup) caster (superfine) sugar. When the mixture is thick and creamy, pour in 225 g (8 oz, 2 cups) rice flour, 200 g (7 oz, 1 cup) melted butter and 2 tablespoons Maraschino or rum. Mix thoroughly, then pour into a well-buttered trois-frères mould. Roll out the dough to a round shape 5 mm (¼ in) thick and a little larger than the mould. Place on a buttered and floured baking sheet. Bake both the pastry dough and the egg mixture in a preheated oven at 200°C (400°F, gas 6) at the same time, the former for 45 minutes and the latter for 20 minutes. Remove from the oven, turn out of the mould and allow to cool. Set the crown-shaped cake on the pastry base, cover generously with apricot syrup, sprinkle with chopped shredded (slivered) almonds and decorate with diamond shapes of candied angelica.

Vanilla mille-feuille with a strawberry coulis

Prepare 3 rounds of puff pastry 22 cm (8½ in) in diameter and bake in a preheated oven at 220°C (425°F, gas 7) for 15 minutes. Bring to the boil 1 litre

(1¾ pints, 4⅓ cups) milk with 2 vanilla pods (beans), slit open and scraped. Mix 10 egg yolks with 150 g (5 oz, 1¼ cups) icing (confectioner's) sugar. Add 50 g (2 oz, ½ cup) plain (all-purpose) flour, 50 g (2 oz, ¼ cup) custard powder and 2 teaspoons cornflour (cornstarch). Add the milk and stir well. Simmer gently for 2 minutes, stirring all the time. Allow to cool. Then place in the refrigerator.

Soften 200 g (7 oz, 1 cup) butter and whisk in the custard mixture. Spread a layer of this mixture on one of the pastry rounds. Place the second round of pastry on top and spread another layer of creamy mixture on it before covering it with the third round. Sprinkle the latter lightly with icing sugar. Crush 500 g (18 oz, 3½ cups) strawberries with a whisk or in a blender or food processor, adding the juice of ½ a lemon and 100 g (4 oz, 1 cup) icing sugar. Serve with the mille-feuille.

Walnut and honey tartlets

Line some greased tartlet tins (pans) with shortcrust pastry (basic pie dough). Sprinkle them with crushed walnuts and arrange some narrow strips of pastry in a crisscross pattern on the top. Brush with beaten egg and bake in a preheated oven at 220°C (425°F, gas 7) for about 15 minutes. When they are cooked, coat them with acacia honey.

Sweet breads

Bireweck

Cook 500 g (18 oz) pears, 250 g (9 oz) apples, 250 g (9 oz) peaches, 250 g (9 oz) dried figs and 250 g (9 oz) prunes in a little water, but do not allow them to become pulpy. Mix 1 kg (2¼ lb, 9 cups) sifted plain (all-purpose) flour and 25 g (1 oz, 4 packets) easy-blend dried yeast with enough hand-hot cooking water from the fruit to form a soft dough. Leave to rise until doubled in size. Meanwhile, finely dice 100 g (4 oz, ⅔ cup) candied citron and 50 g (2 oz, ⅓ cup) angelica. When the dough has risen, mix in the diced candied fruit, 250 g (9 oz, 1½ cups) sultanas (golden raisins), 125 g (4½ oz, ¾ cup) hazelnuts, 125 g (4½ oz, ¾ cup) almonds, 125 g (4½ oz, 1 cup) walnuts, 50 g (2 oz) blanched strips of orange zest, 125 g (4½ oz, ¾ cup) stoned (pitted) dates, and the drained cooked fruit. Add 200 ml (7 fl oz, ¾ cup) kirsch and mix well. Divide the dough into 200 g (7 oz) portions (about 28). Shape into rolls and smooth the surface with water. Place on a greased baking sheet, cover loosely and leave to rise until doubled in size. Bake in a preheated oven at 160°C (325°F, gas 3) for about 1¾ hours.

Bottereaux

Stir together 20 g (¾ oz, 1½ cakes) fresh (compressed) yeast and 100 ml (4 fl oz, 7 tablespoons) slightly warm milk. Put in a food processor 400 g (14 oz, 3½ cups) strong plain (bread) flour, a pinch of salt, 3 tablespoons caster (superfine) sugar and 2 tablespoons rum. Add the yeast mixture and process thoroughly to form a dough. Roll out to a thickness of 5 mm (¼ in). Distribute 125 g (4½ oz, ½ cup) butter cut into small pieces evenly over the surface. Fold the dough in two and roll out evenly, then work the dough again to incorporate the butter. Roll into a ball, flatten and roll into a ball again. Leave to rise for 3 hours. Roll out the dough very thinly, about 3 mm (⅛ in) and cut out the shapes with a pastry (cookie) cutter. Fry them in very hot oil, then drain on paper towels before dusting with icing (confectioner's) sugar.

Brioche à tête (Parisian brioche)

Lightly flour the hands and the worktop (work surface), then divide 275 g (10 oz) brioche dough into 2 balls, 225 g (8 oz) for the body of the brioche and the remaining 50 g (2 oz) for the head. Roll the large ball by hand until it is perfectly round. Butter a 500 ml (17 fl oz, 2 cup) brioche mould and place the larger ball inside it. Roll the small ball of dough into a pear shape. Make a hole in the top of the large ball and insert the pointed end of the small ball; press down with the fingertips. Allow to double in volume at room temperature, for about 1½ hours.

Make some small incisions in the large ball, from the edges towards the head, using wet scissors. Brush the brioche with beaten egg and bake in a preheated oven at 200°C (400°F, gas 6) for 30 minutes. Turn out of the mould while still warm.

- *Individual Parisian brioches* These are made in the same way as the large brioches, using small brioche moulds. Bake in a preheated oven at 225°C (425°F, gas 7), but allow only 15 minutes for cooking.

Brioche bordelaise

Lightly flour the worktop (work surface). Place 300 g (11 oz) brioche dough (classic or standard) on the floured surface and flatten with the hand to make a thick disc. Finely chop 65 g (2½ oz, ½ cup) crystallized (candied) fruit and distribute it evenly over the surface of the dough. Bring the edges of the dough to the centre to form a ball. Place the ball of dough on a buttered baking sheet and leave it to rest for 10 minutes. Push both thumbs into the centre of the ball and pull the dough gently into the shape of a ring. When the hole is about 10 cm (4 in) in diameter, leave to rest for about 1½ hours.

Brush the ring with beaten egg. Crush 12 sugar lumps with a rolling pin. Using scissors dipped in water, cut 5 mm (¼ in) deep sloping notches into the surface of the ring. Bake in a preheated oven at 200°C (400°F, gas 6) for at least 30 minutes, then take the brioche out of the oven and decorate with whole crystallized (candied) fruits and crushed sugar.

Brioche mousseline

Cut 2 pieces of foil twice the height of a cylindrical 1 litre (1¾ pint, 4⅓ cup) mould. Line the mould with the double thickness of foil shaped into a cylinder. Butter the bottom of the mould and the full height of the foil. Place a 300 g (11 oz) ball of fine brioche dough in the mould and leave to rise at room temperature until it comes to 1 cm (½ in) below the top of the mould.

Brush the surface with a beaten egg and make 2–4 cross-shaped incisions in the top of the dough using a pair of wetted scissors. Bake in a preheated oven at 200°C (400°F, gas 6) for about 30 minutes. Turn out while still warm.

Brioche polonaise

Make a brioche weighing about 800 g (1¾ lb). Steep 200 g (7 oz, ¾ cup) diced crystallized (candied) fruit in kirsch. Make a syrup with 200 g (7 oz, ¾ cup) granulated sugar, 250 ml (8 fl oz, 1 cup) water and a liqueur glass kirsch. Prepare a confectioner's custard (pastry cream) with 50 g (2 oz, ½ cup) plain (all-purpose) flour, 4 egg yolks, 100 g (4 oz, ½ cup) caster (superfine) sugar, 1 teaspoon vanilla sugar and 500 ml (17 fl oz, 2 cups) milk. Mix 40 g (1½ oz, 3 tablespoons) butter with the custard, then incorporate the drained fruit.

Cut the brioche horizontally into slices, after removing the top. Dip the slices in the syrup and spread each with a thick layer of the fruit custard. Reshape the brioche and put the top back in position. Stiffly whisk 4 egg whites, incorporating 50 g (2 oz, ¼ cup) caster sugar. Completely cover the brioche with the meringue, then sprinkle with icing (confectioner's) sugar – no more than 2 tablespoons – and scatter about 100 g (4 oz, 1 cup) shredded (slivered) almonds over the surface. Brown in a preheated oven at 230°C (450°F, gas 8) for 5 minutes. Cool completely before serving.

Brioche with pralines

Make some leavening dough with 250 g (9 oz, 2¼ cups) strong (bread) flour and 20 g (¾ oz) fresh yeast (1½ cakes compressed yeast) or 2 teaspoons dried yeast dissolved in 150 ml (¼ pint, ⅔ cup) warm water. Roll this dough, which will be fairly soft, into a ball and leave it to rise for at least 30 minutes; it should double in volume.

In the meantime, mix together 800 g (1¾ lb, 7 cups) plain (all-purpose) flour, 1 tablespoon salt, 65 g (2½ oz, 5 tablespoons) sugar and 6 whole eggs. Knead vigorously and then add 900 g (2 lb, 4 cups) good-quality softened butter, a little at a time. Then mix in the leaven and roll the dough into a ball again. Leave this to rise at room temperature for 6–7 hours.

Mix some pink pralines (or candied rose petals) into the dough, then put it into a large brioche mould and bake in a preheated oven at 200°C (400°F, gas 6) for about 1 hour. When cooked, decorate the surface of the brioche with a few crushed pralines.

Brioche with raspberries

Make a large brioche mousseline and allow to cool completely. Slice off the top and scoop out the inside, leaving a thickness of about 1 cm (½ in) at the bottom and sides. Add some kirsch to melted butter and sprinkle this mixture over the inside of the brioche; fill with a mixture of raspberries and whipped cream. (Wild strawberries may be used instead of raspberries.)

Alternatively, the brioche may be filled with confectioner's custard (pastry cream) lightened with whipped cream and mixed with stoned (pitted) cherries, poached in syrup and drained.

Buns

Crumble 25 g (1 oz, 2 cakes) fresh (compressed) yeast into a bowl, then gradually stir in 250 ml (8 fl oz, 1 cup) lukewarm milk. Cover and leave at room temperature until frothy. Mix 675 g (1½ lb, 6 cups) strong plain (bread) flour with 1 teaspoon salt and the grated zest of 1 lemon. Rub in 125 g (4½ oz, ½ cup) butter, then stir in 125 g (4½ oz, ¾ cup) raisins. Make a well in the dry ingredients. Add 500 ml (17 fl oz, 2 cups) lukewarm milk, 1 beaten egg and the yeast mixture. Gradually mix the dry ingredients into the liquid to make a dough. Knead for about 10 minutes, until smooth and elastic.

Place the dough in a bowl, cover with a cloth and leave in a warm place until doubled in volume (about 5 hours). Divide the dough into balls about the size of a tangerine. Place on a greased large baking sheet, brush them with butter, cover with tented foil and allow to rise for a further 5 hours or until 2½ times their original size. Bake in a preheated oven at 200°C (400°F, gas 6) for 20 minutes. Meanwhile, heat 250 ml (8 fl oz, 1 cup) milk with 1 tablespoon sugar and bring to the boil. A few minutes before they are cooked, brush the buns with the syrup and return them to the oven. Cool on a wire rack.

Christmas pompes

Pompe is a sweet or savoury pastry, popular in many parts of Auvergne, Lyon and Provence. In Auvergne, *pompe* (or *pompo*) *aux pommes* is a traditional dish for family celebrations, Christmas and Easter. It is made of buttery rough puff or flaky pastry, spiced with cinnamon and filled with jam (preserve), plums or even cream cheese. In Provence, *pompe à l'huile* is a flat Christmas cake of leavened dough made with olive oil, flavoured with orange-flower water, lemon zest or saffron, and sometimes studded with sugared almonds (dragées). The *pompe à l'huile* is an essential element of the 13 desserts of the Provençal Christmas, which are eaten with mulled wine.

Place 1 kg (2¼ lb, 9 cups) plain (all-purpose) flour in a bowl and add 250 g (9 oz) bread-dough leaven cut into small pieces, 250 g (9 oz, 1½ cups, firmly packed) brown sugar, ½ teaspoon salt, 4 tablespoons olive oil and 3–4 whole eggs. Mix well. Add the grated zest of an orange and a lemon. Knead the dough thoroughly and 'throw' it on the table. When it is very soft, roll the dough into a ball, wrap it in an oiled plastic bag and leave to rise in a warm, draught-free place for about 6 hours. Knead the dough again, divide into 8 pieces and shape into crowns. Place the crowns on a buttered cloth and leave for a further 2 hours. Then place in a preheated oven at 230°C (450°F, gas 8) and bake for 25 minutes. Remove from the oven, moisten with orange-flower water and return to the oven for 5 minutes with the oven door left open.

Dampfnudeln

A sweet dessert, made in Germany and Alsace, consisting of rounds of leavened dough baked in the oven and served either with compote, fruits in syrup, jam (preserve) or vanilla cream, and dusted with sugar and cinnamon.

Prepare a starter dough. Cream 15 g (½ oz, 1 cake) fresh (compressed) yeast in 200 ml (7 fl oz, 1 cup) warm milk until dissolved, or sprinkle 1½ teaspoons dried yeast over the milk and stir until dissolved. Leave in a warm place until frothy. Then mix into 125 g (4½ oz, 1 cup) strong plain (bread) flour. Leave this starter in a warm place until doubled in volume.

Now gradually work into the dough 100 g (4 oz, ½ cup) melted butter, a pinch of salt, the grated zest of 1 lemon, 5 egg yolks, 100 g (4 oz, ½ cup) caster (superfine) sugar and 375 g (13 oz, 3¼ cups) strong plain flour. Roll out with a rolling pin and leave to rest for 5 minutes. Cut the dough into rounds and leave to rise in a warm place for 1 hour. Brush with melted butter, dust with icing (confectioner's) sugar and bake in a preheated oven at 180°C (350°F, gas 4), for about 15 minutes until lightly browned.

Doughnuts

Mix 15 g (½ oz, 1 cake) fresh (compressed) yeast with 150 ml (¼ pint, ⅔ cup) warm milk. (Alternatively, use 1½ teaspoons dried yeast.) Put 500 g (18 oz, 4½ cups) strong white (bread) flour, 100–125 g (4–4½ oz, ½ cup) caster (superfine) sugar, a generous pinch of salt and ½ teaspoon grated nutmeg into a large bowl. Make a well in the centre and mix a beaten egg with the dry ingredients as thoroughly as possible. Add 2 more eggs, one at a time. Work 65 g (2½ oz, 5 tablespoons) melted butter into the mixture, then add the warm yeast mixture. Knead the dough until it becomes elastic. Leave to rise until doubled in size.

Roll out the dough on a floured surface to a thickness of about 1 cm (½ in) and cut it into rounds with a pastry (cookie) cutter 6 cm (2½ in) in diameter. Fry the doughnuts in hot fat – at least 185°C (365°F) – until they swell up and become golden brown. Drain on paper towels, dust with caster sugar and serve hot with maple syrup or a cranberry compote.

Dresden stollen

Similar to brioche and made with dried fruits, this is a German speciality traditionally eaten at Christmas. There are several recipes, the best known being that from Dresden. Some stollens have a filling of marzipan.

Make a well in the centre of 800 g (1¾ lb, 7 cups) sifted plain (all-purpose) flour. Add 20 g (¾ oz, 1½ cakes) fresh (compressed) yeast, 1 table-spoon caster (superfine) sugar and 250 ml (8 fl oz, 1 cup) warm milk. When bubbles form in the mixture, knead it thoroughly, incorporating the flour to make a smooth dough. Cover with a cloth and leave to rise in a warm place free from draughts.

Soak 200 g (7 oz, 1⅓ cups) currants in 3 tablespoons rum. Soften 500 g (18 oz, 2¼ cups) butter at room temperature, then beat it with 150 g (5 oz, ⅔ cup) granulated sugar and 3 eggs until light and creamy; add the currants and the rum, 200 g (7 oz, 1⅓ cups) chopped mixed candied peel, a pinch of powdered vanilla or a few drops of vanilla essence (extract) and 1 teaspoon grated lemon rind (zest).

Add this mixture to the dough with just enough milk to keep it soft but not sticky. Knead the dough well, knocking it back several times, as for brioche dough, and leave to rise under a cloth. When the dough has doubled in size, turn on to a floured work surface, stretch it into a thick sausage shape and fold it in half lengthways. Put on a buttered baking sheet and leave to rise again for 15 minutes in a warm place. Brush with clarified butter and bake in a preheated oven at 180°C (350°F, gas 4) for 50 minutes.

When cooked, brush again with clarified butter, dust with icing (con-fectioner's) sugar and leave to cool before serving.

Fouace

Also known as fouasse or fougasse, these are among France's oldest pastries. They were originally pancakes made of fine wheat, unleavened and cooked under the cinders in the hearth. Nowadays they are usually rustic dough cakes baked in the oven, sometimes salted and flavoured, and usually made for Christmas or Twelfth Night.

Dissolve 15 g (½ oz, 1 cake) fresh (compressed) yeast in a few tablespoons of warm milk or water. Add 125 g (4½ oz, 1 cup) strong plain (bread) flour and then enough milk or water to make a slightly soft dough. Cover the dough with a damp cloth or greased cling film (plastic wrap) and leave to rise until it has doubled in volume. Heap 375 g (13 oz, 3¼ cups) strong plain flour on a work surface. Make a well in the centre and add a large pinch of salt, 100 g (4 oz, ½ cup) softened butter, 1 liqueur glass of rum, brandy or orange-flower water, 4 tablespoons sugar (optional) and 4 beaten eggs. Knead together, adding a little milk or water to obtain a smooth dough. Add the risen dough and (if wished) 150–200 g (5–7 oz, 1¼ cups) crystallized (candied) fruits. Work the dough until it is elastic. Knead it into a ball, cut a cross in the top and leave it to rise, loosely covered until doubled in volume.

Place the fouace on a lightly buttered baking sheet, in a ball, loaf or crown shape. Glaze with beaten egg and bake in a preheated oven at 230°C (450°F, gas 8) for about 40 minutes or until golden; when the dough is cooked through, the base should sound hollow when tapped.

Fruit brioche

Toss prepared and diced seasonal fruit (such as peaches and pears, plums and apricots, or plums and pears) in the juice of 1 lemon. Sprinkle with a little sugar and pour a little fruit liqueur or suitable spirit over and mix well. Cover and set aside to macercate. Prepare frangipane cream and leave to cool.

Line a large mould or individual round moulds or tins (pans) with brioche dough. Spread with frangipane cream, leaving a border around the edge. Drain the fruit (reserve the soaking liquor for a fruit coulis to serve with the brioche) and arrange it in a layer on top of the frangipane cream. Cover with brioche dough, pressing the edges together to seal in the filling, then leave to rise in a warm place for about 1 hour, until doubled in size.

Brush the brioche or brioches with beaten egg and bake until golden. A large brioche will take about 30 minutes in a preheated oven at 200°C (400°F, gas 6); individual brioches will take about 15 minutes in a preheated oven at 220°C (425°F, gas 7). Dust with icing (confectioner's) sugar and serve hot, decorated with pieces of fresh fruit. Fruit coulis goes well with the brioche – prepare it using the same type of fruit as in the filling and flavour the coulis with the reserved soaking liquor.

Fruit croûtes

Cut a slightly stale savarin into slices 1 cm (½ in) thick. Place these slices on a baking sheet, dust them with fine sugar and glaze them in a preheated oven at 230°C (450°F, gas 8). Reassemble the savarin on a large round dish, alternating the croûtes with slices of canned pineapple. Place around this crown, alternately, quarters of pears and apples, cooked in vanilla-flavoured syrup and well drained. Fill the inside of the crown with a salpicon of various fruits cooked in syrup and drained. Decorate the top with glacé (candied) cherries, angelica lozenges, quarters of crystallized (candied) apricots, small golden and green preserved oranges and halved almonds. Warm the crown in a preheated oven at 150°C (300°F, gas 2).

When ready to serve, coat it with apricot sauce flavoured with rum or kirsch, and serve more of this sauce separately. Croûtes containing other types of fruit cooked in syrup (apricot, peach, pear, plum, nectarine) are prepared in the same way.

Fruit savarin

Melt 50 g (2 oz, ¼ cup) butter. In a bowl, mix 125 g (4½ oz, 1 cup) strong plain (bread) flour, a good pinch of salt, 15 g (½ oz, 1 tablespoon) sugar and 1 egg. Dissolve 7 g (¼ oz, ½ cake) fresh (compressed) yeast in 1 tablespoon lukewarm water and add to the dough. Add another egg and work the dough by hand, using a combination of kneading and beating in the bowl, slapping the mixture from the palm of the hand against the side of the bowl. The mixture should be light, smooth and elastic. Beat in the melted butter by hand until well blended. Pour the batter into a buttered savarin mould, 20–23 cm (8–9 in) in diameter, and leave to rise in a warm place for 30 minutes.

Bake in a preheated oven at 200°C (400°F, gas 6) for 20–25 minutes. Turn out on to a wire rack and leave to cool. Pour some rum-flavoured syrup over it. Peel 2 white peaches, 1 pear, 1 orange and 1 banana. Dice the fruit and sprinkle with the juice of ½ a lemon. Wash a small bunch of seedless green grapes, about 75 g (3 oz, ½ cup). Clean 50 g (2 oz, ½ cup) raspberries and 50 g (2 oz, ⅓ cup) wild strawberries (if available). Wash and hull 50 g (2 oz, ½ cup) large strawberries. Put all this fruit in a bowl, pour over the rest of the syrup used to soak the savarin, and leave to steep for 1 hour. Melt 200 g (7 oz, ⅔ cup) apricot jam (preserve) over a low heat and coat the savarin with it. Fill the centre of the savarin with some of the fruit and serve the rest separately.

Kouing-aman

The name of this flat yeasted Breton cake from the Douarnenez region means 'bread and butter'.

Dissolve 15 g (½ oz, 1 cake) fresh (compressed) yeast in 2 tablespoons warm water and mix with 50 g (2 oz, ½ cup) plain (all-purpose) flour. Cover with a cloth and leave to rise in a warm place. When its volume has doubled, sift 200 g (7 oz, 1¾ cups) plain flour and a pinch of salt into a bowl and add the yeast, kneading with the tips of the fingers and adding just enough water to obtain a pliable dough. Knead well, then leave to rise again in a warm place.

When its volume has doubled, place it on a floured working surface and roll it into a large circle. Dot the surface with 125 g (4½ oz, ½ cup) softened butter cut into pieces and sprinkle with 50 g (2 oz, ¼ cup) caster (superfine) sugar. Fold the dough into three, roll it out and fold it again into three. Leave it for 15 minutes. Roll it out into a circle again, fold it into three and leave it to rest. Repeat the operation once more.

Shape the dough into a circle about 23 cm (9 in) in diameter and put it into a buttered and floured flan tin (pie pan). Score the top of the dough with diamond shapes and brush with egg. Bake in a preheated oven at 240°C (475°F, gas 9) for about 20 minutes, basting the top occasionally with the butter that will run out of the dough. Sprinkle with icing (confectioner's) sugar and continue to bake until the cake is cooked (it should still be fairly moist inside). Unmould straightaway and serve warm.

Kugelhopf

A yeast cake from Alsace, of Austrian origin, containing raisins or currants and cooked in a special high, crownlike mould.

Soak 40 g (1½ oz, ¼ cup) currants in a little warm tea and soften 175 g (6 oz, ¾ cup) butter at room temperature. Mix 25 g (1 oz, 2 cakes) fresh (compressed) yeast with 3 tablespoons warm milk, add 90 g (3½ oz, scant 1 cup) strong plain (bread) flour and mix well. Add just enough warm milk to obtain a soft dough. Shape the dough into a ball, put it in a bowl, mark a cross on the top with a knife, cover it with a cloth and leave it to rise in a warm place, away from draughts.

Sift 250 g (9 oz, 2¼ cups) strong plain (bread) flour into a heap on the working surface, make a well in the centre and into this put 2 eggs and 1 tablespoon warm water. Mix these ingredients and knead the dough well. Dissolve 3 tablespoons caster (superfine) sugar and 1 teaspoon salt in a little water and add this to the mixture, together with the softened butter. Finally add 2 more eggs, one at a time, continuing to knead the dough. Roll this out on the board, put the yeast mixture on top, then mix it together by gathering the dough up, kneading it on the board and then repeating the procedure. Finally, add the currants. Put the dough into a bowl, cover it with a cloth and leave it to rise in a warm place until it has doubled in volume.

Butter a *kugelhopf* mould and sprinkle the inside with 100 g (4 oz, 1 cup) shredded almonds. When the dough is ready, shape it into a long sausage and put it into the mould, turning the mould as the dough is fed in (it should half-fill the mould). Leave it to rise again in a warm place until the dough reaches the top of the mould. Bake in a preheated oven at 200°C (400°F, gas 6) for at least 40 minutes. Unmould the *kugelhopf* on to a wire rack. When it is completely cold, sprinkle it lightly with icing (confectioner's) sugar.

Merveilles

Make a dough with 500 g (18 oz, 4½ cups) plain (all-purpose) flour, 4 lightly beaten eggs, 150 g (5 oz, ⅔ cup) softened butter, a generous pinch of salt, 2 tablespoons sugar and 1 liqueur glass of orange-flower water, rum or Cognac. Roll the dough into a ball and leave it to stand for at least 2 hours, covered with a cloth. Roll it out to a thickness of about 5 mm (¼ in) and cut it into various shapes with fluted pastry (cookie) cutters. Deep-fry in oil at 175°C (347°F) until golden brown. Drain on paper towels, sprinkle with a mixture of icing (confectioner's) sugar and vanilla-flavoured sugar, and pile up on the serving dish.

Panettone

A large, round Italian cake which is a speciality of the city of Milan but is made anywhere between Milan and Venice. Panettone is made from a raised dough enriched with egg yolks (which give it its colour) and contains raisins and candied orange and lemon peel. The dough is traditionally kneaded three times a day for several days to give the characteristic light texture, then it is placed in a cool oven to rise and cooked in a cylindrical mould. Traditional Christmas fare, this cake is also eaten for breakfast, with coffee, and it is sometimes served as a dessert, accompanied by a liqueur wine.

Mix 3 tablespoons water, 50 g (2 oz, ¼ cup) butter and 75 g (3 oz, ½ cup) soft brown sugar in a saucepan and place over a moderate heat, making sure the mixture does not come to the boil. Sift 300 g (11 oz, 2¾ cups) plain (all-purpose) flour and 20 g (¾ oz, 3 packages) dried yeast at least four times. Put into a mixing bowl. Add 25 g (1 oz, 2 tablespoons) raisins and 50 g (2 oz, ⅓ cup) diced candied citron peel. Mix together thoroughly and incorporate 2 egg yolks. Slowly add the melted butter mixture. Work the dough thoroughly with a wooden spoon until it leaves the sides of the bowl. Then place the dough on a lightly floured work surface and knead it for another 1–2 minutes. Mould the dough into the typical dome shape of panettone, making an incision in the shape of a square with a cross in the middle. Leave to rest in a warm place for 30 minutes. Bake in a preheated oven at 180°C (350°F, gas 4) for 45 minutes, wrapping the panettone in foil for the first part of the cooking process to prevent the dough from spreading. Just before the end of the cooking, spray a little water over the incision in the panettone, which will give it a glossy surface.

Pastis bourrit

In south-western France, the term *pastis* is used to refer to various pastries.

Make some leaven with 25 g (1 oz, ¼ cup) plain (all-purpose) flour, 7 g (¼ oz, ½ cake) fresh (compressed) yeast and 100 ml (4 fl oz, 7 tablespoons) water. Leave to rise. Make a well in 1 kg (2¼ lb, 9 cups) plain flour in a very deep mixing bowl and add 150 g (5 oz, ⅔ cup) melted butter, a pinch of salt, 250 g (9 oz, 1 cup) sugar, 6 egg yolks, 4 teaspoons vanilla sugar and

3 tablespoons rum or anisette cordial. Stir and add 7 g (¼ oz, ½ cake) fresh (compressed) yeast and the leaven. Beat everything well. Whisk 6 egg whites into stiff peaks and add to the dough. Leave to rise.

When the dough has doubled in size, butter some moulds, half-fill them with dough (this quantity of dough is enough for 2 or 3 pastis) and leave to rise to the top. Cook in a preheated oven at 220°C (425°F, gas 7) for 45 minutes until the pastis are golden. Serve with caramel custard. Sliced and toasted, it may also be served with fois gras.

Pogne de romans

Also known as *pognon* or *pougnon*, this is a type of brioche that is sometimes filled with crystallized (candied) fruit and served either hot or cold

Arrange 500 g (18 oz, 4½ cups) plain (all-purpose) flour in a circle on the worktop. In the middle of this circle put 1½ teaspoons salt, 1 tablespoon orange-flower water, 25 g (1 oz, 2 cakes) fresh (compressed) yeast, 250 g (9 oz, 1 cup) softened butter and 4 whole eggs. Mix together thoroughly, working the dough vigorously to give it body. Add 2 more eggs, one after the other, and finally incorporate 200 g (7 oz, ¾ cup) caster (superfine) sugar, little by little, kneading the dough all the while. Place this dough in a bowl sprinkled with flour, cover with a cloth and leave it to rise for 10–12 hours at room temperature away from draughts.

Turn the dough out on to the table and knock it back with the flat of the hand. Make into 'crowns': shape two-thirds of the dough into balls, then use the remainder to shape smaller balls to place on top, like brioches. Place these crowns in buttered baking tins (pans). Leave the dough to rise for a further 30 minutes in a warm place. Brush with beaten egg and bake in a preheated oven at 190°C (375°F, gas 5) for about 40 minutes. Serve with redcurrant jelly.

Rolled brioche with raisins

Soak 75 g (3 oz, ½ cup) raisins in 4 tablespoons rum. Butter a 20 cm (8 in) Genoese mould (a sponge cake mould with sides sloping outwards towards the top) and line it with 150 g (5 oz) flattened brioche dough. Cover with a thin layer of confectioner's custard (pastry cream). Lightly flour the worktop (work surface). Place 165 g (5½ oz) dough on the floured surface and roll out to a rectangle 20 × 12 cm (7 × 4 in). Cover this rectangle with confectioner's custard, then spread with the drained raisins. Roll the rectangle into a sausage 20 cm (8 in) long and cut into 6 equal portions. Lay these portions flat in the lined mould and leave to rise for 2 hours in a warm place.

Brush over the entire surface of the brioche with beaten egg. Bake for about 30 minutes in a preheatted oven at 200°C (400°F, gas 6). If the brioche colours too quickly, protect it with a sheet of foil. Take the cooked brioche out of the oven, sprinkle with vanilla or rum syrup, then turn out of the mould while still warm. When the brioche is cold, brush with syrup made from 65 g (2½ oz, ½ cup) icing (confectioner's) sugar with 2 tablespoons hot water.

Ruifard

Ruifard is a dessert that is typical of the Dauphiné region of France, particularly the Valbonnais area. It is a large pie made from yeast dough, filled with sliced pears, apples and quinces cooked in butter, and sweetened and flavoured with Chartreuse.

Dissolve 15 g (½ oz) dried yeast (2 packages active dry east) in 2 table-spoons warm water. Sift 250 g (9 oz, 2¼ cups) strong plain (bread) flour into a heap and pour the dissolved yeast into a well in the centre. Mix in a little of the flour to make a thick cream. Leave it to rise for 10 minutes. Then add 1 egg, 20 g (¾ oz, 1½ tablespoons) softened butter, 1 tablespoon oil, 100 ml (4 fl oz, 7 tablespoons) double (heavy) cream, 15 g (½ oz, 1 tablespoon) sugar and ¼ teaspoon salt. Work with the hands to incorporate all the flour and knead until the dough leaves the fingers cleanly, then put it in a bowl and leave to rise for 30 minutes at 25°C (77°F).

Peel and slice 5 large apples, 5 pears and 2 small quinces. Cook them for 10 minutes with 50 g (2 oz, ¼ cup) butter and 150 g (5 oz, ⅔ cup) sugar; flavour with 2 tablespoons Chartreuse. Butter a 20 cm (8 in) sandwich tin (layer cake pan) and roll out half the dough to a thickness of 5 mm (¼ in). Line the base and sides of the tin with this dough and pour in the cooked fruit. Roll out the remaining dough a little more thinly and cover the fruit, sealing the edges with a little cold water.

Leave to rise for a further 10–15 minutes, then brush the surface with egg yolk. Bake in a preheated oven at 190°C (375°F, gas 5) for 30 minutes.

Rum babas

Soak 100 g (4 oz, ¾ cup) raisins in 300 ml (½ pint, 1¼ cups) rum and soften 100 g (4 oz, ½ cup) butter at room temperature. Mix 25 g (1 oz, 2 cakes) fresh (compressed) yeast or 2 teaspoons dried yeast with 2 tablespoons warm water. Make a well in 250 g (9 oz, 2¼ cups) sifted strong plain (bread) flour and add 2 tablespoons sugar, a generous pinch of salt, 2 eggs and the yeast mixture. Mix with a wooden spatula until the ingredients are combined, then add another egg. Work this in, and then add a further egg and work that in. Finally add the softened butter and work the dough until elastic before adding the drained raisins. Reserve the rum from the raisins.

Melt 50 g (2 oz, ¼ cup) butter over a low heat and use to brush the insides of 16 dariole moulds or individual ring moulds. Divide the dough among the moulds. Leave in a warm place until the dough has risen to fill the moulds. Bake in a preheated oven at about 200°C (400°F, gas 6) for 15–20 minutes. Turn the babas out immediately on to a rack and allow to cool.

Prepare a syrup using 1 litre (1¾ pints, 4⅓ cups) water and 500 g (18 oz, 2¼ cups) sugar. Place each baba in the boiling syrup and leave submerged until no more air bubbles are released. Drain and place on a wire rack resting over a dish. When the babas have cooled slightly, soak them in the reserved rum, adding extra rum as necessary to soak the babas generously. As the rum syrup collects in the dish repeatedly spoon it back over the babas to ensure they are very moist.

Serve the babas topped or filled with whipped cream and fresh fruit, such as raspberries. Crème anglaise may be served with the babas: streak the sauce with a little chocolate sauce and add a few rum-soaked raisins for decoration.

Savarin with confectioner's custard

Melt 50 g (2 oz, ¼ cup) butter. In a bowl, mix 125 g (4½ oz, 1 cup) strong plain (bread) flour, a good pinch of salt, 15 g (½ oz, 1 tablespoon) sugar and 1 egg. Dissolve 7 g (¼ oz, ½ cake) fresh (compressed) yeast in 1 tablespoon lukewarm water and add to the dough. Add another egg and work the dough by hand, using a combination of kneading and beating in the bowl, slapping the mixture from the palm of the hand against the side of the bowl. The mixture should be light, smooth and elastic. Beat in the melted butter by hand until well blended. Pour the batter into a buttered savarin mould, 20–23 cm (8–9 in) in diameter, and leave to rise in a warm place for 30 minutes. Bake in a preheated oven at 200°C (400°F, gas 6) for 20–25 minutes. Turn out on to a wire rack and leave to cool. Make a syrup with 500 ml (17 fl oz, 2 cups) water, 250 g (9 oz, 1 cup) sugar and a vanilla pod (bean). Pour the syrup over the savarin. Prepare some confectioner's custard (pastry cream) with 250 ml (8 fl oz, 1 cup) milk, 3 egg yolks, 50 g (2 oz, ¼ cup) sugar, 100 g (4 oz, 1 cup) plain (all-purpose) flour and 2½ tablespoons rum. Spoon into the centre of the savarin and serve well chilled.

Swiss wine tart

Mix 350 g (12 oz, 3 cups) plain (all-purpose) flour, a pinch of salt and 1 tablespoon caster (superfine) sugar. Add 75 g (3 oz, 6 tablespoons) softened butter and 15 g (½ oz, 1 cake) fresh (compressed) yeast mixed with 3 tablespoons milk. Alternatively, sprinkle 1½ teaspoons dried (active dry) yeast over the milk, whisk with a balloon whisk until dissolved and leave in a warm place until frothy before adding it to the other ingredients. Rapidly work the ingredients, then roll the dough into a ball and set aside for 2 hours. Roll it out and use it to line a buttered tart tin (pie pan). Beat 3 eggs with 100 g (4 oz, ½ cup) sugar until the mixture becomes thick and creamy, then add 100 ml (4 fl oz, 7 tablespoons) dry white wine. Pour the mixture into the tart case (shell). Bake in a preheated oven at 220°F (425°F, gas 7) for 20 minutes. Take out the tart, sprinkle with caster sugar and knobs of butter, then return it to the oven for a further 15 minutes. Serve lukewarm.

Tourtes à la mode béarnaise

Melt 500 g (18 oz, 2¼ cups) butter and pour it over 100 g (4 oz, 8 cakes) fresh (compressed) yeast in a bowl. Mix together. Add 500 g (18 oz, 2¼ cups) caster (superfine) sugar, 12 eggs, 1 small glass rum, the grated zest of 2 lemons, a pinch of salt and enough flour to obtain a firm mixture. Leave to rise for 24 hours. Divide into balls and put into buttered moulds. Bake in a preheated oven at 220°C (425°F, gas 7) for about 45 minutes.

BASIC RECIPES & CLASSIC ADDITIONS

Batters

Coating batter

This batter is suitable for coating food before deep-frying. Sift 200 g (7 oz, 1¾ cups) plain (all-purpose) flour into a bowl. Add 2 teaspoons baking powder, 2 tablespoons groundnut (peanut) oil, a pinch of salt and 250 ml (8 fl oz, 1 cup) warm water. Mix the ingredients thoroughly and beat until smooth, then leave the batter to rest in a cool place for at least 1 hour. Just before using, fold in 2 stiffly whisked egg whites.

Fritter batter (1)

Sift 250 g (9 oz, 2¼ cups) plain (all-purpose) flour into a bowl. Heat 200 ml (7 fl oz, ¾ cup) water until lukewarm. Make a well in the flour and add 150 ml (¼ pint, ⅔ cup) beer, the warm water and a generous pinch of salt. Mix, drawing the flour from the sides to the centre. Add 2 tablespoons groundnut (peanut) oil and mix. Leave to rest for 1 hour. When required, stiffly whisk 2 or 3 egg whites and fold into the batter. Do not stir or beat.

For sweet fritters, flavour the batter with Calvados, Cognac or rum. The batter may also be sweetened with 1½ teaspoons sugar and the oil replaced with the same amount of melted butter.

Fritter batter (2)

Put 250 g (9 oz, 2¼ cups) sifted plain (all-purpose) flour in a mixing bowl. Make a well in the centre and add 1 teaspoon salt, 2 whole eggs and 300 ml (½ pint, 1¼ cups) groundnut (peanut) oil. Whisk the eggs and oil together, incorporating a little of the flour. Add 250 ml (8 fl oz, 1 cup) beer and, stirring well, gradually incorporate the rest of the flour. Allow to stand for about 1 hour. A few minutes before using the batter, whisk 3 egg whites stiffly and fold into the batter using a wooden spoon or rubber spatula.

Sweet crêpe batter

Mix 500 g (18 oz, 4½ cups) plain (all-purpose) flour with 1 tablespoon vanilla-flavoured sugar (or a few drops of vanilla extract), 5–6 beaten eggs and a small pinch of salt. Gradually stir in 750 ml (1¼ pints, 3¼ cups) milk and 250 ml (8 fl oz, 1 cup) water. Flavour with a small glass of rum, Cognac, Calvados or Grand Marnier, depending on the recipe. Finally, add 40 g (1½ oz, 3 tablespoons) melted butter or a mixture of 25 g (1 oz, 2 table-spoons) melted butter and 2 tablespoons oil. Leave the batter to stand for 2 hours. Just before making the crêpes, dilute the batter with a little water or milk – 100–200 ml (4–7 fl oz, ½–¾ cup).

It was formerly the custom to add 2–3 tablespoons caster (superfine) sugar to the batter, in addition to the vanilla-flavoured sugar. Today, the crêpes are usually sprinkled with sugar when cooked, according to taste.

Butters & creams

Almond butter

Cream 225 g (8 oz, 1 cup) butter until softened. Blanch 100 g (4 oz, 1 cup) sweet almonds and reduce to a paste in a blender with 1 tablespoon cold water. Add to the softened butter and press through a sieve. Very fresh ground almonds can also be used. This butter is used in the preparation of petits fours and cakes. Make walnut butter in the same way.

Chantilly cream

Chill some double (heavy) cream and some milk in the refrigerator. Mix the well-chilled cream with a third of its volume of very cold milk and whisk until frothy. Add 65–75 g (2½–3 oz, 5–6 tablespoons) caster (superfine) sugar to each 500 ml (17 fl oz, 2 cups) cream, flavour with vanilla extract or vanilla-flavoured sugar and continue to whip until the cream remains in the coils of the whisk. Return to the refrigerator immediately and chill until ready to use.

Chiboust cream

Soak 4 leaves of gelatine in cold water, then dissolve over hot water. Boil 500 ml (17 fl oz, 2 cups) milk with ½ vanilla pod (bean). Beat 4 egg yolks with 125 g (4½ oz, ½ cup) caster (superfine) sugar until the mixture lightens in colour. Add 75 g (3 oz, ¾ cup) plain (all-purpose) flour and mix well. Gradually pour in the boiling milk, whisking continuously. Pour the mixture into a saucepan, add the dissolved gelatine and heat gently, stirring continuously. Remove from the heat as soon as it begins to boil. Add a pinch of salt to 4 egg whites and whisk into stiff peaks. Reheat the cream until it

293

starts to simmer and pour it immediately over the egg whites. Mix with a spatula, lifting the whole mixture, but taking care not to beat it, so that a smooth cream is obtained.

Chocolate crème au beurre

Follow the recipe for *crème au beurre* (with custard), but dissolve plain (unsweetened) chocolate in the milk, using 100 g (4 oz, 4 squares) chocolate to 500 ml (17 fl oz, 2 cups) milk. For *crème au beurre* made with sugar syrup, dissolve the chocolate gently in a bain marie and incorporate in the finished crème au beurre.

Coffee crème au beurre

Add coffee essence (extract) or instant coffee to the milk used when making a custard base. To flavour cream made with sugar syrup, blend the coffee essence or instant coffee with cream, using 1 teaspoon coffee essence to 300 ml (½ pint, 1¼ cups) double (heavy) cream; the mixture should mix thoroughly when heated.

Crème au beurre (with custard)

Prepare the recipe for crème anglaise (see custards). Bring 225 g (8 oz, 1 cup) butter to room temperature, then cut it into small pieces. Blend the butter with the custard cream, working with a whisk, and flavour as desired with coffee, chocolate, liqueur, praline, lemon zest or orange zest.

Crème au beurre (with sugar)

Beat together 250 g (9 oz, 1 cup) caster (superfine) sugar and 6 egg yolks. Then blend in a few drops of vanilla extract and 100 ml (4 fl oz, 7 table-spoons) double (heavy) cream until the mixture is quite smooth. In a separate bowl, work 225 g (8 oz, 1 cup) butter into a soft paste using a wooden spatula. Place the first basin in a bain marie and whisk the mixture until it becomes white and foamy. Remove it from the bain marie and continue to whip until the mixture is completely cool. Then gradually blend this mixture with the creamed butter.

Crème au beurre (with syrup)

Boil 125 g (4½ oz, ¼ cup) caster (superfine) sugar in 500 ml (17 fl oz, 2 cups) water for 10 minutes at a temperature of 120°C (248°F). Meanwhile, beat 4 egg yolks in a small bowl. Gradually pour on the boiling syrup, whisking for 3 minutes. Continue to whisk until the mixture has cooled to lukewarm. Then whisk in 125 g (4½ oz, ½ cup) butter cut into small pieces and whisk for a further 5 minutes.

Frangipane cream

Boil 750 ml (1¼ pints, 3¼ cups) milk with a vanilla pod (bean) or 1 teaspoon vanilla sugar. Put 100 g (4 oz, 1 cup) plain (all-purpose) flour, 200 g (7 oz, 1 cup) caster (superfine) sugar, 4 beaten eggs and a pinch of salt in a heavy-based saucepan and mix together thoroughly. Gradually add the hot milk and cook slowly for about 3 minutes, stirring all the time, until the cream thickens. Pour the cream into a bowl and stir in 75 g (3 oz, ¾ cup) crushed macaroons and 50 g (2 oz, ¼ cup) softened butter. Mix well.

Ganache

Melt 250 g (9 oz, 9 squares) plain (unsweetened) chocolate over a low heat and add 65–75 g (2½–3 oz, 5–6 tablespoons) unsalted butter. Cool, then fold in whipped cream, either 250 ml (8 fl oz, 1 cup) whipping cream or 200 ml (7 fl oz, ¾ cup) double (heavy) cream whipped with 3 tablespoons milk.

Whipped ganache

Bring 100 ml (4 fl oz, ½ cup) double (heavy) cream to the boil. Remove from the heat and add 225 g (8 oz, 8 squares) plain (unsweetened) chocolate, broken into squares. Stir until the chocolate has melted and is thoroughly combined with the cream. Leave until cool, but not set, then whip until pale, thick and light. Alternatively, the cooled, but not whipped, ganache may be stirred and poured over cakes as a chocolate icing (frosting).

Custards

Caramel custard

Add caramel to the boiling milk used for preparing a crème anglaise.

Chocolate confectioner's custard

Use 75–100 g (3–4 oz, 3–4 squares) cooking chocolate for 500 ml (17 fl oz, 2 cups) confectioner's custard. Cut the chocolate into small pieces, add them to the hot custard and stir until they have melted completely.

Confectioner's custard (1)

In a heavy-based saucepan, place 50 g (2 oz, ½ cup) plain (all-purpose) flour, 175 g (6 oz, ¾ cup) caster (superfine) sugar, a pinch of salt, 15 g (½ oz, 1 tablespoon) unsalted butter and 4 eggs. Work this mixture with a whisk. Infuse a vanilla pod (bean) in 500 ml (17 fl oz, 2 cups) milk, bring to the boil and add it to the mixture. Stir well, place the saucepan over the heat and boil for a few minutes, stirring all the time to prevent the custard from sticking to the bottom. Remove the vanilla pod, pour the custard into an earthenware dish and allow to cool, stirring from time to time.

Confectioner's custard (2)

Split a vanilla pod (bean), boil it in 500 ml (17 fl oz, 2 cups) milk, then remove it. Beat 3 egg yolks with 75 g (3 oz, 6 tablespoons) caster (superfine) sugar; when the mixture has turned white, add 40 g (1½ oz, ⅓ cup) cornflour (cornstarch). Then gradually add the boiling vanilla-flavoured milk, whisking all the time. Put the mixture in a saucepan over a gentle heat and boil for 1 minute, whisking vigorously. Pour the custard into a deep bowl and leave to cool.

Crème anglaise

Blend 250 g (9 oz, 1 cup) caster (superfine) sugar, a pinch of salt and 8 egg yolks in a pan using a whisk. Boil 500 ml (17 fl oz, 2 cups) milk flavoured with vanilla or the zest of either 1 lemon or 1 orange. When the sugar-egg yolk mixture forms ribbons, gradually add the warm (not boiling) milk. Mix well, keeping the pan on the heat and stirring continuously until the first signs of boiling. At this point the yolks are sufficiently cooked and the custard should cling to the spoon. Press the hot custard through a fine sieve or a silk strainer. Keep it hot in a bain marie if it is to accompany a hot dessert; otherwise pour it into a basin, stir until it is completely cool and keep it in a cool place.

A simpler and lighter version of this can be made by reducing the number of egg yolks to 5–6 and adding ½ teaspoon arrowroot, starch or cornflour (cornstarch) to the eggs and sugar. This gives a slightly thicker consistency and helps to prevent the custard from curdling if allowed to overheat.

Icings & pastes

Almond paste

Grind 250 g (9 oz, 2 cups) blanched sweet almonds in a blender, in small quantities, as they turn oily if too many are worked together. Cook 500 g (18 oz, 3 cups) caster (superfine) sugar, 50 g (2 oz, ⅓ cup) glucose and 150 ml (¼ pint, ⅔ cup) water to the 'small ball' stage. Remove the saucepan from the heat, add the ground almonds and stir briskly with a wooden spoon until the mixture becomes granular. Leave to cool completely, then knead the paste by hand in small quantities until it is soft and easy to work.

Chocolate icing

Sift 100 g (4 oz, 1 cup) icing (confectioner's) sugar. Melt 125 g (4½ oz) bitter (bittersweet) chocolate in a bain marie, working it with a wooden spoon. Add the sifted icing sugar, then 65 g (2½ oz, 5 tablespoons) softened butter cut in small pieces. Continue to stir until the mixture is completely melted and remove from the heat. Gradually stir in 100 ml (4 fl oz, 7 tablespoons) cold water. Use the icing (frosting) when slightly warm.

Condé icing

Chop 250 g (9 oz, 1½ cups) shelled almonds finely in a blender, without reducing them to a paste. Mix 350 g (12 oz, 2 cups) icing (confectioner's) sugar, 1 tablespoon vanilla sugar and the chopped almonds in an earthenware dish. Beat 2 egg whites and a small pinch of salt with a fork until fluffy but not stiff, and add them little by little to the sugar – the mixture should be liquid enough to spread easily over the cakes, without overflowing while cooking.

Fondant icing

Put the following ingredients in a heavy-based saucepan: 2 kg (4½ lb) lump sugar, 75 g (3 oz, 6 tablespoons) glucose and 120 ml (4½ fl oz, ½ cup) water. Cook over a high heat, skimming regularly. Take the pan off the heat when the sugar reaches the 'soft ball' stage, at about 118°C (245°F). Oil a marble slab, pour the sugar mixture over it and allow to cool until just warm. Working with a metal spatula, alternately spread out and scrape up the fondant until the mixture is uniformly smooth and white. Place in a bowl, cover and keep cool. When it is needed, heat the fondant gently in a small saucepan and add a little syrup cooked to the 'short thread' stage – 101.5°C (215°F) – and the selected flavouring (coffee liqueur, essence or extract, or melted chocolate). Alternatively, add a few drops of edible food colouring.

Marzipan (1)

Blanch 250 g (9 oz, 1¾ cups) sweet almonds and 2 or 3 bitter almonds and pound them in a mortar (or use a food processor), moistening from time to time with a little cold water. When the almonds have been reduced to a fine and fairly firm paste, put them in a heavy-based pan with 500 g (18 oz, 2¼ cups) caster (superfine) sugar, a pinch of powdered vanilla or vanilla extract, and a few drops of orange-flower water. Dry out over a gentle heat, stirring with a wooden spoon.

Put the paste back into the mortar and grind it with the pestle, then work it with the hands on a marble slab until smooth, adding a small handful of sifted icing (confectioner's) sugar. Use the paste as required.

• *marzipan sweets (candies):* to make sweets, roll the paste out to a thickness of 2 cm (¾ in), lay it out on a sheet of rice paper, and cut it up into various shapes with a cutter. Lay the pieces on a baking sheet lined with rice paper and dry out in a very cool oven.

Marzipan (2)

Take 1.4 kg (3 lb) sweet almonds, blanch and peel them; drain and wipe them. Pound them in a marble mortar, sprinkling them from time to time with a little water, so that they do not become too oily (or use a food processor). When they are pounded to a smooth paste, cook 675 g (1½ lb, 3 cups) sugar to the small thread stage, 101°C (214°F). Add the almonds to the sugar and mix together with a spatula, carefully scraping the bottom and sides to prevent sticking, which may occur even when the pan is removed from the heat. The paste is ready when it does not stick to the back of the hand when touched. Place the paste on a board. Sprinkle with caster (superfine) sugar on both sides and leave it to cool.

• *baked sweets:* roll out the paste to a moderate thickness and cut out different shapes with cutters, pressing them gently with the fingertips on to sheets of rice paper before baking. Cook on one side only, then ice (frost) the other side and bake in the same way.

Nougatine

Put 200 g (7 oz, 1 cup) caster (superfine) sugar and 4 teapoons liquid glucose into a copper pan. Melt over a fairly high heat, stirring constantly with a wooden spoon. When the mixture turns a light brown, add 100 g (4 oz, 1 cup) ground almonds. Stir well, then pour on to an oiled baking sheet. Keep this hot until it is to be used, by placing it at the front of an open oven. Then allow the nougatine to cool and set slightly.

Using a lightly oiled rolling pin, roll out the nougatine on the baking sheet to the desired thickness and cut it into the required shapes with a biscuit (cookie) cutter. Alternatively, if the nougatine is to form the base of a cake, pour it into an oiled cake tin (pan) the same size as the cake, or cut it to shape with an oiled knife.

Royal icing

Gradually add icing (confectioner's) sugar to lightly whisked egg whites, stirring continuously and gently until it forms a mixture that is thick enough to spread without running. Stop stirring when the mixture is smooth. Strained lemon juice may be added (10 drops for 2 egg whites). Keep the icing cool, covered with damp greaseproof (wax) paper. To cover a Genoese cake 20 cm (8 in) in diameter, use 1 egg white, 175 g (6 oz, 1¼ cups) icing sugar and 1 teaspoon lemon juice. If a piped decoration is to be used, the icing must be firmer, so use 300 g (11 oz, 2¼ cups) icing sugar per egg white.

Pastry & dough

Brioche dough (classic)

Soften 225 g (8 oz, 1 cup) butter at room temperature. Crumble 7 g (¼ oz, ½ cake) fresh (compressed) yeast and stir in 1 tablespoon warm water. In a separate container stir 1 tablespoon sugar and a pinch of salt into 2 tablespoons cold milk. Sift 250 g (9 oz, 2¼ cups) strong plain (bread) flour, make a well in the centre, and add the yeast mixture and 1 lightly beaten egg. After working in a little flour, add the sugar and salt mixture, and another lightly beaten egg. Continue to work the dough until it becomes smooth and elastic. It should stretch easily. Mix a third of the dough with the softened butter, then add the second and finally the remaining third of the dough to the mixture.

Put the dough in a 2 litre (3½ pint, 9 cup) container, cover with a cloth, and leave to rise in a warm place until it has doubled in volume. Then separate the dough into 3 pieces, knead lightly and leave to rise again. Leave to rest for a few hours in a cool place: the dough is now ready to be shaped and baked.

- *standard brioche dough:* this is prepared in exactly the same way, but the quantity of butter is reduced to 175 g (6 oz, ¾ cup).
- *pâte levée pour tartes:* this yeasted brioche dough is used for tarts and flans. Prepare as for brioche dough, but use 250 g (9 oz, 2¼ cups) plain (all-purpose) flour, 7 g (¼ oz, ½ cake) fresh (compressed) yeast, ½ teaspoon salt, 2 teaspoons caster (superfine) sugar, 2 eggs, 100 g (4 oz, ½ cup) butter and 6 tablespoons milk.

Choux buns or fingers

Make the choux paste and transfer it to a piping bag fitted with a plain nozzle, 1 cm (½ in) in diameter. Pipe small balls, 4–5 cm (1½–2 in) in diameter, on to a lightly oiled baking sheet, spacing them out so they do not stick to each other as they swell during cooking. Alternatively, pipe the paste into larger buns or fingers to make éclairs.

Bake choux pastries in a preheated oven at 220°C (425°F, gas 7) for 10 minutes. Reduce the temperature to 180°C (350°F, gas 4) and continue to cook, allowing a further 10 minutes for small buns or up to 25 minutes for large puffs. Transfer cooked choux pastries to a wire rack to cool and split them immediately to allow steam to escape, so that they stay crisp outside, but slightly moist on the inside.

Choux paste

To make about 40 small buns, 20 larger buns or éclairs, measure 250 ml (8 fl oz, 1 cup) water or milk and water (in equal proportions) into a saucepan. Add a large pinch of salt and 65 g (2½ oz, 5 tablespoons) butter cut into small pieces. Add 2 teaspoons caster (superfine) sugar for sweet choux.

Heat gently until the butter melts, then bring to the boil. As soon as the mixture begins to boil, take the saucepan off the heat, add 125 g (4½ oz, 1 cup) plain (all-purpose) flour all at once and mix quickly. Return the saucepan to the heat and cook the paste until it thickens, stirring: it takes about 1 minute for the paste to leave the sides of the saucepan. Do not overcook the mixture or beat it vigorously as this will make the paste greasy or oily. Remove the saucepan from the heat and allow to cool slightly. Beat in 2 eggs, then 2 more eggs, one after the other, continuing to beat hard until a smooth glossy paste is obtained.

Flaky pastry

Mix 75 g (3 oz, ⅓ cup) butter with 75 g (3 oz, ⅓ cup) lard or white vegetable fat (shortening) by chopping both types of fat together in a basin. Divide into quarters and chill well. Rub a quarter of the mixed fat into 225 g (8 oz, 2 cups) plain (all-purpose) flour, then mix in 7–8 tablespoons cold water to make a soft dough.

Knead the dough lightly on a lightly floured surface, then roll it out into a long rectangle measuring about 15 × 35 cm (6 × 14 in). Mark the pastry across into thirds. Dot another quarter of the prepared fat in lumps over the top two thirds of the pastry. Fold the bottom third over the fat on the middle third, then fold the top third down on top of it. Press the edges of the pastry together and give the pastry a quarter turn in a clockwise direction. Chill the pastry for 15 minutes, then roll it out as before and dot with another portion of fat. Fold and chill the pastry for 30 minutes. Repeat the rolling and folding twice more – once with the remaining portion of fat and once without any additional fat. Chill the pastry in the refrigerator for 15–30 minutes between each rolling out and at the end, before finally rolling it out and using as required.

Lining pastry (pâte à foncer)

This is a lining pastry for flans and tarts; it is a basic shortcrust made by the French method. Sift 250 g (9 oz, 2¼ cups) plain (all-purpose) flour on to a board. Make a well in the centre and add ½ teaspoon salt and 125 g (4½ oz, ½ cup) butter (softened at room temperature and cut into pieces). Start to mix the ingredients and then add 2 tablespoons water (the quantity of water required may vary depending on the type of flour used). Knead the dough gently, using the heel of the hand, shape it into a ball, wrap it in foil and set aside in a cool place for at least 2 hours if possible.

For a richer pastry increase the quantity of butter to 150 g (5 oz, ⅔ cup) and add 1 small egg and 2 tablespoons caster (superfine) sugar.

Pâte sablée

This is a rich, sweetened short pastry, flavoured with vanilla and used for sweet flans and tarts. Sift 250 g (9 oz, 2¼ cups) plain (all-pupose) flour. Cream 125 g (4½ oz, ½ cup) butter. Quickly mix the flour and butter by hand, draw the mixture together and make a well in the centre. Add 1 egg, 125 g (4½ oz, ½ cup) caster (superfine) sugar and a few drops of vanilla essence (extract). Quickly blend the ingredients together, roll the pastry into a ball and chill for 1 hour.

Alternatively, the pastry can be made by first mixing the egg and sugar, then rubbing in the flour, and finally kneading in the butter.

Pâte sucrée

Heap together 250 g (9 oz, 2¼ cups) plain (all-purpose) flour, a pinch of salt and 75 g (3 oz, ⅓ cup) caster (superfine) sugar and make a well in the centre. Put 1 large egg (or 2 small ones), 100 g (4 oz, ½ cup) softened butter and 1½ teaspoons orange-flower water in the middle of the well and work all the ingredients together, drawing the flour into the centre. Knead the dough quickly and gently with the heel of the hand, form it into a ball, cover and keep cool until required.

Puff pastry

The preparation of puff pastry is a lengthy and complicated procedure in which butter is incorporated into rolled-out dough. The dough is then folded, turned at right angles, rolled and folded again, up to 8 times.

Put 500 g (18 oz, 4½ cups) plain (all-purpose) flour on a board in a circle, making a well in the middle. Since flours differ, the exact proportion of water to flour is variable. Into the centre of this circle put 1½ teaspoons salt and about 300 ml (½ pint, 1¼ cups) water. Mix and knead until the dough is smooth and elastic. Form into a ball and leave to stand for 25 minutes.

Roll out the dough into square, mark a cross in the top and roll out the wedges to form an evenly thick cross shape. Put 500 g (18 oz, 2¼ cups) softened butter in the middle of this dough. (The butter should be softened with a wooden spatula until it can be spread easily.) Fold the ends of the dough over the butter in such a way as to enclose it completely. Leave to stand for 10 minutes in a cold place, until rested and firmed slightly.

The turning operation can now begin. Roll the dough with a rolling pin on a lightly floured board to obtain a rectangle 60 cm (24 in) long, 20 cm (8 in) wide and 1.5 cm (⅝ in) thick. Fold the rectangle into three, give it a quarter-turn and, with the rolling pin at right angles to the folds, roll the dough out again into a rectangle of the same size as the previous one. Again fold the dough into three and leave to stand for about 15 minutes and chill if too sticky. Repeat the sequence (turn, roll, fold) a further 4 times, leaving the dough to stand for about 15 minutes after each folding. After the sixth turn, roll out the dough in both directions and use according to the recipe.

Shortcrust pastry

Sift 225 g (8 oz, 2 cups) plain (all-purpose) flour into a bowl and stir in a pinch of salt, if required. Add 50 g (2 oz, ¼ cup) chilled butter and 50 g (2 oz, ¼ cup) chilled lard or white vegetable fat (shortening). Cut the fat into small pieces, then lightly rub them into the flour until the mixture resembles breadcrumbs. Sprinkle 3 tablespoons cold water over the mixture, then use a roundbladed knife to mix it in. The mixture should form clumps: press these together into a smooth ball. Chill the pastry for 30 minutes before baking. Roll out and use as required.

Preserves & jellies

Apple conserve

Marmelade de pommes. Peel and core some apples, cut into quarters and weigh. For 500 g (18 oz) apples, allow 300 g (11 oz, 1⅓ cups) sugar. Put the apples and sugar in a preserving pan with 2 tablespoons water. Cook gently until the apples crush under a spoon. Rub them through a strainer over a bowl. Put the purée back into the pan, bring to the boil, stirring continuously, and cook until the purée reaches a temperature of 106°C (223°F). Pot.

Blackcurrant jelly (1)

Wash, dry and stalk some blackcurrants. Weigh them, place in a saucepan and add 150 ml (¼ pint, ⅔ cup) water per 1 kg (2¼ lb) fruit. Heat until the berries burst (if a perfectly clear jelly is required), then place the fruit in a cloth and wring to extract the juice. (If a thicker jelly is preferred, rub the contents of the saucepan through a sieve or mouli.) Measure the liquid obtained, then, for every 1 litre (1¾ pints, 4⅓ cups) fruit juice, put 850 g (1 lb 14 oz, 3¾ cups) preserving sugar into a saucepan together with the juice of a lemon and 175 ml (6 fl oz, ¾ cup) water. Heat to a temperature of 109°C (228°F), then add the blackcurrant juice. Stir thoroughly over a high heat until the jelly coats the back of the spoon. Skim and pour the boiling jelly into sterilized jars. Allow to cool completely. Cover, label and store in a cool place.

Blackcurrant jelly (2)

Prepare a blackcurrant jelly as described in the previous recipe but using 1 kg (2¼ lb, 4½ cups) sugar per 1 kg (2¼ lb) of fruit. Cook the sugar in the same way, then take the saucepan off the heat, add the juice and stir thoroughly. Then pour the jelly into sterilized jars, leave to cool and proceed as in the previous recipe.

Blackcurrant syrup

Crush the blackcurrants, put into a muslin (cheesecloth) bag and leave to drain; do not press. The pulp is very rich in pectin, which turns the syrup into jelly. Measure the juice and allow 800 g (1¾ lb, 3½ cups) sugar per 500 ml (17 fl oz, 2 cups) juice. Put the sugar and juice into a saucepan and heat, stirring well until the sugar has completely dissolved. When the temperature reaches 103°C (217°F), skim and pour into sterilized bottles. Label and store in a cool dry place.

Candied angelica

Cut some young angelica stems into 15–20 cm (6–8 in) lengths. Soak them for 3–4 hours in cold water, then plunge into boiling water until the pulp softens.

Drain, cool and peel carefully to remove all the stringy parts. Macerate the stems for 24 hours in a syrup of 1 cup sugar to 1 cup water. Drain. Boil the syrup to 102°C (215°F) and pour it over the pieces of angelica. Repeat this operation once a day for three days. On the fourth day cook the syrup until it reaches the 'pearl' stage, 105°C (221°F). Add the angelica and boil for a few moments. Remove the pan from the heat, cool and drain the angelica in a sieve. When the angelica pieces are dry, lay them out on a slab, dust with caster (superfine) sugar and dry in a slow oven. Store in sealed containers.

Candied orange peel

Choose thick-skinned oranges. Peel them, scrape off all the white pith from the peel and cut the peel into strips. For each orange, put 250 ml (8 fl oz, 1 cup) water, 125 g (4½ oz, scant ⅔ cup) sugar and 6 tablespoons grenadine syrup into a pan and bring to the boil. Add the peel, half-cover the pan and let it simmer gently until the syrup is reduced by three-quarters. Leave the peel in the syrup until it is quite cold, then drain it. Sprinkle a baking sheet thickly with icing (confectioner's) sugar, roll the pieces of peel in the sugar and dry off under the grill (broiler).

Chestnut preserve

Peel 2 kg (4½ lb) chestnuts, cover them with cold water in a saucepan, bring to the boil and cook for 40 minutes. Drain and press them through a sieve. Weigh the resulting purée and add an equal quantity of granulated sugar. Put the sweetened purée in a preserving pan with 100 ml (4 fl oz, 7 tablespoons) water per 1 kg (2¼ lb) sweetened chestnut purée and 2 vanilla pods (beans). Heat the mixture fairly gently, stirring continuously. The preserve is ready when it comes away from the bottom of the pan when stirred. Remove from the heat, take out the vanilla pods and put into jars.

Mincemeat

Combine the following ingredients in a large mixing bowl: 450 g (1 lb, 3 cups) shredded suet, 450 g (1 lb, 3 cups) currants, 450 g (1 lb, 3 cups) seedless white raisins, 450 g (1 lb, 4 cups) chopped apples, 450 g (1 lb, 2 cups) sugar, 450 g (1 lb, 3 cups) sultanas (golden raisins), 100 g (4 oz, ⅔ cup) chopped mixed candied fruit peel, 3 tablespoons brandy or rum, the juice and zest of 1 lemon and 1 teaspoon each of cinnamon, nutmeg, cloves and mace. Pack closely in jars and cover. This yields about 2 kg (4½ lb) mincemeat.

Redcurrant jelly (1)

Use either all redcurrants or two-thirds redcurrants and one-third white currants. Weigh 100 g (4⅔ oz) raspberries for each 1 kg (2¼ lb) currants.

Crush the currants and raspberries together and strain them through a cloth which is wrung at both ends. Measure the juice. Allow 1 kg (2¼ lb, 4½ cups) granulated sugar for each 1 litre (1¾ pints, 4⅓ cups) fruit juice. Heat the sugar in a pan with a little water – just enough in which to dissolve the sugar. Add the fruit juice and cook until setting point is reached, then pot and cover as usual.

Redcurrant jelly (2)

Put the prepared and weighed currants in a pan, add a small glass of water for each 1 kg (2¼ lb) currants, then heat them gently until the skins burst and the juice comes out. Add raspberries (the same proportion as in the previous recipe) and boil for a few seconds only. Strain the fruit and filter the juice. Continue as described in the previous recipe.

Sauces, coulis & purées

Apricot sauce (1)

Stone (pit) 12 apricots and reduce to a pulp in a food processor or blender. Put the pulp in a thick copper saucepan and add 500 ml (17 fl oz, 2 cups) light syrup. Bring to the boil, skim and remove from the heat when the sauce coats the back of a spoon. Strain. Flavour with 1 tablespoon kirsch or brandy.

Apricot sauce can be served hot or cold. If served hot, it can be made smoother by adding a little fresh butter. When stewed apricots (fresh or preserved) are used, the syrup can be used to dilute the sauce.

An apricot sauce can also be made by mixing about 3 tablespoons of the good apricot jam (preserve), 1 tablespoon lemon juice and a few spoonfuls of water. Heat, strain and flavour with kirsch or brandy, as described above.

Apricot sauce (2)

Purée 500 g (18 oz) stoned (pitted) apricots in a food processor or blender. Put the purée in a saucepan with 500 ml (17 fl oz, 2 cups) water and 500 g (18 oz, 2¼ cups) granulated sugar and boil for 5 minutes. Add 1 tablespoon cornflour (cornstarch) mixed with cold water. Bring to the boil again, stirring. Remove from the heat and add 3 tablespoons kirsch.

Blackcurrant sauce (1)

Put 10 lumps of sugar into a saucepan with 5 tablespoons water. Heat to dissolve the sugar and then boil to make a syrup. Wash 250 g (9 oz, 2 cups) blackcurrants in cold water, wipe them and reduce to a purée in a food processor or blender. Rub the purée through a fine sieve. Mix the syrup with the purée and add the juice of 1 lemon. Pour the sauce into a bowl and chill in the refrigerator.

Chilled blackcurrant sauce can be served with baked apples, floating islands, pineapple water ice or fruit salad. It can also be served hot with a rice dessert, apple charlotte or cold lemon mousse.

Blackcurrant sauce (2)

Blackcurrant sauce can also be made quickly by mixing 500 ml (17 fl oz, 2 cups) blackcurrant cordial with 2–3 liqueur glasses of raspberry brandy or plum brandy. A generous handful of whole blackcurrants may be added if they are in season. This sauce can be used for pouring over sorbets or ice cream sundaes.

Caramel sauce

Make a pale caramel with 150 g (5 oz, 1 cup) icing (confectioner's) sugar and 120 ml (4½ fl oz, ½ cup) water. Boil 500 ml (17 fl oz, 2 cups) milk with a vanilla pod (bean), remove the pod and whisk the milk into the caramel. Put 3 egg yolks into a bowl and whisk in the caramel mixture. Pour the sauce back into the saucepan and heat gently, stirring, until it thickens. When the sauce has reached a pouring consistency, remove from the heat and allow to cool, stirring continuously.

Chestnut purée

Boil some peeled chestnuts, drain them, press them through a sieve and place the purée in a saucepan. Add 150 ml (¼ pint, ⅔ cup) double (heavy) cream per 1 kg (2¼ lb) chestnuts and reheat, stirring constantly. Then add 50 g (2 oz, ¼ cup) butter and adjust the seasoning. If the purée is too thick, add a little of the strained cooking liquid.

Chocolate sauce

Melt 100 g (4 oz) bitter (bittersweet) chocolate in a bain marie with 100 ml (4 fl oz, 7 tablespoons) milk and 20 g (¾ oz, 1½ tablespoons) butter. When the mixture is completely smooth, add 40 g (1½ oz, 3 tablespoons) caster (superfine) sugar and 1 tablespoon double (heavy) cream. Stir until smooth, then remove at once from the heat.

Fruit coulis

Prepare 1 kg (2¼ lb) fresh fruit (apricots, strawberries, peaches, redcurrants or any other suitable fruit in season). Chop into pieces where necessary, and purée in a blender with some caster (superfine) sugar – use 575–800 g (1¼–1¾ lb, 2½–3½ cups) – depending on the acidity of the fruit. Add the sugar a little at a time while blending.

Raspberry coulis

Sort, clean and wipe 1 kg (2¼ lb) raspberries. Reduce to a purée in a blender together with about 500 g (18 oz, 2¼ cups) caster (superfine) sugar.

Sugar

Caramel

Caramel can be prepared either by heating sugar in a dry pan (or with a little water) until it melts and then boiling until it caramelizes or by dissolving the sugar in water to make a heavy syrup, then boiling until the syrup is reduced and caramelized.

Heat the sugar and water gently at first, stirring occasionally, until the sugar has dissolved completely. When stirring, try not to splash the syrup around the sides of the pan as it may form crystals and encourage the rest of the syrup to crystallize before it cooks to a caramel. Bring to a full boil and stop stirring. Stirring will encourage the syrup to form crystals.

Continue boiling until the syrup turns a pale golden colour. If there are any signs of white crystals forming around the inside of the pan at any stage during cooking, use a pastry brush to trickle a little cold water down the side of the pan to dissolve them. Continue boiling until the caramel is as dark as required – this may be a light golden colour, a medium or dark rich brown. Take care when making a dark caramel as cooking it for a few seconds too long will make it too bitter or burnt.

Pour the caramel out of the pan immediately into a heatproof dish or container. Alternatively, for pouring caramel, carefully add a little hot water to the pan. To coat a dish, protect your hands with an oven glove or folded tea towel (dish cloth) and tilt the dish until the caramel coats it completely inside.

When dipping ingredients, such as choux buns or fruit, in the caramel, submerge the base of the pan in cold water to arrest the cooking process and to prevent the caramel from overcooking from the heat of the pan.

- VERY PALE CARAMEL: almost white and used to glaze petits fours and sugar-coated fruits. Stop heating as soon as the syrup starts to turn yellow at the edges of the pan. A teaspoon of vinegar will help it stay liquid for longer.
- PALE CARAMEL: used to caramelize choux pastry, coat citrus fruits and bind meringues and other items. Make only small quantities at a time since, once hardened, it changes colour if reheated.
- MEDIUM CARAMEL: mahogany in colour and used to coat moulds, make nougatine, and flavour puddings, creams, compotes and ice creams. Never make the caramel directly in the cake mould.
- SLAKED CARAMEL: a small quantity of cold water is carefully added when the caramel has turned a mahogany colour, in order to stop the cooking process. Some of the syrup solidifies immediately. Used for flavouring, it is put back on a low heat and melted while stirring.
- BROWN CARAMEL: amber-red and used to colour consommés, sauces and stews.
- DRY CARAMEL: cooked without water, but with a few drops of lemon juice. Used in a few recipes, including nougatine and caramel ice cream.
- LIQUID CARAMEL: sold ready for use, in bottles or sachets, to flavour desserts, yogurts and ice creams, or to caramelize moulds or cover desserts.

Cooking sugar: the different stages

Definitions of stages and temperatures vary slightly. Specialist chefs adjust the cooking for delicate procedures according to the precise results required and their experience of handling the syrup. The following are typical stages and temperatures.

- COATED 100°C (212°F): absolutely translucent syrup about to come to the boil. When a skimmer is dipped in it and withdrawn immediately, the syrup coats its surface. It is used for fruits in syrup.

- SMALL THREAD OR SMALL GLOSS 103–105°C (217–221°F): professional chefs test the consistency of this sugar by plunging the fingers first in cold water, then quickly in the sugar syrup, which has become thicker; on parting the fingers carefully, short threads will form, about 3 mm (⅛ in) wide, which break easily. It is used for almond paste.

- LARGE THREAD OR LARGE GLOSS 106–110°C (223–230°F): the thread obtained between the fingers is now stronger and about 5 mm (¼ in) wide. This syrup is used in recipes requiring 'sugar syrup' (without any further qualification) – for butter creams and icings (frostings).

- SMALL PEARL 110–112°C (230–234°F): a few minutes after the large thread stage, round bubbles form on the surface of the syrup; when a little is collected on a spoon and taken between the fingers, it forms a wide solid thread. It is used in jams and *torrone* (a type of nougat).

- LARGE PEARL OR SOUFFLÉ 113–115°C (235–239°F): the thread of sugar between the fingers may reach a width of 2 cm (¾ in); if it drops back, forming a twisted thread (at 1° higher) it is described as 'in a pigtail'; when one blows on the skimmer after plunging it into the syrup, bubbles are formed on the other side. It is used in jams, sugar-coated fruits, marrons glacés and icings.

- SMALL OR SOFT BALL 116–118°C (241–244°F): when a little syrup, which has obviously thickened, is removed with a spoon and plunged into a bowl of cold water, it will roll into a soft ball; if one blows on the skimmer dipped into the syrup, bubbles break loose and blow away. It is used in jams and jellies, soft caramels, nougats and Italian meringue.

- LARGE OR HARD BALL 121–124°C (250–255°F): after several boilings, the previous operation is repeated and a harder ball is obtained; if one blows through the skimmer, snowy flakes are formed. It is used in jams, sugar decorations, Italian meringue, fondant and caramels.

- LIGHT, SMALL, OR SOFT CRACK 129–135°C (264–275°F): a drop of syrup in cold water hardens immediately and will crack and stick to the teeth when chewed. (A saccharometer cannot be used above these higher temperatures.) It is used mainly for toffee.

- HARD CRACK 149–150°C (300–302°F): the drops of syrup in cold water become hard and brittle (like glass), but not sticky; the sugar acquires a pale straw-yellow colour at the edges of the saucepan; it must be watched carefully to avoid allowing it to turn into caramel, which would spoil it at this stage. It is used for boiled sweets and candies, spun sugar decorations, icings, sugar flowers and candy floss.

- LIGHT CARAMEL 151–160°C (304–320°F): the syrup, which now contains hardly any water, begins to change into barley sugar, then into caramel; yellow at first, it becomes golden and then brown. It is used in the caramelization of crème caramel, sweets and nougatine and for flavouring sweet dishes, puddings, cakes, biscuits (cookies) and icings.

- BROWN OR DARK CARAMEL (BLACKJACK) 166–175°C (331–347°F): when it has turned brown, sugar loses its sweetening power; extra sugar is added to preparations with a basis of dark caramel. As the last stage of cooked sugar before carbonization (sugar burns and smokes at about 190°C, 375°F), brown caramel is used mainly for colouring sauces, cakes and stocks.

Praline

Praline is a mixture of toasted nuts in caramel. It is widely used in sweet cookery, for desserts and cakes. Blanch 200 g (7 oz, 1½ cups) almonds and toast them under the grill (broiler) or in a frying pan without fat (they should be golden brown but not burned). Put 200 g (7 oz, ¾ cup) granulated sugar and 1 tablespoon water into a copper pan and melt over a brisk heat. When the sugar bubbles, add a few drops of vanilla extract; as soon as the sugar has turned brown, add the almonds and mix all together briskly for 1 minute. Pour on to a greased baking sheet, spread out and leave to cool. Pound the praline very finely in a mortar as required.

Sugar for decorating

There are several methods for fashioning sugar, for making confectionery and decorating pastries and cakes.

- BROWN SUGAR: cooked to nearly 145–150°C (293–302°F), which may be coloured and is blown like glass.

- FASHIONED, DRAWN OR PULLED SUGAR: cooked so that it loses its transparency. It is then cooled, poured on to a greased marble slab or other cold surface, and then pulled, kneaded or moulded into flowers or sweets (candies) with a satinized finish. (These should be stored in an airtight container.)

- POURED SUGAR (SUCRE COULÉ): cooked to cracking point, possibly coloured, then moulded into cups, pompons, little bells and other decorative shapes.

- ROCK SUGAR (SUCRE ROCHER): cooked to nearly 125°C (257°F), emulsified with royal icing (coloured or otherwise), then used especially to give a rocky effect. It keeps well when exposed to the air.

- SPUN SUGAR (SUCRE FILÉ OR ANGELS' HAIR): cooked to nearly 155°C (311°F). The pan is taken off the heat and left to cool for 1–2 minutes, then placed in a saucepan of hot water to keep the syrup hot. Two forks are dipped into the syrup and flicked quickly backwards and forwards above a lightly greased rolling pin; the threads obtained are then spread over a marble slab and flattened lightly with the blade of a knife in order to make 'ribbons', or collected and used decoratively like a veil. The spun sugar may be coloured. The strands should be used within an hour, or they will melt.

These types of sugar are used in pâtisserie, mainly for constructing *pièces montées*: flowers and leaves, ribbons, knots and shells of drawn and coloured sugar; flowers of fashioned or pulled sugar (rolled out into thin sheets); moiré ribbons (in strips shaped over a spirit lamp and flattened by hand on a board); various types of baskets of plaited sugar (sugar spun into the shape of small cords, plaited and cooled); objects made of cut, compacted or pressed sugar (moistened and moulded, then dried out in a closed container); and plumes of spun sugar. Coloured sugars are made from granulated or coarse caster (superfine) sugar, which is heated, then sprinkled with colourings soluble in alcohol.

For making biscuits (cookies), pastries and petits fours, sugar may be flavoured with citrus zest, cinnamon, aniseed, clove, ginger or dried and pounded flower petals (orange blossom, thyme, lime, violet or rose).

Vanilla sugar

Split 50 g (2 oz) vanilla pods (beans) and chop them finely. Pound them finely in a mortar with 500 g (18 oz, 5 cups) lump (loaf) sugar and sift through a fine sieve. Store in a tightly corked jar, in a dry place. Use as required.

INDEX

Picture acknowledgements

Cabanne P. et Ryman C. *Coll. Larousse* colour plates 1, 2, 3, 5, 9, 10, 11, 12, 13, 16; **Kiefer H.** *Madame Figaro* colour plate 6; **Magis J.-J.** *Coll. Larousse* colour plates 8, 15; **Sudres J.-D.** *Coll. Larousse* colour plates 4, 7, 14.

Editorial Director **Jane Birch**

Executive Editor **Nicky Hill**

Design Manager **Tokiko Morishima**

Editorial team **Anne Crane, Lydia Darbyshire, Bridget Jones, Cathy Lowne**

Index **Hilary Bird**

Cover design **Tokiko Morishima**

Senior Production Controller **Ian Paton**

Picture Research **Jennifer Veall**

Typesetting **Dorchester Typesetters**